A SEMINAR ON TIME

A SEMINAR ON TIME

By A.G.E. BLAKE

Illustrations By Phyllis Peltz Bolton

Claymont Communications

Copyright © 1980 by A.G.E. BLAKE
ISBN 0-934254-00-1
Library of Congress Catalog Card Number: 79-52756
All rights reserved.
This edition is published by Claymont Communications
Box 112 Charles Town, West Virginia
Manufactured in the United States of America

Library of Congress Cataloging in Publication Data

Blake, Anthony George Edward.

A seminar on time.

Bibliography: p. 196.
1. Time. 2. Gurdjieff, Georges Ivanovitch, 1872-1949. I. Title.
BD638.B57   115   79-52756   ISBN 0-934254-00-1

NOTE TO THE READER

This text, as stated in the introduction, is not entirely the verbatim presentation of the seminar. Although some development and modification were required, the whole of the book remains true to the original intent and spirit of the talks as they were given.

Inherent in an oral communication may be an inexactness in various quotations and citations not permissable in a work originally prepared for publication. For the same reason, the footnotes are not extensive and the bibliography is selective.

In the dialogues of chapters 3, 6, and 9, the initials are identified as:

A.G.E.B. — Tony Blake
J.W. — John Wilkinson
Q. — Questioner or Student

Contents

Note to the Reader   v
Introduction   xi

PART ONE — THE ORDER OF TIME

1. In Hope and Fear We Live   3
2. Space, Time, and Existence   19
3. The Drawing of a Line   33
4. The Third Dimension   37
5. Time Past and Time Future   40
6. Observations on the Feeling of Time   49
7. Time Out of Time   53
8. A Note on Space   76
9. Dreams   77

PART TWO — THE ORDER BEYOND TIME

10. Time and Energies   89
11. Hazard   101
12. What Makes the Future?   108
13. The Pentad of Time   125
14. The Qualities of Time   130
15. Living Time   150
16. Making Progress   151
17. Freedom   170
18. The Greater Present Moment   179
19. The Cosmic Present Moment   186
     Notes   193
     Select Bibliography   196

List of Illustrations

The Order of Time	1
Garden Aroused	39
The Order Beyond Time	87
A Chance Moment in Time	88
Untitled	107
Unstuck in Time	169

ILLUSTRATIONS BY PHYLLIS PELTZ BOLTON

Phyllis Peltz Bolton is an artist and teacher-therapist. She believes in the healing properties of art, and sees the explorative process as a key to self awareness.

She has had two one-person shows, has been in numerous group shows and her work is part of many private collections.

Her pen and ink drawings combine a love of classical drawing with a weaving of pyschic material from the unconscious.

Introduction

While staying in a country cottage in Somerset, I had a telephone call from Dr. Pierre Elliot, Director of Studies of the Claymont School for Continuous Education. Would I like to go over to West Virginia and give a seminar on time? I knew I was hooked, however reluctant I felt at that time to travel abroad. It did turn out that it landed me and my future wife in all sorts of unforeseen difficulties, but perhaps they were to our benefit.

Pierre gave me a very open brief: "Do something on time that shows where it fits into our work." He was referring to the tradition of search and experiment that was transmitted to us mainly by J.G. Bennett and which came out of Gurdjieff's researches. It has always been very striking that all of the major exponents of ideas derived from Gurdjieff have made deep studies of the meaning of time: Ouspensky, Nicoll, Collin, and Bennett.

I enlisted the aid of John Wilkinson and was promised help from two sensitive musicians: Susan Lipman, a resident of the Claymont Community, and Elan Sicroff, a concert pianist, who flew down from Alaska to join the seminar.

Nearly every lunch-time Elan gave us a piano recital to make a balance with the words, the practical activities, and the exercises. He is a very gifted performer of the music of Thomas de Hartmann and during the week gave some astonishing interpretations of the music de Hartmann wrote – both his own and that composed with Gurdjieff. Susan took us through sound experiments to develop our sensitivity to the phenomenon of rhythm and duration. John led various exercises and gave the talk "Time and Energies."

When we first gathered together, we joined in various experiments and games with John. One of these experiments plunged us straight into the heart of our investigation. It is the experiment of stopping the second hand of a watch. You look at the watch and bring your attention into yourself. Much to your surprise you will find a moment at which the hand ceases to move. This was the first experiment into what I later called 'being-time'.

Every day we had a reading from some major piece of writing on the meaning of time. Each day I gave at least one long talk on a key idea, developing an analysis and a language step by step.

What is written here is not a verbatim report of these talks. When I came to edit the transcripts, I found myself impelled to develop the ideas. I have no remorse about doing this. The whole spirit of the seminar was to *go on* and not stay still.

Many things came out of the seminar which went far beyond a discussion of ideas. The seminar was an event and its prime reality was as an action. I have increasingly felt that action is primary, experience secondary, and thought comes trailing after. People's lives were affected by this seminar. Some crucial decisions were shaped. The seminar, I know, helped John Wilkinson to take the big step of initiating the formation of the new College for Continuous Education in England. The College is a center for people who truly wish to "investigate their situation."

The words recorded were therefore the lesser part of the seminar. They are offered to the reader as a trace of the action. The book ought to be rewritten entirely, but there is no time. Maybe it is an advantage that the explanations are not neatly sewn up, the loopholes are left uncovered, and many barbarisms of expression are left untouched by the cosmetics of bon-ton — it is more "like it is." Already my own thought is changing, and I would not repeat the same ideas if I were to do another seminar on time.

But an important thing was this: ideas came which were not expected. If this had not happened, I would have been in despair. The unexpected is a sign of significance that one is not simply going through the same damned thing again. It gives life.

I did not know what I would say during the seminar. I had the valuable resource of my years spent studying with Bennett, but I was not about to repeat his words if I could help it. I set for myself to see what I would have to say next.

The seminar taught me something about the meaning of the discipline of *Systematics* which Bennett had tried to communicate to people but failed. I refer to three kinds of time, five modes of time, seven stages of progress, and so on. This way of speaking comes out of the conviction that the world is really complex, but there are ways of understanding it. These ways take us through the valleys of ambiguity and even the peaks of conflict, but they leave far behind just about everything that is fixed and lifeless. Ideas do not have to be fixed, they do not have to be divorced from feeling and action. But to think for real does mean to take a risk.

I am still surprised at the idea, which relates the human to the divine, that emerged in the final session. The greatest truth for me is that God and Man are *almost* incompatible

The seminar period included the summer solstice. On the Tuesday when the solstice came, we all experienced a most extraordinary change in the quality of our perception. To many, including myself, it was a sign of our connection with a greater present moment.

Where do ideas come from? I do not know. It was Eivor, now my wife, who gave me most of the major clues — as well as ending up typing most of the manuscript. Even the horrifying attack on her by a man who gave her a lift from the nearby town contributed a much needed shock at one point, when I was in danger of dreaming my way through the ideas.

I asked Rosa, another resident of Claymont, to prepare an astrological reading for the seminar. I found this to be of practical use in helping me to become sensitive to the changing color of events.

Every incident had some influence. It was not necessary to talk about them; though, sometimes we did, as the reader will find out.

As someone once said, "I came, I saw, I wondered."

A.G.E. Blake
Oxford, England
January 1978

PART ONE

THE ORDER OF TIME

In Hope and Fear We Live

"But what in discourse do we mention more familiarly and knowingly than time? And we understand, when we speak of it; we understand also, when we hear of it spoken of by another. What then is time? If no one asks me, I know; if I wish to explain it to one who asketh, I know not."
                                        St. Augustine, Confessions, Book XI, Chapter 4.

There are very good reasons why we should regard time as an enigma as St. Augustine does. Time is a test case for our *understanding*. What we know about time is not time. If we start our investigation believing that we know what time is, our possibilities of understanding are stifled. What gets in the way is not what we know, but the beliefs we have about what we know.

As St. Augustine says, we have a kind of knowledge of time, but if we try to take this out of ourselves and look at it, we find that it disappears. It is something that is in the living of our lives. Our words and concepts and all the apparatus of thinking and experience cannot take hold of this life in us. As long as we hope to pin down and define what time is, we shall end up with nothing of value: either we will draw a blank, or worse, invent some substitute which is really just moonshine.

To work at understanding we have to ground ourselves in the state of ignorance in which we exist. Our culture encourages us to fill our minds with concepts and images in the place of real understanding. There are not only intellectual abstractions, there are also emotional pictures which trigger off satisfying emotional associations. The former are called scientific or philosophical and the latter artistic and personal. Both are fairy gold and both turn to ashes in the light of the morning. The feeling and direct consciousness of our human lives is the greatest instructor in the meaning of time. The problem is that we are rarely conscious of our lives. We live in shadows made of the fantasies of mind and the turbulence of emotions. Consciousness of our lives is extraordinary. To come to that we have to go beyond thought and emotion.

I have called time a test for our understanding. This is because it is there 'all the time', it is inescapable and applies to everything we can experience. Because it is so universal — really, in an abstract sense as we shall see, it is *cosmic* — we cannot see it for what it is. It takes a very great deal for us to become aware of the air that surrounds us and to know what it is. Yet air is the medium in which we exist. Time may be a deeper thing than air. We can be aware of air, and even to some degree of what air does in us; but maybe we can never be aware of time. Maybe time is an illusion as some people say, maybe it is an absolute, maybe it is relative. None of these words can be taken for granted. To see an illusion we must be able to see reality. To see the relative for what it is, we need to see the absolute. If anyone wants some definition of time which pleases them, it will not be hard to find, but it will not be understanding.

If only we could begin with all the aspects of time all together. All the questions, feelings, cognitions, theories, stories, sources, intuitions, experiences, attitudes, information, experiments — all as one! But we cannot do this. We have to start somewhere and go on to somewhere else. When we pass on, what we leave fades, and where we are going already conditions us in anticipation. We can have all the possible knowledge of the universe at our disposal, but we ourselves cannot experience it all at once. Experience comes in bits. The content of experience comes and goes. What comes expels what has come. This is as true of emotions as it is of thoughts. Sadness gives way to cheerfulness, and it is very rare that both are experienced together. This is part of the real problem we face. Not only the active presence of knowledge is temporary, but also the feeling, the state we're in, is fleeting. All this is obvious to everyone, but very few people take it into account when trying to understand something. Understanding cannot be got by a succession of bits of experience. Unless *I myself* enter into it, there is not understanding. The brain and the unconscious can be as clever as they like, but this makes no difference to *my* understanding. What do *I* understand of what my brain is doing — or the hairs on my chest for that matter? What matters for my understanding is my own act, my own living of my life. And I want to say this in the same breath as saying, "I have no idea of what 'I' is, or even whether there is an 'I' or not."

It seems that time is against understanding. In speaking or writing or simply in feeling, we are constantly losing what we have gained. To come into a state is to lose it. To say something is to separate it from all the other things that have been said or will be said. What can possibly come out of this millstream of flotsam? Maybe it can turn the mill wheel that grinds us into the material of understanding. The ordinary vision of understanding as having a comforting mental image of something is not only incorrect, it is almost blasphemous.

I shall accept the millstream of time for what it is, and not pretend to some impossible timeless overview of the universe from which it is possible to pontificate on the 'nature of time'. I am in the stream and so are you and so are these words. Isaac Newton taught that (absolute) space and time were the sensorium of God. Put in another way, they were the way in which God experienced. This is close to the Islamic view that 'natural laws' are "the habits of Allah." These are quite sensible views — if we can understand them. For that we need to understand mind, experience, God, laws . . . The real understanding is *all at once,* and it is *open, not closed.* We cannot get to a terminal point in understanding; we cannot get to understand half of something. So we neither finish understanding nor come to it by parts, steps, or degrees. This is what I mean by understanding being open not closed, while having an 'all or nothing' character.

I will be describing what I take to be the significance of certain ancient writings. Needless to say, my descriptions are going to be terribly crude. I do not want to give an account of ancient mythologies. What is needed is to get what is said right enough in the right way to contribute something to this event of ours: a venture into the meaning of time. To get it right is a matter of understanding. And to paraphrase St. Augustine: "Imperfection and inaccuracy: they also serve."

Some of the oldest records we have of man's feelings about himself and his destiny come from the Sumerian civilization that Gurdjieff called the Tikliamishian. As a boy, living in the region which once belonged to ancient Armenia, he often heard his father singing of the hero Gilgamesh. In particular he remembered his father reciting the story of the flood that Utnapishtim told to Gilgamesh. Many years later, just before the First World War, Gurdjieff came across the very same story which had just been translated from a cuneiform tablet recently excavated in Mesopotamia.[1] His father was an *ashokh,* a bard who belonged to an oral tradition. This tradition had evidently preserved stories for more than two thousand years. The Sumerian and Babylonian civilizations deeply affected Armenia and the Anatolian civilization of the Hittites. It is difficult to trace in any detail the way in which ideas were transmitted from culture to culture, but what is always left out of account is the kind of understanding of those who made use of the stories and literature. The Sumerian civilization has been recognized by Prof. Samuel Kramer as highly original. It is still not very clear who the people were that drained the great marshlands of the Tigris and the Euphrates and founded the first cities. Soon after the emergence of writing in Mesopotamia, 5,000 years ago, the original Sumerians were invaded by the Semitic people. We have a scarcity of literature that goes back beyond 2400 B.C. But the civilization of the Sumerians — that led later to the Babylonian culture that figures so largely in Gurdjieff's writings — was responsible for all kinds of inventions in building, agriculture, and mathematics, as well as in the sphere of ideas. *How* they used ideas is not understood. The ordinary view is that these were part of a system of indoctrination that took its images from the environment and historical memories. The ideas were simply beliefs, often inculcated into people for political reasons. The objective content of these ideas is hardly ever considered.

The story of Gilgamesh has been put together from numerous fragments, mostly drawing on the remains of the collection of Ashurbanipal, the late Assyrian ruler whose capital was Nineveh. Inscriptions tell us that there was an actual ruler called Gilgamesh, who lived in Uruk a few generations after 'the flood'. The flood was an event around 3000 B.C. when a discontinuity was experienced in the organization of human life.[2] Certain tablets speak of the coming of the power of kingship, represented as the 'tiara from above', after this event. It probably has nothing to do with actual flooding. In the succeeding millenium, there were several local floods that destroyed cities. Whatever the actual events, the epic of Gilgamesh is one of the most extraordinary stories the world has ever known. It would be foolish to attempt a complete interpretation. But this can be said: the story belongs to a time when exceptional people made journeys in *other worlds*. These journeys were represented in stories just as they are today, only the forms of expressions are different. Today such journeys are described in the language provided by religions. Religions as we know them did not exist 5,000 years ago.[3]

According to J.G. Bennett, the time period 3000-500 B.C. was characterized by an attitude of mind in which ordinary people looked for the meaning of their lives through exceptional, semi-divine personalities. He calls it the *Hemitheandric Epoch*. It was the time of the Pharaohs of Egypt, the priest kings of Lagash, and the great Emperors of China. All of them represented as semi-divine, endowed with their power to rule 'from above'. An understanding of this power persisted into recent times where it appears in Christianity through the image of the halo surrounding a spiritualized man, and in Sufism as *Baraka* or 'enabling grace'. In Zoroastrian times, it was called *farrah* and *hvareno*. It was probably a certain kind of substance.

Gilgamesh, as the great hero, is able to do what is beyond the power of the ordinary man, but his story goes beyond heroics to an encounter with the problem of human life: death. His beloved companion, Enkidu, dies. Like the Buddha, thousands of years in the future, he becomes aware that nothing in this human life is immortal. He goes into the worlds beyond death to seek an answer. "Because I am afraid of death, I will go as best I can to find Utnapishtim whom they call the Faraway for he has entered the assembly of the gods."[4] In a fit of rage and despair, he destroys the buckle of the boat of Urshanabi, the ferryman who can cross the ocean of death, and has to use his own energy to propel the boat. Utnapishtim gives him no solace. "There is no permanance. Do we build a house to stand forever?...From the days of old there is no permanence. The sleeping and the dead, how alike they are, they are like a painted death." Gilgamesh asks him how it came about that the gods gave him immortality, and here Utnapishtim tells the story that Gurdjieff heard from his father. The gods decided to liquidate man as a failed enterprise. Only Ea, the Lord of Wisdom, has mercy. Ea whispers to Utnapishtim and tells him to build an ark and how to survive. Because Utnapishtim obeys, he is rendered deathless. There are strange pre-echoes here of Solomon and his obedience to wisdom, the creative power that dances before the Lord.

Utnapishtim challenges Gilgamesh to stay awake for six days and seven nights, but Gilgamesh does not have this strength and is even unaware that he fails. Incidentally, this is a direct teaching on the nature of consciousness in man. Man does not *have* consciousness. Once a woman said to Gurdjieff that she had a state of unbroken awareness for fifteen minutes. He said, "Impossible. Not even Mother of God capable." True consciousness is beyond life and, therefore, beyond death.

Out of compassion Utnapishtim tells Gilgamesh of a plant under the water that can restore youth: "The Old Men are Young Again." Gilgamesh takes the plant, but while bathing in a pool, a serpent comes and takes the flower. Immediately it sloughs its skin and disappears into the pool. Obviously, all this is talking about *self-renewal.* Gilgamesh laments, "I found a sign and now have lost it." I believe this sign to be the principle that Gurdjieff constantly referred to in *All and Everything* in his cosmology of reciprocal maintenance and in the meaning of the name of one of his most sacred characters Ashiata Shiemash.[5] It is the whole question of how the creation renews itself, the secret that every man has to find in order to be immortal.

Gilgamesh returns to Uruk worn out with labor, and inscribes his story on a stone. Enlil, the god, tells him that his destiny is to rule, not to gain everlasting life.

During his search for immortality Gilgamesh meets Siduri, the woman of the vine, the maker of wine. She tells him, "When the gods created man, they allotted to him death, but life they retained in their own keeping. As for you, Gilgamesh, fill your belly with good things; day and night, night and day, dance and be merry, feast and rejoice. Let your clothes be fresh, bathe yourself in water, cherish the little child that holds your hand, and make your wife happy in your embrace; for this too is the lot of man."

The terror and despair of Gilgamesh belongs to us. But we must remember the point made by Gurdjieff, (it is made at the climax of *All and Everything*), that is illustrated by one of Idries Shah's stories. Someone asks Uwais about his condition. He replies: "When I wake up, I know that I could be dead before the day is out." His interlocutor objects that this is the condition of every man. "But," Uwais replies, "how many people are aware of it?"[6] The fear of death is only part of the awareness of death, but it is probably a major factor in beginning to understand time. If death is not serious for us, then we are probably in a state of dream. I know that a clear and sudden awareness of death had a critical effect on my future life.

The Sumerian material and its transformations in Babylon thousands of years later could well have provided the background for the researches of the Sãrmãn Society that Gurdjieff often refers to as the group that preserved real understanding of the purpose of human life.[7] One of the major pieces of literature of Babylonian times was the creation epic, *Enùma Elish*, "When on High." I can only give the barest impression of this stupendous work. It is very important for understanding the background of ideas we are plunging into. In the beginning there is the state of chaos. Tiamat, the bitter waters of the ocean, and Apsu, the sweet waters of the abyss, are mingled together, and with them is Mummu, mist. Here is the statement of the primal triad in the state of unconditioned being in which spirit (Apsu) and matter (Tiamat) are not distinguished. Then the gods are 'named'. That means that there is a step of *conditioning*. After Lahmu and Lahámu come Anshar and Kishar. Shar means 'horizon', An 'above' and Ki 'below'. This is the division between higher and lower, and An is also the name of heaven and Ki, of earth. Then come other differentiations including the creation of Ea, the Lord of Wisdom.

In the later work done in the Old Testament "Genesis," creation is represented in terms of partition and blending. In the *Enùma Elish*, there is partition, or separation of the elements, but their recombination is represented in terms of struggle in which the world situation is drastically changed. The gods make such a 'commotion' that Apsu goes to Tiamat and urges their destruction. Tiamat will not hear of this, but Apsu and the wazir Mummu plot to destroy the gods. Ea comes to the rescue and subdues Apsu and Mummu. He 'kills' Apsu after casting a spell on him. I interpret this to mean that there is a barrier between the unconditioned and the conditioned. Later Tiamat and some of the gods again find the condition intolerable, and Tiamat prepares to destroy the creation. She becomes a source of monsters. The gods are terrified, and this time Marduk, the son of Ea, assumes the task of fighting Tiamat in exchange for absolute authority. He overcomes her and divides her into two to form the fabric of the heavens and the substance of the earth. This is the ordered world of existence.

Tiamat has a consort Kingu. His fate is to provide material for the fashioning of lullu, or man. It is from the blood of Kingu that man is made, therefore, there is something of the gods in him. But Marduk says, "Yes, I will create lullu: Man! Upon him shall the services of the gods be imposed that they may be at rest."[8]

This is the incredible proposition: man is an instrument in involuntary service to the gods (usually called the Annunaki). He is a sort of kitchen boy of the universe. As Gurdjieff was to say: "Man serves the purpose of Great Nature, willy-nilly!" From another creation account, part of a birth incantation, we read: "Create man that he may bear the yoke."[9] From a Babylonian tablet containing a ritual for the restoration of a temple: "He, (Anu, the sky god in this case), created mankind for the doing of the services of the gods."[10] And there are many references to sacrificial offerings and the performance of rites and ceremonies. Offerings and ceremonies, I believe, signify the release of energies. In another tablet which ends with the words, "Let the wise teach the mystery to the wise," the inscription is more subtle. Man is depicted as the creation of the Annunaki. His role is to maintain order on the earth and: "Day and Night to celebrate the festivals of the gods."[11]

There are some extraordinary hints here about the background of Gurdjieff's ideas. *Man has to work.* This is largely represented as an imposition concerning which he has no choice. The objective is the maintenance of order. Man, by providing order on the earth and 'worshipping the gods', provides something that enables the gods, the Annunaki, to rest.

In *All and Everything* Gurdjieff describes how there is an inevitable tension between the requirements for order and the higher principle of compassion. Order is the responsibility of what Bennett was later to term *Demiurgic Intelligence,* in Sumerian times, the Annunaki. These intelligences, though higher in the scale than man, are yet limited and fallible. Gurdjieff says that a possible threat of disorder led the higher intelligence to implant the organ *kundabuffer* which prevented man from seeing reality. He then saw reality upside down. Later when the threat passed and the organ was removed, man had somehow acquired the habit of blindness and perpetrated an insane attitude toward his life. Yet, willy-nilly he serves, and things adjust so that he provides the energy required, consciously or unconsciously.

Seeing reality upside down may be, in part, a reference to the fact that it is impossible for the mind to represent spiritual reality. Hence, the tradition was advocated by René Guénon, for example, that spiritual teachings represent reality by way of *inverse analogy*. The *Enûma Elish* typifies this: for example, in representing the conquest of Apsu and Tiamat by their progeny. It also means that when man wakes up to his situation, he must become aware of *the inevitable need to labor.* His task is then to find out how to do this in such a way that he can gain immortality for himself. This corresponds to a higher aim than the maintenance of order. It is represented in all the teachings of the Age of

Revelation from Buddha to Muhammad. Above all, however, the upside downness of man's perceptions means that he can hardly be aware at all of the reality of his own death, which Gurdjieff says is the only way he can become free of egoism. As he is, man is a sheep looked after for the sake of his 'mutton' and 'wool' by a 'magician'.

The way out of the situation in the Hemitheandric Epoch was through the mysteries for the few and through the divine leader for the many. At the end of this epoch, the Old Testament speaks of the special few who after death would be gathered into the bosom of the Fathers, who included Abraham. Abraham is associated with the extraordinary and enigmatic figure of Melchisedic of Lagash. There are both pessimistic and optimistic views of life after death, usually presented to persuade the majority to adhere to moral principles. When it was optimistic, as in many of the Egyptian writings, it was nothing but a presentation of the paradise of the inner *spirit world*. This world is free of the constraints of space and time, but it is not the spiritual reality. Only in the latter revelations was there declared the reality beyond Paradise, which is really the place of union between man and his source.

To come to a realization of the spiritual reality, man had probably to be released from feeling himself the lackey of superior forces. By and large, these superior forces, such as the Annunaki and Mesopotamia and the Neter in Egypt, were the sole creatures of immortality. According to Rudolf Steiner, man was made insensitive to the great presences of the spirit world so that he could develop his own individual powers. This brings us into what Bennett called the *Megalanthropic Epoch* which extended roughly from the time of Buddha to the last century. The opening up of the sense of individual human power, which led to human self-aggrandizement and technology on a vast scale, was the visible counterpart to the inner message that the true individuality of every man was god-like. Gurdjieff emphasizes the Christian form of this when he says, "We are all equally children of the Common Father." The Father is beyond the gods!

What opened up with Buddha, and to a lesser degree with Socrates and other extraordinary figures of the time around 600 B.C., was a radically new attitude to the world. The world was *something to be understood*. Let me make this clear. It is a matter of the individual directly contemplating the world in which he exists and asking, "What kind of world is this? What is possible in it, and what is impossible?" Buddha can be said to have inaugurated vast study programs into the nature of existence itself. There came the great pronouncements, "Impermanent are all component things. Everything that comes into existence also passes away." Even the gods, insofar as they exist — which Buddha did not deny — are perishable. The spirit world, the world of the heavens and the hells, is not an abode of the imperishable. What has to be done is to *go beyond time*.

Time is the representative of the conditions under which we exist, not only as bodies, but also as minds. "Early-lately" we are bound to disintegrate. This raises the question, "Is there anything in us which will not disintegrate?" Buddha refused to answer this question directly. The mind is unable to see what is involved because it belongs to the perishable. Religion was to teach that the imperishable in man was that which came directly from God. It then got itself into endless muddles giving an image of what this could be. The Sufis were to say, "That which does not perish, is that which does not dream!"

It is possible that the promise of religion — in Buddhism, Judaism, Christianity, Zoroastrianism, and Islam — was not fulfilled. People still talked of "life after death," which, though valid enough after we have discovered what "after" means in this context, misses the point. When the Megalanthropic Epoch finally eroded man's sensitivity to the spirit world, the place of the "life after death," his hopes of Paradise and Heaven were eroded too, and he was left with a world view imprinted with the sense of impermanence and extinction. Needless to say, he invented all sorts of ways to "eat, drink, and be merry," including all sorts of mental masturbations in art, politics, and philosophy.

The search for immortality is linked to the search for meaning. I remember the agnostic astronomer Fred Hoyle, writing that the idea of immortality did not appeal to him, because he could stand living as he was for about only three hundred years. This is the crude version of immortality as something static. The problem in getting beyond this is that the immortal seems to us as changeless, and thus, utterly boring, *unless the changeless is at the very peak of our experience.* This is the attitude in the immortality claims of art and romantic love. It was this that Shakespeare brought to a high level of expression that served also to transform the use of English.

>Since brass, nor stone, nor earth, nor boundless sea,
>But sad mortality o'ersways their power,
>How with this rage shall beauty hold a plea,
>Whose action is no stronger than a flower?
>O, how shall summer's honey breath hold out
>Against the wrackful seige of batt'ring days,
>When rocks impregnable are not so stout,
>Nor gates of steel so strong, but Time decays?
>O fearful meditation! where, alack,
>Shall Time's best jewel from Time's chest lie hid?
>Or what strong hand can hold his swift foot back?
>Or who his spoil of beauty can forbid?
>>O, none, unless this miracle have might,
>>That in black ink my love may still shine bright.
>
>(SONNET 65)

Here the symbol of black ink is that of the action stronger than time. The moments of meaning — a state of love, a work of art, a breath of summer — are ephemeral and we lose them. "I wrote her name upon the sand. Came the waves and washed it away." The whole of the *Sonnets* is concerned with time. Probably not until the *Four Quartets* of T.S. Eliot was there anything of an equivalent level of insight.

Anything that we can have as an experience is subject to interaction. What is completely outside this world is completely outside our experience. This means that as we are we cannot know the immortal.

The fear of death, when it did not lead to resignation and fatalism as it turned to in the East, energized all kinds of enterprise. Voltaire said, "If God did not exist, Man would have to invent him." This is really what he did. Man spent thousands of years inventing God, because he could not accept what had been revealed from above. In Europe, perhaps, a few great figures such as Dante and Leonardo da Vinci understoood the situation. Leonardo wrote in his diaries, "I thought that I had been preparing for life, but now I see that I am preparing for death."

On the side of studies of the physical universe, the notion of time as the condition of dissolution reached a climax in the nineteenth century. In 1854 Lord Kelvin declared the inevitable 'heat death' of the whole universe. Whatever the organization of matter, it must in the end disintegrate into a state of disorder. This was almost an exact replica of Buddha's declaration of more than two thousand years before. We can believe that present science has a different view, but what this view is nobody has convincingly declared. Different people latch on to different pieces of science to make their interpretations. One thing that is interesting, however, is how astrophysics has destroyed even the notion of the permanence of atoms, to which Lord Kelvin's contemporaries, (I believe he was agnostic about atoms), were rigid adherents. There is even talk in the big bang theory of the *hadron horizon*, a time period 10^{-23} seconds after the creation of the universe when the fundamental particles were formed. This was quite a different stage from the creation of the elements which is attributed largely to stellar transformations. For fun we can call the atomic and fundamental particles the scientific equivalent of the gods — which is really what they were — and say that modern astrophysics has 'done a Buddha' on them. They are real enough but not the essential thing. The essential thing is hidden in the big bang or somewhere inside a black hole!

Instinctively many scientists felt that something was missing from thermodynamics and the view that everything is running down. There was, after all, the evolutionary evidence of things running up the scale of organization. No matter how much this was labelled a 'temporary fluctuation', it had to be accounted for. The great scientist, Charles Maxwell, stepped in and described an imaginary device for the creation of order which became known as *Maxwell's Demon*. Maxwell was responsible for the discovery of the electromagnetic character of light, and he had a very extraordinary intuition.

His 'demon' worked in the following way. We have to imagine a box containing gas and a partition dividing the box into two halves, which we will simply call 'left' and 'right'. A gas in equilibruim is made of molecules moving about, bouncing off walls and occasionally each other. Roughly speaking, the faster the average speed of the molecules, the hotter the gas. Now, in the dividing partition there is a demon perched by a little shutter. The demon is able to detect the speed of molecules. When he sees a fast one coming from the left, he lets it through; and when he sees a slow one coming from the right, he lets it through. The net result is that the right side gets hotter and the left cooler. With this arrangement it is possible to drive a heat engine and get work out of the system. The energy has not been created. It has been *organized*.

As people rushed to point out, the demon, if he actually does anything, must expend energy, and the way in which he does this is bound to use up the energy made available by his enterprising activities and more. "You can't cheat the system." Whatever we do can only make the situation worse. The objection is valid, but probably misses the clue which is hidden in Maxwell's ingenious model: what appears to do very little may radically change the organization of the system. This is the principle of catalysis where structures facilitate the formation of complex molecules.

It may be one of the keys to understanding evolution, though we must remember, that besides smallness, Maxwell's demon has the property of *intelligence*.[12] In human life the message is pretty clear; if you try to create order by massive effort, you are a fool. Everything that is done creates disorder in its wake. No activity subject to time can get us out of time.

We can imagine our own experiences as a kind of gas, and picture to ourselves the separation of the 'quick' and 'slow'. This is the intelligence in us. This may be the way to overcoming time. Orage had this intuition, but he put it in a totally misleading way.

"Time is the most important thing next to awareness. The flow of time through us gives us an opportunity to extract what we can. Time is the three-fold stream . . . what we catch is ours, but what we don't is gone. Time does not wait for us to catch everything in the stream, but if we catch enough we shall have enough to form higher bodies — and thereby become enduring."[13]

What is misleading is this picture of time as a flow external to us. This is just a belief element that gets in the way. If we try to build on it, we will be doing worse than building castles in Spain; yet, the intuition is there. We have to be patient with our minds and their habits. But there is no need to indulge in pictures. We can come to understand if we bring ourselves to be true to what we know.

Besides the time of fear, there is the time of hope. Jesus taught that amongst those who were with him, there were some who would not taste death before the coming of the Kingdom of Heaven. In the *Revelations* of St. John the Divine, an angel appears who declares that there shall be time no longer. In a *Hadith* of Muhammad, God speaks of the day of resurrection when even the body will be restored and all will come to the final judgment through which the worthy will find Allah.

These teachings inspired the most intense hope. The early Christians waited for the end of the world and the coming again of Christ in glory. After centuries of disillusionment and compromise, the message of *Revelations* inspired innumerable 'cults of the millenium' in Medieval Europe. Mystics, such as the fourteenth century anchorite, Julian of Norwich, in *The Revelations of Divine Love* spoke of an ultimate fulfillment. "And all shall be well and all manner of thing shall be well."

We ourselves know that we need to hope, and that if we cease to hope, life is meaningless and even hellish. If we do not persistently align ourselves to 'tomorrow', our lives fall apart. It is the hope of the "life to come" that has supported countless human beings in their strivings to live well. But it is not only a matter of a reward system: if we are good we will get to heaven. It is far more complex than that. There is the need we have for tomorrow to be in some way different from yesterday. This is a hunger for new impressions based on the hardly thought-out realization that we cannot come to understand the world and our situation in it without experiences coming to us that we cannot engineer for ourselves. It is connected with all the beliefs we have that there is somehow or other, somewhere or other, a real wisdom which knows where things are going and what to do with our lives. People have invented all sorts of pictures about 'God' or 'spirit powers' or 'historical forces' because of the endemic disease of having to produce something in which to *believe*. But the feelings we have about tomorrow are very direct. If it is totally unknown, it is liable to plunge us into anarchy and fear. If it is predictable, it is liable to drag us into depressive states. Hope means that something can happen tomorrow that can get us somewhere: that something will be nearer achieved, that new awareness of life will open up, that problems will be resolved. All this is so obvious, but we do not understand it. If we understood it, we would be in a position to understand the teaching of Jesus and the Revelations of St. John.

The extreme form of hope on the historical scale is *messianism*: a Savior will come. According to Bennett, this image originated with the Savior God culture of the Indo-Europeans, and came first to expression in the teaching of Zoroaster in the notion of the *Saoshyans*. One will come who will set us free. Free from what? From political oppression, from poverty, from sin, from blindness — all these are common attitudes. I will suggest that behind them all is the hope of release from conditioning. We must realize that this release is *not* something that can be done by one person to another. It is this crucial point that is usually missed, and as a consequence, what a messiah can do is totally misunderstood. This was the situation of the politically-minded Jewish zealots in the time of Jesus.

The image of some great future event has been with us for at least two thousand years, and it has had a profound effect. It has entered into the cult of progress that increasingly dominated European thinking before this century. Whether the context is technological, religious, or political, the significant aspect is the state of mind of 'living in expectation'. The state of expectation we are in has an effect on our lives: how we deal with experiences or relate ourselves to them. The form of expectation is the form of our efforts. If we expect the world to end tomorrow, we are going to do such things as get blind drunk or repent of our sins. When we go outside the sphere of natural events, such as the destruction of cities or planets, and also leave behind the 'carrot phenomenon' of expecting some future reward for good behavior in the past, the situation becomes very hazy.

The Day of Resurrection is a good example. There will be a day when all mankind will be resurrected and come to judgment. It is easy to criticize the notion that each person's body is to be reassembled by divine fiat, and there is a mode of explanation in which it is said that this really refers to some 'inner body'. Really, this argument in itself is limited. It presupposes that what is being talked about belongs to some succession of events analogous to those we experience in this life. Let us turn it around; the Day of Resurrection is 'to come', simply because mankind has not got there. And we need to add the following. The imposition of ordinary ideas about succession make us believe that the creation of the world *was in the past*. This is probably quite mistaken! Many people, for example, have had the intuition that the creation began with Christ, and, so to say, proceeded both 'backwards' into the past and 'forwards' into the future from the time of Christ. Similar descriptions have been given centered on Muhammad.

That mankind has not reached the Day of Resurrection is much the same as the fact that mankind *has forgotten how itself had originated*. In Sufism this condition of mankind is called *Nāsūt*, humanity, from the word *insān*, man. It is talked about in contrast to the divine world, *Lāhūt*, from *ilāhī*, divinity. The Day of Resurrection and the creation of souls are the same kind of event, and they cannot be described in the language suitable for material processes. They have to do with the world of the imperishable. The Day of Resurrection is no more — but no less — impossible to understand than how a spiritual reality can be welded to a physical body to create man.

Further, the *Quran* is full of references to the omnipotence of God's will, even to the point of suggesting that the unbeliever has been led to unbelief by Allah. Yet for this the unbeliever shall be judged and purged! This makes no sense other than as the portrayal of human life as a meaningless puppet show, unless we understand that all decisions come from will — and will is God. (Rumi understood this better. In the *Mathnawi*, after giving a story containing a long dialogue between an advocate of free will and a compulsionist, he adds that the argument will not be resolved until the Day of Judgment, and what is needed is Love to dissolve our perplexity.) The Day of Resurrection and Judgment is the Day of Will. If this is a real event, it is an event of a totally different character from those we believe we know. I must add that it is also different from events to do with life after death. Perhaps we will be able to come to some real understanding of 'another life' and theories of reincarnation during our investigation. But all the great religions distinguish this sphere from the coming 'face to face' with God.

If only we had a language that did not carry with it all the clutter of unintelligent associations that have assembled around such words as "God" and "life after death!" Really, we have no idea what these things mean. The way to get to an understanding about these things is illustrated by one of the stories that Idries Shah has collected: a country bumpkin goes to a city and is utterly bewildered by the impact of so many people and so much activity. His senses reel, and he wonders how he is going to identify himself when he wakes up the next day. He hits upon the idea of tying a balloon to his foot, and goes to sleep with peace of mind. A practical joker removes the balloon, however, and ties it to his own foot. In the morning, the yokel wakes to find the situation. Seizing hold of the joker, he yells, "If you are me, then who am I?"

The problem with philosophy is that it is a specialized activity and ends up with philosophy talking only to philosophers. Philosophers produce words about such things as 'identity', and omit the practical side of learning how to hear the identity of a melody, for example, or to see what happens in their own changes of state. Philosophers, like most people, imagine that they are in contact with their experience. I do not know whether we can avoid such an illusion ourselves. I speak about hope and fear, but am I in contact with that when I speak? We can study the material of ancient legends, of sacred books, or of modern science, but are we really in touch with what is being said? There's no certainty at all in this business, but one thing we can hope for: to open up something unexpected.

Already unusual things are appearing in our exploration, and already we need to let ourselves assimilate the material without interference from belief.

Gurdjieff's teachings on creation and time are some of the most difficult materials with which to grapple. But we are capable of absorbing more than we believe, once we can bring ourselves to abandon rigid mental images and slavish emotional associations. Throughout *All and Everything* there is a teaching on the realm of the imperishable, or on 'higher worlds'. It is not surprising that time appears as a major protagonist in the cosmic drama, almost personified as the *Merciless Heropass.*

In a beautifully comic version of the second law of thermodynamics, Gurdjieff describes how God came to realize that the place of His dwelling, the Holy Sun Absolute, is almost imperceptibly, but inevitably, decreasing in volume. This, according to Gurdjieff, is the background of the creation, something prior to the creative act. What on earth is he talking about? According to J.G. Bennett, he is saying that *time destroys possibilities*: if anything is started, it must inevitably become more and more conditioned until it is completely determined and fixed.[14] This is a statement about the conditions which the creative act cannot annihilate, but must somehow 'get around'.

If we look at the creation from the other side, for example, of human beings attaining immortality or evolving, then similar considerations apply. What is it that through experience associated with time can escape the ravages of time? It is all very fine to say that man does not have to build a soul, that all he needs to do is divest himself of the veils of illusion including the illusion of time – what on earth is an illusion and how is it so *effective?*

Gurdjieff's account of the creation describes how His Endlessness manages to create a truly independent world, which, by its striving to return to Him, the Source, provides a counterbalance to the destructive consequences of time. This is an astonishing version of the religious view of 'God as Love' and the notion that God created the world in order to 'love Himself'. If we assimilate what Gurdjieff is saying, we can begin to see; firstly, that Love is not a sentiment, but the very source of the Creation; and secondly, that Love itself is not the ultimate reality. The ultimate is 'beyond God'. J.G. Bennett many times has referred to the Zoroastrian teaching on *Zurvan*, absolute time, as the origin of Gurdjieff's *Heropass. Zurvan* is even once represented as the source of both Ahura Mazda, the Good Spirit, and Ahriman, the Spirit of the Lie. The Good Spirit, His Endlessness in Gurdjieff's *All and Everything,* does not have absolute power. There is something beyond Love, the 'merciless', within which God, Will, and Love have to operate. Many people have puzzled over this cosmology and wondered how it can possibly be asserted that 'time' is prior to God. There is something tremendous here. If we look at our experiencing, if we can bring ourselves to be able to do this, which is Gurdjieff's *contemplation*, we can see that time enters as the factor of *evacuation*. Locke, in his phrase, "Time is a perpetual perishing," got very close. Time means that we lose whatever we gain. It is the taste of *nothingness* in us. We can not be anything in time. This is not because time is simply a condition of 'matter', as taught in ancient philosophies, it is a condition of reality.

The exercise of will requires existence, and existence requires time. To *do* anything, there has to be the risk of conditioning, illusion, and death; otherwise, there is no doing. The image of God is the image we have of real doing.

We end this first exploration with some of Gurdjieff's own words. "Time itself, no being can understand by reason or sense or by any other inner being function. It cannot even be sensed by any gradation of instinct which arises and is present in every more or less independent cosmic concentration."[15] ". . . it does not issue from anything, but blends always with everything and becomes self-sufficiently independent; therefore, in the whole of the Universe, it alone can be called and extolled as the 'Ideally-Unique-Subjective-Phenomen'."[16]

Space, Time, and Existence

Quite often the picture we have of space is of a box of nothing into which one can put things, and of time, as a kind of flow which is a flow of nothing but carries everything with it. Of course, these images are not usually put in such a crude way, but something like them is behind most of the thinking about space and time.

If I just said that space and time are not material objects, it would obviously be true; and if I say that they are not spirits or kinds of superghost, that may seem obvious too. Yet, when we come to the question of time and space, we always say, "What is it?" as if such a question could be answered. If we talk about a man, we can say he has such and such characteristics, is made up in a certain way, and, historically speaking, came from such a place and so on. But we cannot say anything like that about space or time. All we can say about space is 'space' and about time, 'time'. We cannot describe them as things or beings to be given a name or ascribed properties, but we fall into the way of trying to do just that. When Bennett, in *The Dramatic Universe,* Vol. I, talks about time in terms of irreversibility, successiveness, endurance, continuity, etc., it is liable to seem that he is talking about *something.* It is not true. There *is* irreversibility, successiveness, and so on, but these characterize everything that we can observe and know; they do not characterize time itself.

When we think, it seems that we have to think about something. This makes thinking very limited. When we try to think about time, we are led to invent something to think about. We get no understanding because all we are doing is dealing with an artificial invention.

There are many alternative theories of space and time around. Modern physicists begin to get the feeling that space and time are not separable from energy. They start thinking that there are energies out of which time and space emerge.[1] It all sounds very fascinating and seems to be a great advance. But what they have done is to turn energy into a thing they can think about, just as people turn time and space into things to think about. Nobody has seen an energy and nobody has seen time or space. All that we see are just things happening.

Of course, there is 'something behind' the things happening and the way in which they happen; but where are we going to put this something behind, and how are we going to describe its operation? It all gets into a tangle in which we try to explain what we know in terms of what we do not know. Clearly, this is absurd, but it is what people do. So they invent something quasi-knowable — something that appears to be knowable and describable — and think and talk about that and argue this way and that way. This is all described in *All and Everything* where the great, learned being Hamolinadir gives a talk in Babylon on whether man has a soul or not and is reduced to gibbering frustration.

We do not have to get into such a predicament which is really a defect in our understanding of reason. We can simply look at what we know, the facts of our experience, and through this find a way. I am going to say that what we call 'time' and 'space' are the names for our understanding of the 'limitations of existence'. Unless we have a sense of these limitations, the meaning of space and time is impossible to grasp. This is the whole crux of the matter which is constantly being missed.

It is a very big thing to realize how true it is that existence is limited. To the ordinary view, such a thing is nonsensical. Here is the world; isn't it *something*? Isn't being something, *something*? If this were taken away, there would only be nothing; without space and time, there would be a blank. And so on. This is the ordinary view, the view of thinking. But if we go into our whole experience, there is something else: all the feelings of incompleteness, separation, longing, and anxiety without which our lives would be 'firm — calm'. I am talking about psychological states. I am talking about the very stuff of our experience and what it is like. It has often been said that feelings choose the philosophy one believes in with the mind, and it is true. But go deeper. See how it is that the regions of experience which we vaguely indicate by the word "feeling" lead us, as common humanity, to seek all sorts of explanations, to dwell in images and pictures, to find some release from a strain that is inescapable. We can look at this simply and not wiseacre about it, not waste time discussing the mechanics of other folks' beliefs. Discussing mechanics is madness, a deep sickness that has fallen on us all. We have got to *see how it is,* not talk to each other about the mechanics of our conditioning.

If I said that every theoretical physicist is lonely and strives to find an image to cover his loneliness, it might appear very stupid or judgmental. It is not. There is loneliness, and it is in us all. We hardly realize what it is. Only the very profound, such as Rumi, could bear to see it directly.

If you ask, "What is space? What is time?" you say nothing at all, because they are not there. Set yourself to answer the question, "Where is space?" Where are you going to point to?

In this room there are pillars that support the roof. What is between these pillars? Please ask yourselves that question. So often people will say, "There's a space between them" or "There's a distance between them." Indiscriminately, they picture a distance, a gap, a something that *is* space between separate things. Of course, the pillars are separated from each other, and this is an important fact. But we get into much trouble and confusion if we want to think about something between the pillars which is their separation. Separation isn't anything, so we develop the contortion in thinking about two things separated by something which isn't anything. If we start from the question: "If two things are separate, what is between them, what is separating them?" we have already said too much.

There is separation and this is a manifestation of the condition of space. That there is separation I am sure of in all sorts of ways. I am sure by the experience that comes through my eyes: I scan from left to right, focussing on this pillar and then on that pillar. There is a movement in my eyes or a movement in my attention. I feel that there is some work to be done in overcoming the separation of two places, a feeling that comes from the experience of the muscles moving my eyes. There is not only the side to side experience of scanning, there is the experience of depth. I know that if I see a distant hill, I have a long way to go in order to reach it. I am aware of 'far-awayness' and degrees of 'far-awayness' through the organ of sight. What this means for me and my experience is realizing how much or how little effort I've got to expend to get to that point which is far away. All these things are correlated and measured and made precise in the natural sciences. It all has to do with the effort or work required to overcome separation. This is the primary thing. Science really talks about this rather than some kind of landscape called space, littered with objects of various forms kept apart by nothing at all, by this space. The language of science consists of rules that govern the getting from one place to another.

Whatever I believe, however I talk, I am still going to have to sweat up that hill or turn my head to see what is behind me. Space is not the 'betweenness' between things. Space is a condition of bodily existence.

René Descartes had this argument about the ordinary view of space as the 'nothing-between-things'. He said that if you have a round vessel, a cylinder which does not contain anything, then there is nothing between the walls of the vessel and they must be in contact. But, obviously, they are not in contact; so there must always be something between the walls. Descartes used this argument to sell his idea of an omnipresent ether. What he failed to understand was that there are words like 'space' which are meaningful but do not have to refer to anything. Space is the name we give to the situation that he describes, such as that of a vessel. Space is part of the possibility of there being containers.

What is the possibility of a container? A container is a very good example to choose for talking about space. There is inside and outside; but what does that mean? It means again, simply, separation, *but not unlimited separation*. There is a boundary between inside and outside, but this boundary can be connected with itself. Integral to the condition of separation is the condition of connecting or togetherness.

Look at these pillars again. The ceiling is holding them apart and the floor is holding them apart. But the floor and ceiling are also connecting them. If we take them away, the pillars might topple towards each other and 'make contact' or they might just fall down separately. But whether they are a thousandth of an inch apart or a thousand inches, it is all the same: they preserve their separation so that one is 'here' and the other 'there'.

Why don't the pillars come together? Let us ask this question. Talk of intramolecular forces and crystal structures just takes the question further back. Whether we talk about pillars or molecules is really irrelevant. As long as we are talking about something, then this question remains. The one thing we can be sure of in the material world is that it is a world of separation. Separateness, apartness, is a prime fact — a law — of material existence. If we chase after forces and interactions, we can do some interesting physics and chemistry, but fail to see the wood for the trees.

What if everything came together? This would be like the initial state of the universe as it is described today by big bang theorists — the state before there were any particles, before what is called the *hadron horizon* 10^{-23} seconds after the creation. If everything came together, then everything would be where everything else is, and there would be one presence. In fact, this is something stronger than what is pictured in the big bang theory, where the initial states are pictured as relatively inchoate. The theoretical physicists do not know whether to call the initial state more organized, more structured, more positive, or less organized, structured, positive than the succeeding stages. It is connected with the problem of space and time. When did these emerge? They do not apply to a world where there are not even particles.

The idea of everything being in the same place is the idea of a *total presence*. In both separation and connectivity there is a manifestation of presence. Presence is simply being somewhere. This is the most common fact of all to do with space. We may not grasp what this is, because it is a universal fact which enters into all experience. Gurdjieff wrote about the utter state of single presence as the 'Holy Sun Absolute', in which all presence is "there" with quotation marks around the word 'there'. It is totally different from the world we know in which the presence of one thing, which we describe as 'being somewhere', excludes the presence of other things. A gaseous presence may exclude other bodies differently from a rock presence, but it is not surprising that the mode of exclusion should depend on what the thing is.

The mutual exclusion of presences is the world of connectivity and separation that we describe as 'spatial'. It is the world of material bodies which is characterized by solids that exist outside each other. It is arranged so that the presence of one thing shall exclude the presence of another. That is why I mentioned loneliness before and tried to say how wise our common feelings are. The law of space is loneliness, and our entanglement in the world of bodies brings us into suffering, into what the Buddhists call *dukkha*. Somehow we realize that space ships and motor cars do not overcome separation and that no technology ever will, because it must always operate and can only operate in a spatial world. That is why images and beliefs become so powerful in us. We cannot face the incompatibility between this world and what is behind our feelings.

The pillars stand as they do because of all the interactions through the floor and ceiling and the whole building and the earth itself. They stand because of their own structure of crystal domains. In it all is the mutual exclusion of bodies. Perhaps we can begin to feel why it is that such things as neutron stars and black holes are so significant; because in them the condition of mutual exclusion is partially overcome. In an uncanny way they suggest the condition of men who have acquired souls. Maybe we shall be able to see this without fantasy if we are able to get beyond the ordinary mental world of things and possessions.

All that we have said so far has come from contemplating the facts which we can associate with the idea of 'betweenness'. Now, I want to look at the idea of space as something which is there. We talk about 'inter-galactic space'; this means the regions — which are far from empty — between the galaxies. It contains all kinds of radiation and dust and probably things that have not been discovered yet. It gives us the idea of a 'background stuff': what is left behind when every conceivable thing has been removed. However far away we go from solid bodies, stars, and dust, there still seems to be something. Physicists talk of the 'background radiation' of the universe corresponding to thermal energy in equilibrium at $4°K$. This is thought to be a residue of the big bang. But let us get rid of everything including background radiation. After all, does not this radiation permeate something, some medium? Does it not make sense to say that the 'where' of this radiation is itself something?

This is the question of the *ether*, the ultimate substance which we cannot say exists or does not exist. Gurdjieff uses this idea in a crude way, picturing the word-god, or *theomertmalogos*, emanating from the Sun Absolute into the 'surrounding space' and producing all the suns and the rest of it. He uses the word *etherokrilno* to indicate that he means something with creative potential.

According to Mr. Bennett's explanation, the root '*krr*' signifies in Arabic a creative action. The etherokrilno represents the prime source substance out of which existing things can be formed. It is the *denying force* in the cosmic triad. In itself the etherokrilno has no presence. Presence is entirely the Sun Absolute. Then there is produced the *concentrations* which are called the second order suns. Presence is brought into the creation, but it is a limited form of presence. The field of presence of all the other suns becomes the denying force for the individual sun, and other tertiary concentrations or presences are formed, which we know as planets.

Such ideas were commonplace in ancient times, though expressed in different ways. In Europe the scholastics of the Middle Ages took it for granted that there was a prime Matter, matter with a capital M, out of which everything was made. This matter could not be known, because it had no form. All that we know is the world in which Form and Matter are coalesced to produce things. Nowadays, university philosophers are scandalized that anyone took ideas such as these seriously. These ideas came from the old myth of Nature as the Mother, the Matrix, in which the creatures are fashioned. Plato played a big part in putting this myth into philosophical language, and the Arabs did their bit as well. Now, in modern physics you find a lot of reference to the 'vacuum state'. It is an extraordinary kind of nothingness, this vacuum state, and produces all sorts of effects on the quantum mechanized level. You have particles disappearing into it and reappearing from it and having all kinds of communications inside it which are not directly observable, associated with very high energy thresholds.[2]

The idea I want to focus on is that when we eliminate every conceivable body, i.e. everything which is at all spatial, we come across something very powerful and strange. The vacuum state is the ultimate in homeopathy. It is the name given to the threshold of existence, not to any thing or substance.

The trouble with taking examples from modern physics is that one can always find something to illustrate any idea no matter how wild or absurd. We do not know, I do not know, how the physicists came to speak of the vacuum state, and what forced them to use such a word when dealing with certain problems. So we cannot claim to understand it at all; it is just a 'Scientific American' illusion or an addition to Capra's *Tao of Physics*. There is something we *can* do that is genuine. Just as the physicists use mathematics to 'go through the motions' of world laws, so we can use the forms of our attention. We know there is presence, and we also know that what we experience is presence under limitation (and this 'is space'). What happens when these limitations are transcended? We have seen that one form of transcendence is the 'Sun Absolute' state of utter presence. Another form of transcendence is in the elimination of presence as such. Then there cannot be any stuff we can picture: what is left is not even like a gas, not even like a ray of light; it is even more tenuous than radiation. You cannot apply to it any of the criteria of space and time, because it is prior to space and time. There is not the property of mutual exclusion; there are no places, no directions, no rotations, no accelerations, no successiveness, it is utterly unthinkable.

I remember a time when some of us were working with Mr. Bennett and Professor David Bohm, and we looked at various modes of *sub-existence* lacking in one, two, three, or more of the conditions that characterize existing things. It did seem that what we were looking at were very much like the things being suggested in modern sub-nuclear physics.[3] It also seemed that we were looking at the kind of realm where ghosts come from.

I mentioned just now 'forms of attention' and did not explain what I meant. What I meant was *how we look*. Usually we look through, or by means of, images. Then we can somehow get hold of what is going on in doing this, (this is what Wittgenstein was sweating over in *The Philosophical Investigations*), and something else begins to operate. We no longer need to be looking at things, whether material bodies or the thought of material bodies. We are in contact with the world of feelings and can even begin to see directly how the world works.

We can see directly that *absence is powerful*. It allows something to be present. This perhaps, is the whole secret of the ancient idea of the Prime Matter; it is not the stuff of stuff, but the absence of stuff. If it were not like that, then we would simply have the world being made out of some stuff like pots out of clay; and that is not it at all.

The ancients used to say that Matter is a 'privation' or a lack. They expressed it very well — though all the modern commentators presume they were idiots looking for a universal stuff with impossible properties, monumental defectives who could not understand that there must be an atomic structure to material bodies. The power of privation is the power of the denying force. Without it, nothing can happen; there can be no *coming to presence*. In our experience we can surely see that it is only absence which makes it possible for a creative step to be made.

So perhaps we have discovered some very remarkable things. We start from the ordinary naive images of space as 'betweenness' or as 'ether' and come to the immense significance of presence and absence. But we will go terribly wrong if we start playing around with 'presence' and 'absence' as if they were anything at all significant apart from our experience. With great attention we can come to see their reality — but only through the substance of our total experience, especially what I call the world of feeling.

We are trying to get beyond all images, but we can do a lot with images as long as we look into them and 'see through' them. We have traced the naive images of space further back until we begin to see something real. In the first image we found that instead of talking about a distance between things, we need to talk about the condition operating upon the presence of everything, the presence of every whole to exclude other wholes from its own presence. In the second image, about space as a medium, we found a reference to some extraordinary intuition of a pre-existence or sub-existence which becomes subject to form the world such as we know. The point is that things are not 'in' space. They are, if you like, 'from' space; they come out of the absence.

All we are trying to do is to get the machinery of our heads, where all the words and concepts are, a bit more in alignment with what we know already, with what we experience already, so that it is not going on about silly things all the time.

I haven't defined 'presence' at all. We have said that any particular presence implies the exclusion of other presences. There is also some kind of relativity of presence. This is something we can easily get at through an examination of our various senses. It is sight that mostly leads us to the image of a distance between things, simply because our eyes do not see the air. Sound fills the room and connects us in a different way from sight. There is still direction, but the sound comes to us more from around us, and we can be aware of the secondary reverberations which give the quality of sound corresponding to a room just as you can now in hearing my voice. There is something more intimate in sound than sight.

This is not an absolute thing. We can have the experience of sight in which there is no difference between near and far, only what appears to us. This requires a particular sensitivity. But if we close our eyes and listen, we can see that all the time we are imposing a picture of things existing in various directions and at varying distances as the sources of sounds. For this picture we rely on sight. If we just listen, what is direct is an intimacy of contact. It is only because we strain to hear or move our head from side to side that we come into the realm of space. If we just listen, there is only sound. Sound has more presence in it than sight. It is even more so with smell. Smell is very intimate. Scientists have even discovered that this is so. We are surprised that butterflies can recognize the smell of a mate a mile away. But the mile we think of is a visual one, linked to displacements of our body. What we smell becomes very much part of 'us', that is, the sense of our own presence.

Here is the thing we have been skirting around. In the midst of our experiencing of the world is the experiencing of our own existence. Every contact we have has something of our own existence in it. We go from sight, to sound, to smell, to taste, to pain, and begin to enter into the realm which includes the kinesthetic sense, that is, the sense of muscle tone, the tension of the skin, the pressure on the walls of blood vessels, etc. This sense merges into what we call the sensation of our own bodies. It is an experience of a contact with a body which can no longer be called 'other body', but is still in the realm of spatial presence.

All the sensory experience we have is experience of bodies, and this must always include experience of our own bodies. How we are in our own bodies influences how we are in the world of bodies. I do not want to talk about any self or being 'in' a body. In this world there are just bodies, but in the experience of our own bodies there is some kind of culmination of our sense of presence. Here it is. When I say my arm, my heart, and so on, there is something utterly extraordinary. *Here* is the sense of being somewhere which is part and parcel of everything we know through our senses. How absurd is the picture of the world of men who believe they can pretend to be just 'minds' coupled to telescopes and gauges, the measuring sticks of modern science. We know that there are worlds upon worlds of beings in this body of which we are scarcely aware. Do we sense the creatures that eat the dead skin in our beds, the bacteria that live in the lining of our intestines, or the battles of our white cells? We do not. Our experience only takes us so far; that is to say, that our 'inner' only meets the 'outer' so far.

What am I talking about here? You can all see it directly! There is not just a world to be observed, looked at; the world is also being made what it is by how we look at it. (We cannot afford to let any of these ideas take root in our minds. They will poison us and make us think in silly ways. Keep it moving!)

We are turning towards time. If we have been talking about presence and absence, now we must talk about the movement, the action, in which the forms of presence change. Can we contemplate this: that there is no world 'out there' to be looked at independently of the world 'in here' which is trying to get out?[4] It is about this I want to say that in the experience we have of ourselves being here, there is a meeting of inner and outer. The inner is *not* just a hidden outer, but it is not higher or better, or more spiritual than the outer; all of which are just associations which we tend to have. The inner is simply inner. It is towards oneself rather than towards other, whether the other is a person or a thing or a thought. Towards other and towards self meet in an awareness of one's own body. This is why it is such a strange and important element in our experience. The experience of being in a body enables one to understand that every being, every entity, high or low, whatever it is, *manifests what it is*: a mountain by staying still, a bird by flying. Everything manifests what it is, so that the bird flies and does not swim, the mountain stays still and does not fly. This may sound very obscure and dark, but it is simple. We have to ask (just as we asked what kept the pillars apart), what keeps the mountain the mountain and the bird the bird?

The manifestation of things is sometimes called *actualization*. It is, if you like, the stuff of our knowledge and experience about time. No actualization, no time, but also no knowledge, no experience. If we cease to actualize, we cease to experience. It is hard not to ask, "What is it that is actualizing? Where is it coming from?" It is not coming from anywhere. It is there, but it is not there all the time.

So we come to the world of past and future: what has been actualized and what will be actualized. We know that everything does not happen all at once. It is rather like we found in our discussion of presence — that there is no single complete presence which does not exclude other presence. So there is no single, super event which does not exclude other things from happening.

We are bound to start thinking about some totality or whole which is brought out in bits according to the condition of time. Plato tried to get hold of this in his cosmology, but he was intelligent enough to call his description a useful myth rather than a factual one. He realized that he could only speak about images, not as things really are. He spoke of time as the image of eternity, of movement as the inferior reflection of the eternal circle, and the whole visible world as a darkened inferior version of a higher one. This led people to picture everything on this earth as a grotty substitute for the divine archetype up there in heaven. They introduced two different places, earth and heaven, which was not really part of Plato's intention in the *Timaeus*. Something was missing in the language of Plato that has misled people ever since when they talk about the timeless and other worlds. The problem is this: where are we going to put what is not subject to time? Where is there room for it?

If there is something which is not actualizing, we have no way of knowing it, and probably there is no experience corresponding to its own presence. The wholeness that is mythological in the Platonic archetype belongs to the *inner*, but this is not an inside space. An inside space would just be another form of separation. Space is always outside. The 'inner is time', but it is more than actualization, because actualization shows us events that exclude each other. The timeless, I want to say, is a kind of time because it is inner.

There is this body; it is our prize instrument of manifestation. We can say that this body is our actualization; and whether we have an 'I' or 'self' is quite besides the point. These bodies move around, they talk and produce all sorts of chemicals, emotions, images, and so on. All of this is an actualization of what a man is or what a member of the human species is. The two regions, the outer and the inner, meet in this body. The body is spatial and interacts under the condition of space with other bodies. It is also 'my place'. As my place it is the localization of my actualization. Everything that I do, (not that we need to suppose anything about 'I' or 'doing' besides that there is something happening), is done here or through here; and without the body I would not exist. You see, the body is not just the thing I look at in the mirror or know about, it is the location of my living. It does not matter whether there is also a mind, or a mind in this body with all sorts of super-powers. All of what is here is body, and without it there would be no actualization. The phenomenologists such as Merleau Ponty got hold of this and called the inner aspect of the body 'intentionality'. What I want to get at is that the inner side is simply *time* and the outer is simply *space*.

Things are only there if they are doing something. The vast, silent mountain may not be dancing a jig, but it is doing an enormous amount to the local climate; it is producing stresses and strains in geological strata, it is eroding and changing shape. Nothing can be pointed to unless it is in actualization.

Let us go back to the ordinary image of the 'flow of time'. It is a beautiful image which Isaac Newton did much to propagate. There is something behind it which is right, because it must be impossible to create a mental picture of anything which is totally wrong. We know that there isn't anything flowing, because time is not a gas or a liquid. Yet we feel there is something like a continuous movement. There is movement, because there is actualization which is always incomplete; and there is also continuity, because there are no gaps in actualization. It is like saying that there is always change, and the actualizations of all the things of the world mean that the world is a place of change. Knowledge of this comes through some center of actualization, so we have the subjective sense of time passing slowly or quickly; our experience of other things is *felt* to be slower or faster according to our own state of actualization.

"Time is passing," we say. What is passing? What is flowing? Nothing. How can a nothing flowing do anything, produce anything, make any difference to how things are? Perhaps it can do a great deal. Perhaps the power of time is connected with negation. The nature of time is *not*.

Mr. Bennett spoke of time in *The Dramatic Universe* as 'selective actualization'. Out of all that might be only this bit is let through. In speaking to you there are all sorts of things I could be saying, but, in fact, only one thing can be said at once. Time is a gate that lets only one thing through, one out of a multitude. The tension or feeling about this is our inner life. On the one hand, there is the potential with its manifold content, and on the other, is the actual, the one thing which can have an effect in space. Actualization is therefore almost wholly denial of what might be.

What might be is the *potential*. We can see that what is potential has a kind of existence; otherwise, there would be nothing to actualize. There are very simple situations where there is only one potential, only one thing can happen or actualize. All that a swinging pendulum which has reached the limit of its arc can do is to swing back again. Such situations are completely determined. Where there is more than one potential, there is not a complete determination of what will happen. As the ratio of potential to actual increases, we approach something which looks like awareness. I mention this, because in awareness there is something which *does not happen*, yet is felt in our presence. We can go on to think of the possibility of choice which presupposes that the quality of our awareness has an influence on actualization.

Time is a multitude of noes to a single yes. Potential is a multitude of yeses to a single no, the no being what loses potential existence to become actual. Time is both very poor and very precious. It is poor because it is poorer in content than what is potential. It is rich because it is actual. What becomes actual can take part in the infinite complexity of interaction which is the process of the universe.

The medieval Scholastics felt the importance of actuality. They wanted to make God wholly actual, because He could not have the imperfection of nonactualized potential. Almost in the same language as determinism, they would say that God *has* to be wholly actual. But this is the picture of the super event we mentioned earlier in which something happens which does not exclude anything else happening. This is the picture of God's activity: it cannot be in bits, successive or lacking in anything. But it is not just the sum total of everything that happens. There is the question of what it is that *chooses* what is actualized. God might be a certain direction of choice.

If we look at any whole and put our attention on this 'direction of choice', then I think we can see that this is what we mean by the independence or freedom of the whole, its kind of self-determination. But there is also the interaction between wholes. What you say to me will influence what I say to you. The rock falling down the mountain will erode the mountain and be eroded. There is a reciprocity of actualization in which wholes have some kind of self-determination, dependent on what they are.[5]

Without actualization wholes would be like dreams. Imagine me dreaming of you and you dreaming of me. Nothing happens between us. We can't learn anything from each other or do anything in cooperation together. There is no external common reference, therefore no shareable knowledge and no possibility of common action. Really, this was the picture of Leibnitz's *monadology*, a tremendous insight into the potential existence of things. The monads were wholes lacking in external windows. They apprehended each other, so to say, on the inside. This totally fails to account for the reciprocity of existence in which everything interacts with everything else through intermediaries.[6] The negativity of time opens the universe and everything in it to risk. This is the guarantee that it is no dream. Risk makes existence concrete.

We need to look again at the image of the flow of time. The continuity implied by a flow of time is quite spurious. Imagine actualization as a set of points. Each point is the result of an act of choice, a selected actualization. By thinking of a set of points, we do not impose any order or structure. It is easy to see that, as we are constituted, we would not be able to tell whether it was like that or like a continuum. What would there be between the points? Non-actualization. Dream. Trance. Emptiness. As far as our senses and thinking and knowledge go, there would be no gaps even if there were gaps! If we are only geared to registering actualization, then there is actualization 'all the time', a continuity and hence a 'flow'.

We do not notice any intervals there might be between actualizations. But if we are right in understanding actualization to be a selection out of the potential, then there are non-temporal kinds of intervals. I am not talking about spatial, outer intervals, but 'inner intervals'. Maybe we do not have the power to notice these, because as yet it is uneducated in us.

If I said that time was an order imposed on actualization — so that it is restricted, successive, irreversible, and so on — it would seem something spatial to you and nothing like a flow. But to say this is right, the feeling of this order is the feeling we call 'time'. *We* are constrained by this order, so that *we lose ourselves in yesterday and tomorrow*. 'Self remembering' is going beyond the limiting order of time and discovering what we are.

What we are is in the intervals which are not of actualization, intervals in other kinds of inner conditions. Without actualization we are isolated dreams; with actualization we are all the time losing ourselves.

What is in this inner determination of our actualization? No, let's get away from ourselves with all our ridiculous images of being a person and look at every kind of existence and ask the same question. Let us ask the question of existence itself.

The selection of actualization is the move that can be taken in the game of existence. As in any game there are rules. Perhaps the scientists have discovered a few elementary rules which fit a small proportion of the possible moves. Perhaps the rules are not utterly fixed, and the very playing of the game modifies the rules that hold. But there are rules. There are rules of presence and actualization which are evident whenever we look at how very limited existence in space and time is. Presences exclude each other in a certain way; actualizations exclude each other in a certain way. Wholes are separated from each other and from themselves, yet not totally.

What I am talking about here is so very simple and obvious and yet so hard to grasp. It is that everything that exists has a certain power of self-determination, of selective actualization. This power is possible, because *the whole of existence is self determined*. Everything is playing by the same rules, but the rules are, so to say, interpreted differently for every different kind of thing. The overall result of this is uncertain.

What exists is the state of play, not the player or the creator of the game. What is setting up the game and, in everything, playing the game? The name Mr. Bennett gave to this is *will*. Not Mr. God's will or your will or the will of anybody or anything, but simply will.

If you get a glimpse of how space and time arise, it is incredible. If there were only will, nothing could happen, there would be no creation, no risk, and no existence. Some extraordinary act of privation takes place to produce conditioning and limitation which can only be 'self-limitation'. That is why Jesus Christ is identified with the world and represents the creation rather than the creator. To be here He had to undergo the privations which make existence possible.

Without the limitations of existence, there would be nothing at all. The rules are not arbitrary, they are in the very fabric of existence. Without them there would be no existence.

The Drawing of a Line

We asked people to take a piece of paper and for one hour and a half to draw a single line on it. The line was not to cross itself, nor should the pen or pencil ever be lifted from the page. Whenever the person doing this exercise realized that he or she had 'drifted off', stopped moving the pencil, or lifted it from the page, a dot should be made to mark that lapse of attention.

This simple exercise typifies certain kinds of training having to do with developing attention. But we let the observations speak for themselves. They certainly show that undertaking such a task is a real encounter with time and with oneself.

A.G.E.B.   I had the most peculiar experience in the middle, no, about a third of the way through the time. I was struggling to keep awake and trying to put what I could into drawing the line. I suddenly realized that it was rather like a stripping away process. The thing that came to my mind at that moment was that this was sort of a torture. I had this strange wish to confess, you know, to become really sincere and realistic about how I really was and everything really was. It was amazing. A wish to be exposed came that I've never had before in that way.

J.W.   It is well known in torture that after a certain time of mistreatment the subject begins to like it. This is why the techniques keep changing. The most favorite technique is to rough up subjects, beat them up, and then to treat them very kindly; otherwise, it cancels itself out. There's a very good example of it in Lawrence of Arabia's *Sevenfold Pillars of Wisdom*. He is caught by the Turks and is beaten and tortured, but he comes into a state where he wanted more.

Q.   When I started out I limited myself simply to being aware of my feet and being present to that while I was drawing the line. Whenever I saw that I'd forgotten that I'd become unpresent to my feet, I made a dot. I went on for quite a while like that, and then I tried being aware of bird sounds and two other sensory type things — trying to be aware of three things at once and stopping whenever I saw that I'd become unpresent to one of them. The frequency increased, and it became a very subtle thing to make sure one was aware of these different things; I'd try to hold them together, and they'd constantly slip. I'd be aware of one and realize that I'd forgotten another, and I'd have to try to collect myself and come back to it again. Even sometimes in that effort of collecting myself, I would start with one, make sure I had that, then I'd go to the next one, try to hold those together, and sometimes I'd lose the first one right there. It's a very subtle play of attention.

J.W. When you stopped and made the dot, had you lost one or two?

Q. Yes.

J.W. I pronounce you de-conditioned. This is a de-conditioning process.

Q. I found that it made me more creative, because as I was trying to do it, I had to trick myself along the way to bring my attention back. First I tried to see what I could do with mazes — which worked for a short while. Then I tried to see if I could freely associate in some way with the line drawn, but I had lots of dots and different designs then. The last thing that I did was to write 'hello', and then I was pretty anxious for tea time. So, in a continuous flow, hello, tea, and then a curve, and next to the curve at the end of the 'A', a dot.

J.W. That was the hour and a half?

Q. Also I found myself really tense, and I was in a peculiar state.

J.W. What was your state?

Q. It was like I felt exposed; a lot of aspects of my personality became exposed, and I didn't care.

Q. After I'd filled about half the piece of paper, I thought, "Gosh, this looks awfully feminine and irrational. I'm going to try something very logical." So I did straight lines, squared the corners, and made triangles, and it felt like that was a kind of irrationality in itself. I went back to doing the curved, pointed lines and filled the paper quite closely, about twenty minutes before four o'clock. Later I saw that somebody had done the same thing, but they had thought to turn the paper over. It was as if the four sides of the paper were a boundary that I shouldn't go beyond.

Q. I found that I reached a certain point where it was almost impossible to stay awake. In fact I went to sleep for a few minutes. Then I realized this is pretty much like doing a lot of other things. If I visualized what I was going to do before I actually did it, then I could be aware while I was doing it. If I just pushed the pencil along instead of knowing where I was going with it, it soon became very monotonous and other things would take over my attention. But as long as I presented myself with an image or a challenge, then I could keep my attention on it until I finished that particular concept, and then I would have to stop and dream up another one.

J.W. Did you stop the line then?

Q. Yes, I did, but not always. Sometimes I could continue and something would come.

Q. I didn't try to be creative and didn't set a pattern, I started out that way and very slowly. The first thing that I noticed after a bit of time, not necessarily when I lost contact with the present moment, was the outside noises. After a while they seemed just to go away, and I didn't notice them anymore. I kept my eye contact right on the tip of the pencil, and it seemed that the present moment just rolled off the tip of my pencil right onto this paper. But when I noticed it, I lost contact with it. I found that my mind just started to think about what it was doing. It almost became a meditation. That's all in the first half; in the second half I was falling asleep. The last thing I did was I went backwards. It seemed like quite a long time, and then I lost all contact with time. I didn't know if ten or twenty minutes had gone by.

Q. I noticed a difference in quality in what came out of the pencil. I was really confused in the beginning about where the presence should be. I started really close, then expanded into an awareness of the whole paper, the quality of the drawing, and an awareness of the space. When I had a place in mind to go to, I could continue much further without a dot. At one point towards the end it got really hard, and the only way I could do it was to breathe with it. There was only one place where I kept going around and around; it was all filled up and it was like a maze that I couldn't get out of. It got harder and harder to go along, because it was the same path, and then I discovered after going around three or four times that I was really feeling desperate about it. I put it down and discovered that I could escape at that point where the dot was.

Q. I noticed that my awareness had a cyclical nature. I kept expecting that I would come out of this dream-like state, it would pass, and I would be out of it. I'd think, "I'd better keep my attention on it," but it kept happening that I'd drift into it, and towards the end I discovered that if I speeded up my pencil, my attention was better. It seemed that if I went too slow, it tended continually to lead me into a dream-like state.

Q. When I started out I thought my attention was at least in harmony. I knew that I was interested in the idea of how I was going to fill up that piece of paper, and how intricate, how small, I was going to make my lines, and how long I could pay attention to detail. What I was thinking of lasted for a long time, and then I started going nuts. I thought, "My God, I'll be doing this for an hour and a half. I'm going to drift off now, I'll put down a dot." I think that, except towards the end of it, I was pretty constant all the way through. I'd think, "I can't take putting my attention on this line anymore; it's time to put down a dot." I'd put down a dot, and think about something else. After a while the line was wandering, and I only had a tiny corner of the thing filled up. So I drew something in the middle of the paper, and I thought I'd see how intricate I could make that. The lines made a Chinese Dragon, and then all of a sudden I panicked. I had this thing in the middle of the paper, and I was afraid that in an hour and a half all the lines that I would make would eat it up; I wouldn't be able to see anything. I spent the rest of the time trying not to eat up this dragon. Finally, all of a sudden, I found a way to make more combinations than I ever could have thought possible just in trying not to eat up the space in the middle of the paper without stopping. The other thing I noticed was that there were places that the pencil would go much faster than I wanted it to. I was scared — as if the line were almost some kind of a vehicle which was going too fast. Then I would slow down and really feel like I had nothing to do with it. I don't know why, but there was this very panicky feeling that this line was getting out of control and then coming back.

J.W.   Have you read *Zen in the Art of Archery?* In it Herrigel describes spending an awfully long time learning to draw the bow and letting the string go. It has to let go, but the master is not satisfied, and it takes several months to do. Did you get a taste of it doing it.

Q.   Well it was definitely doing it, but it didn't feel like the experience of actually letting go. It was almost an experience of the mechanics of the whole ... it didn't feel right. It was almost an experience of the way when you're feverish or sick and time is separate, and whatever it is speeds up, and you get that panic feeling. It was just that the line itself took over and was going faster than I could do anything about.

Q.   A real interesting point for me came, when I said, "I'm just going to sleep, to hell with it for a while; I'm getting so tired." I threw down the pen and said to myself, "This is torture. I'm just going to cave in to my body and go to sleep." I must have fallen out for a while, and then I got up and realized that I could go back to it or I could just stay down. Then finally I got up, and there were a few minutes of a very interesting state which I got into. I had no idea of the time at that point, but I was determined to go ahead with it. I wasn't asleep to what I was doing, but I wasn't satisfied with where I was. In a sense, it was all a continuous dot. It was almost as if I weren't looking. I was there watching the line. I was aware of the line, but I wasn't satisfied with my state, and I didn't do anything about it either. It lasted a couple of minutes, and then it went back to the same old tricks.

J.W.   It is not the same as when it's extended beyond two hours. Under an hour and a half is not the same. The extension of an activity like this for a longer period is needed to break through something.

Q.   I heard a lot of people say they tried to trick themselves into being creative or something. How does this relate to being in the present moment?

A.G.E.B.   The tricks make it interesting. Interest is an energy that brings us into a certain relationship with time. Tomorrow, John is going to tell us about time and energies.

The Third Dimension

The nature of our investigation requires us to be able to *see experience*. We fail to understand our situation, only because we do not bring ourselves to see. The material we need is there for everybody, but in the ordinary course of life it is left unused.

One way into seeing is to set ourselves to see a particular phenomenon of our experience. A good instance is the phenomenon of the third dimension of space — as *experienced depth*. There is up and down and right and left, but there is also far and near. What is the experience of that? And what does this experience teach us about our presence in the world?

If I say that in ordinary experience we are hardly aware of depth, this is for you to verify. People such as painters or photographers are trained to be aware of depth, but do this from a limited perspective, because their intention is to produce something in a certain form using certain techniques. They have what is called 'professional sensitivity'. The wholeness of the the phenomenon is lacking. Quite possibly the men and women who reach mastery in their field are able to see the whole and reveal something to us, but this is not ordinary.

With the advent of the hologram in which the depth of field can be accurately recorded on a piece of film we have a marvelous way in to an awareness of the third dimension. Holographic images have an unusual power. Nevertheless, we have to make the step of bringing ourselves to see. And we have to shake ourselves out of being satisfied with the second-hand product.

From your observations it seems that some progress was made. The first thing to realize, which most of you did, is that, in fact, our ordinary looking is almost two dimensional; in it there is very little sense of depth. We talk of the ordinary 'personality' world where we are occupied with thoughts and reactions as *flat* — with good reason. But when the transition comes and there *is* depth, we find ourselves in a different state. We feel different. Indeed, the feelings become awakened, and a freshness comes.

At the same time we realize how terribly restricted the world was for us. In reality we saw very little to right or to left, let alone above and below. We saw only a cramped little world often lacking in color. The change involved can be likened to going from a small, black and white, flickering image to a full-scale, cinerama, color picture (even to that new five story high screen used in the National Air and Space Museum in Washington, D.C.). The analogy is useful, because there is a factual change which comes into the transition to an awareness of depth, as well as a change in the quality of feeling.

But then there is a puzzle. At first the ordinary state seems like watching a movie in comparison to the new, fresh state that has substance and a reality-feeling to it. What we are aware of is much richer than before, and there certainly is a depth. But if we look more deeply, the feeling of depth somehow goes inside out and no longer gives us any sense of solidity. Instead the whole perceptual field suddenly looks to be a paper-thin depth.

You may not have experienced it exactly like this, but many of you saw something similar. What is this?

It is associated with changes in our feeling of potential. What has happened is that we have come into a state in which we can be aware of potential as well as actual. Because of this the actual looks and feels very tiny and insubstantial.

The feeling of potential influences our feeling of time; they go together. There is a somewhat timeless sense. A few of you reported that by working on an awareness of depth in your environment, a clearer and deeper awareness of the aim and possibilities of your own activity came to you. We would not have predicted that, but we can see how it fits into a state of 'connection with potential'.

The actual world dominates our sense perceptions, but it is very far from the whole story. There is an immense world out of which a tiny fragment comes into the state of actuality.

There is something more to add. Besides the various transitions which influence our experience of the world, there are changes in our experience of our own *presence*. The awareness of depth helps to bring us into our own presence — we are here. When we work on being aware of various parts of our body, there can be an even stronger experience. What we call 'sensation' is the means of realizing our own presence. It enters into our awareness of the world about us and into our physical activities.

The hidden message in working out the exercise of awareness of the third dimension is what it means to *be in a body*.

Garden Aroused

Time Past and Time Future

In both ancient teachings and modern mathematics, we can find the same idea: that the way in which we see and experience the world and how things work is a fragmentation of something that is whole. It has such a wholeness that we cannot comprehend it. We always miss the point of the whole. We are living in a world of trees completely unaware that there is a forest and that we ourselves are a tree.

I want to approach this idea through our ordinary concepts of the past and the future. We separate the past and the future. It seems that what goes into the past is lost, certainly lost as an experience. As for the future, we are unable to experience it, because there is nothing there at all.

The past leaves its traces in us, so we are able to perform a kind of cinematic replay of things that have happened. But we cannot really live through a past event again. The actuality has gone out of it. The experience of meaning which I had last week or ten years ago or at the moment of joy as a child of four, what is it now? It is only an echo. The echoes can be experienced so that I can remember and form a representation in my mind of what happened, but the experience that was the source of the echoes and memories is gone. There is an enormous difference between the pen that writes and the mark on the piece of paper that is left behind. One is an action that is able to accomplish something; the other is simply a material trace.

Why do we give a special meaning to the present? What is it that makes now, now? There is a feeling of actualization. Herein lies all the source of our confusion and blindness about freedom and the ability to do. The feeling of actualization requires no agent to be present. All that is required is the condition of successiveness and the energy of feeling.

When we look to the future, we look towards what has not yet been actualized. Therefore the future is not an experience for us, and since it has not happened it has produced no traces, so we cannot think about it. The only kind of future we can possibly reach is that which is just like the past. This explains a great deal about the fact that ordinary thinking keeps us in hell!

What comes out of this state of thought and emotion is the view that there is a 'now' or an 'I' travelling through a region of space-time. The space-time region, in some muddled way, is thought of as 'the world', or what there is. This picture renders invalid any possibilities of freedom and reduces the now and, hence, human life, to a bit of the general world action.

The surface of the blackboard represents space-time. Here is the line of actualization of someone. His 'now' is represented by a circle, and I am putting a whole series of circles in a sequence.

Fig. 1

What we are representing by the place of the circles is, of course, the state of the physical body. The path taken may be very complicated indeed, but the basic idea is that of a tube traversing space-time. In the language of physics the tube is called a 'cosmodesic'. The weird thing we have to take into account is that the circles represent the *nowness* of any cross section of the cosmodesic. This nowness is a feeling, not a bodily condition, something subjective, whether we use this word to be pejorative or complementary. To represent the body as such, we would just have the tube; cross sections would have no special meaning at all.

If we start supposing that the subjective feeling component, or mind, is something that can be represented on the space-time region, then it is just like anything else and its significance disappears. On the other hand, if it cannot be represented at all, then what difference does it make? Either way it goes out of the window as irrelevant. The reason for this is that the space-time region, represented as all there, is fixed and past; present and future are indistinguishable. In this picture then, there is no nowness at all.

There can be a multitude of cosmodesics somehow connected to a mind, but the mind can only be thought of as a useless observer, having no effect on the economy of the world. Even sensitive, perceptive people accept such a view and cheerfully suppose that the mind, in its own quixotic fashion, goes through various experiences of things happening − quite unable to do anything at all except satisfy its own perverse requirements for a contentment of dreams.

Taken at face value the passive mind is the most useless thing imaginable. It is busily engaged in combining and fragmenting cosmodesics within a world completely fixed. This is Gurdjieff's image of man in quotation marks, man the dreamer, the one who sees reality upside down. His now is just subjective reaction to the state of the body.

But if there is a reaction in the one way, can't there be a reaction in the other way too? Or can there be a useful reaction as well as a useless one?

You see, this is Gurdjieff's conundrum which the Sumerians well knew: everyone and everything serves the purposes of Great Nature, but man *can* serve voluntarily, consciously, and gain something for himself. It all has to do with the role he plays in the economy of the world.

The beginning of our work is with developing our contact with being here and now. It is not easy. We all have the sense of being trapped in a fragment of the whole. Something in us desperately wants to flee from the fragment. We want to get away from the conditioned, but we cannot bear the unconditioned. We reject this moment, this state, what we are; we reject words, bodies; we reject working with the material world and other people. We want to be spiritual and fly away. It is a primitive feeling. It is what we have to live through and beyond. In our work we try to go the other way. We try to get inside what is here and now. We begin to see that we are not in contact with what should be most accessible. Suddenly, it all looks very strange and turns inside out.

One of our first efforts is to come into contact with here and now. There is work on sensation and there is work on presence. We begin to learn what gives us presence and robs us of presence. But there are hazards. We can work in a stupid way, and then we find ourselves in a cul-de-sac.

There is an experience of now which comes by rejection of past and future. We judge the past and fear the future. Memory and expectation crush us into a tiny, hateful now. There is another experience in which entering into now releases us from the rejection of yesterday and tomorrow. Instead, it brings us more closely into contact with them.

Let us look at nowness. Here we are and yet we all lived yesterday. Somehow we know that to be true, but we do not see what it means. During yesterday there was a feeling that it was in the now.

Here we are in the now of Friday. Yesterday evening, about the same time of day, we were sitting here and I was also giving a talk, and at that time there was the now of Thursday. In what we call 'tomorrow' there will be the now of Saturday. We can represent now-Thursday, now-Friday and now-Saturday on a diagram like this:

Fig. 2

But the view it produces is quite unlike our own experience of living in a now.

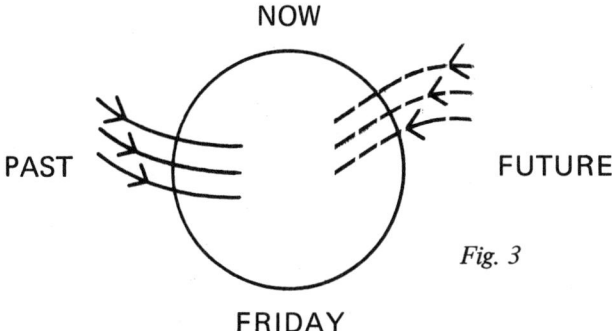

Fig. 3

Here we are in now-Friday. The tracks coming in are traces of the past that become built into our memory. They have to do with causal pushes which are in our bodies, such as the state of health, which carry forward from the causal chain into now. On the other side, we have expectations. The now-Friday is separated by causal action from now-Thursday and separated by expectation from now-Saturday. These other nows are not directly accessible.

But when we are looking at the diagram (Fig. 2), it seems that any now is just as good as any other; they all look the same. The making of the now *now* is not represented.

We know that in reality we are not super-beings now in contrast to being ghosts yesterday and tomorrow. We know that we will be the same kind of being tomorrow and there will be the same kind of experience. Now-Thursday in Thursday is worth just as much as now-Friday in Friday or now-Saturday in Saturday. But now-Thursday feels very thin today, Friday.

What is on the blackboard seems very easy to understand, but, inwardly, to see it like this is a high thing. It is the sort of thing that angels do. We are trying to develop angelic intelligence.

We are using very primitive representations, and I need to explain what the lines mean. The lines represent the order of the material traces. In geological strata the older rocks are lower and the newer ones are higher. The order of the strata is a time-order. This sort of thing is what the lines indicate, one thing happening after another.

There is a sameness in each now that is equivalent to the sameness in every other now. It is not something like a common denominator in the actualizations. It is not something that is conserved so that it passes intact and integrally along the lines of time. It is within each moment, within the mind, within the feeling that it is now. It is what gives the mind a substance and coherence, an order of its own that is quite independent of the order of the lines of time.

Actualization brings us into time. What I have written, I have written. But *what is there* is more than what is actualized; and it is from this that we derive our capacity to see and be aware. It belongs to the side of our being that Bennett called 'eternity'. What is the same in us is what is eternal.

We need to make another diagram which incorporates the line of sameness.

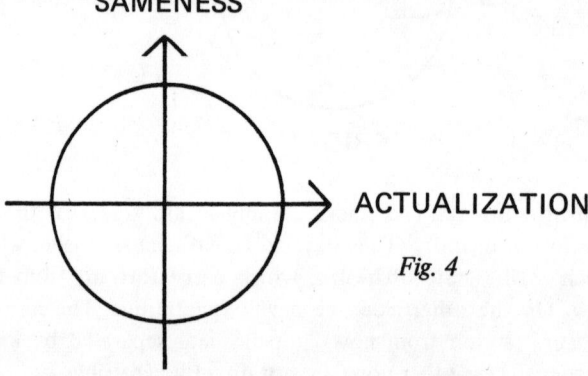

Fig. 4

The direction of sameness is a dimension like that of the time of actualization. More in the direction of sameness means 'more the same'. What does this mean? It means to become oneself, to become more the same as oneself. It is a qualitative kind of quantity.

Eternity is the direction along which the now-Thursday, the now-Friday, and the now-Saturday are the same. Time is the direction along which they become separated. We should not simply think of time as movement and action, and of eternity as lack of movement and powerless. This is hard to see. We have a lot of instrumentation which is designed to deal with time: the going forward in actualization and dealing with the traces left behind. In the other direction we tend to be at a loss. It is a movement out of time.

This does not mean that we float off into another higher world. We can remain in the same world on the same level of existence, but it has a quality that time cannot give. We say that we come into touch with ourselves. There is a stillness. There is quiet.

Bennett said, "Man is eternity blind." Our perceptions are developed along the line of time, not along the line of eternity. Along the line of eternity our experience is enfolded in itself, it is not separated out, nor is it in succession. When we talk about it, we distort.

It is a part of our nature as a self or mind to *suffer* actualization. We do suffer through time, and time is suffering. Even the hope we have along the line of time is suffering.

We are in tension between time and eternity. In certain, completely mechanical states we can be totally unaware of the tension working in us. Then there are different degrees of awareness in which we are partially lifted off the line of time. The balance of time and eternity can shift. We can have the bliss of a timeless state but be unable to act differently. We can have confidence in the unseen regions and sacrifice the demands of time. As we are we know neither time nor eternity. We are their product.

Mind is a mixture, not a whole. There is no stable integration of actualization with sameness. At the moment of actualization mind is 'producing' a separate past and future. At the *same time* it is opening itself to the sameness of what is now. But it does not participate directly in what we call the past and the future.

What would direct participation mean? It would mean that what was yesterday, now becomes now. What will be tomorrow, now becomes now. In other words, we have to speak of a 'greater present moment'.

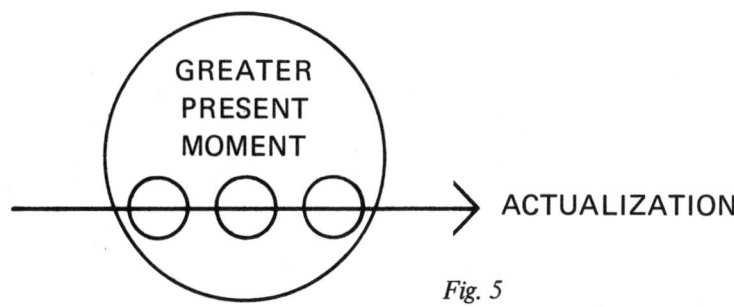

Fig. 5

This representation gives us only a quantitative idea that it is bigger, but this is important. There are states of isolated thoughts, feelings, and so on, but then we 'wake up' and how is it? You get a sense of expansion, of having a bigger experience, with *more past and future contained in it*. What we can learn from changes of consciousness like this is very useful for understanding time.

We also recognize that our experience becomes more whole, more together; we do not have to be in a state of dependence on external forms such as words, tools, and objects. This is our increased extension into the dimension of sameness, eternity.

Through these small excursions into an expanded present moment, we can begin to understand that what past and future mean is relative to the *experi-*

encer. We do not have to suppose somebody or other doing the experiencing. There is the thinking-experience, the bodily-experience, the feeling-experience, also there is the mind-experience, perhaps even the soul-experience.

The distinction between past and future (that we take for granted) arises from the tension experienced between time and eternity by an experiencer. If we could penetrate more deeply into eternity than we ordinarily do, the whole nature of our present moment would change. People touch upon this in deep meditation. It is well described as the *absence* of the consciousness we know. Mr. Bennett used to refer to this kind of experience as a *hiatus*, because our instruments cannot record it and it seems utterly blank.

The picture we had at the beginning of this talk is that of a mind which is totally eternity-blind. There is the body, the cosmodesic. Attached to this body is mind or feeling which keeps on reacting to the body, making the sense of now which we represented by the circles. Such a world can only be a world of horror. There is nothing to be done; every hope is absurd. Nothing really changes because past, present, and future are indistinguishable (except in the subjective way which makes no difference).

It is only when there is a measure of a difference between moments that is not spatial or temporal that hope and fear can refer to something objective, something that will make a difference. Imagine if you like that each moment can be 'weighed' in a special kind of balance. What is being measured by this balance is the degree of sameness. It has nothing to do with the spatial or temporal aspects. In our work it is sometimes referred to as the quality of energy working in us. We do have to learn something about weighing ourselves to live rightly.

In Volume I of *The Dramatic Universe*, Bennett introduced the notion of a universal observer, Q, for whom all events were co-present. Q is the factual or knowable aspect of the Universal Individuality associated with Compassion, in Gurdjieff's language, world 6.[1] Can we make any sense of the world in which Q experiences? This is a world prior to the conditioning of space and time. It is a world of experience, but not experience dependent on conditional forms.

It is. But it subsists by its own act. It is not reflexive of a content that is working according to space and time. Even if there is an inherent shape of our thought, feeling, and sensation, this shape is derivative. World 6 is the origin of all possible form. It is the whole of wholes that Gurdjieff called the Megalocosmos.

We do not know what wholeness is; in the whole, to be means to be all.

You have to picture that within this whole a conditioning comes. The pure affirmation of *it is* is qualified by distinctions. There is the distinction of this and that. It is, by not being anything else. This is the source of the condition of space. There is another conditioning in which to exist means to separate from oneself. This is the conditioning of time, where existence necessitates actualization. It is really the separation of time and eternity, the 'movement of being' divided into actualization and sameness.

So first we have the conditioning in which to be means *not* to be all. Then we have the conditioning in which to exist means to actualize and, therefore, to become separate from oneself. Space and time are images of the conditioning under which we exist.

Wholeness is beyond the mind. The mind is very conditioned. But it is not so conditioned as the events which are recorded by the instrument of mind. The common view is that what is really there are the material events. Mind is only real in that it corresponds to what is materially there. We experience this in terms of the line of traces which is the line of actualization. How mind is connected with them is through the senses. This is what we mean by the senses, instruments through which we can experience what is there. People explain the whole thing by starting with the material substratum and building up into mind.

When other people talk of what is beyond the senses, they do not mean to say that there is another substratum somewhere else for which we need corresponding senses. The true question is hidden in the terms 'we' and 'need'. Mind is a condition of existence, a type of experience. We can look upon it as derived. How we believe it to be derived is largely a matter of prejudice and imagery. We have to find out how a relatively unconditioned experience appears. This experience does not know its own origin, and therefore something is hidden from it. Either we believe this to be hidden in material complexity or in some kind of wholeness beyond imagining. Of course, we can also feel the mind not to be derivative at all, but to be a creative power out of which the complexities of space and time emerge.

To feel that mind is derivative from a great wholeness is only possible if we are able to lose the image of having our own 'I', because this image makes us believe that mind is free and, in being free, incapable of being derived from anything else.

Ask yourself where the nature of mind comes from. And where does your sense of now come from. Can you see what world it is that is enabling you to feel the nowness of this moment.

All we know are the forms of actualization that correspond to our senses. This knowledge exists within a pattern of past, present, and future that is constantly running away with us. But we feel a pull towards a wholeness that the material of the senses cannot give us. Our feeling and knowledge make up what mind is. Yet there is something more to speak about. As we are, we must be involved in actualization and therefore lose ourselves. Yet, if we are, we are constantly entering into ourselves.

Here is a figure showing what we have just talked about. For the sake of completeness and symmetry, I have put the form 'higher intelligence' between 'wholeness' and 'mind'.

        WHOLENESS
  HIGHER INTELLIGENCE
           MIND   *Fig. 6*
         SENSES
     MATERIALITY

There is now as a fleeting moment, as a sense of loss. There is now as a feeling of depth in which nothing can be lost. Time and eternity are incompatible. But what is at the heart of this now? What is it that makes this now a now?

Bennett gave it the name of 'hyparxis'. He meant the *ableness-to-be*, the ableness to reconcile the twin commands of time and eternity. Hyparxis is the answer to the question, "How can we actualize while becoming ourselves?"

Our actualization is needed in the economy of the world we share with other forms of life. This makes us dwell in time. But we cannot be economical without ableness to reconcile the twin commands of time and eternity. Hyparxis is the answer to the question, "How can we actualize while becoming ourselves?"

Our actualization is needed in the economy of the world we share with other forms of life. This makes us dwell in time. But we cannot be economical without organization. This comes from within and gives us eternity. Neither time nor eternity gives us the guts of now. It is a third dimension. It gives us a measure of *will*.

Observations on the Feeling of Time

On Saturday morning I asked people to find experiences having to do with three kinds of time. These three were described as: time passing, having time, and the time that does not pass. I wanted us all to work as much as possible from the feeling of time rather than from concepts about time. These were some of the observations people made later that day.

Q. I came into contact with the feeling of 'time passing' while working in the kitchen. I was at the sink filling something with water, but not wanting to be doing that. I wanted to get back to making bread, and perhaps I was anxious that dinner would not be ready on time. In general I don't have the sense of 'time passing' except when I feel, "I shouldn't be doing this; I should be doing the next thing."

A.G.E.B You are confronted with something that enables the feeling to come. The tap will give water only at a certain rate. Around you things are happening at certain rates of their own. Your environment is actualizing. Your own actualization intersects with the actualization of your environment. It is an emotional thing.

Q. I connect 'time passing' with the past and 'having time' with the future. When I tried to experience time as passing, it seemed it was the moment of actualization sliding behind me. The sense of 'having time' seemed to be connected with an awareness of possibilities and choice. Today there was one occasion when I was doing a breathing exercise while passing somebody. I was startled, because it looked as if they were in slow motion. As I moved past it was like standing alongside a train and not sure of what is moving: you or the train. I was walking, but I was quite aware of not moving. It just seemed that time past was on one side and time future on the other.

A.G.E.B. How do you feel about that?

Q. Somewhat in awe. It wasn't like 'spacing out'. I knew it was something, but I feel that I'm still missing something. There's something I want to see about potential and how purpose comes into it.

A.G.E.B. I myself was noticing this morning how you can make a breakthrough into something and then stop. Really there is no stopping. But every insight you get turns into a barrier between you and a further insight. This is very rarely understood.

Q. I had a time of frustration. Twice this morning I had people suggest I do something when I was in the process of doing something else. I started off confused whether to work in the kitchen or bathrooms and finally worked out that the bathrooms were liable to be more neglected than the kitchen. Just as I was finishing cleaning a bathtub, someone comes and says that help is needed in the kitchen, there's no one. But I chose to finish what I was doing. When I got to the kitchen, the chief cook grabbed me and said, "You don't have anything to do, set up the tables." Again I stopped to think it out. This way, that way, back and forth. I kept wondering why I couldn't get it right. This and that, back and forth, and I go back to the bathrooms. Just as I finished that, two boys came in and in two second the whole place is filthy again. And ...

A.G.E.B There's a nice story of Gurdjieff at the Prieuré. Someone was looking at the vegetable garden when a pig came and started making havoc. The man got into this state, "What shall I do? I must be in the right state. What I do must come from the right place in myself." Suddenly Gurdjieff hurtles past shouting and swearing to drive the pig off.

The heart of it is being in a world of effective action. The usual state is typified by not being there when one is wanted, doing something that has to be undone by someone else, constantly thinking about what to do rather than getting on with something. We feel this disjointedness, and it can be distressing. Again, we can appear to do something, but it's just not real, it doesn't make any contribution.

Q. I had the opposite experience to C——. I got into a real muddle and ended up sweeping a bathroom that was already swept. I was vaguely walking around when I felt something click. I just found myself downstairs sweeping the floor. It was just the right thing for me (as a server) to be doing. But I didn't catch how the transition happened?

A.G.E.B. Do you usually catch it?

Q. No. Yesterday, in the drawing of the line for an hour and a half, I felt I couldn't possibly keep going and I'd have to draw very small. The transition came after I had almost dropped off to sleep. I woke up from that state and I was able to start making designs.

A.G.E.B. One is aware of the two states, but not of the crossover between them. This happens in all sorts of ways.

I'll say some things about it. It is useful to employ two technical terms: 'compresence' and 'coalescence'.[1] Compresence is just existing together, like bodies in a room, nothing more. There is a collection of vegetables on the kitchen table, but there's no unity until there is an action which brings about their coalescence. This action comes from the intelligence of the cook in cutting, mixing, cooking, and blending; then there is a meal. Similarly, one can be a body together with a pan and brush and dusty surfaces, but no blending happens. At other times one really is sweeping the floor, and it has a wholeness and completeness about it. The difference is to do with being in what is called 'world 48' and being in 'world 24'.

The transition happens when escaping a number of laws which have to do with existing as an object in an environment. There are twenty-four laws connected with this which bring us into 'world 48'. When these become suspended, then one comes into one's right place. You may ask, "Well, how are these laws suspended? How does one get free of these laws?" We have vague words for it like letting go, which is not bad, actually. This morning I was thinking, "Will I have time to wash? Will I have time to prepare what I want to say this evening (which I'm not very sure about)?" Then I realized that I have a tendency to be lazy and continued to dawdle. Then I came down to the kitchen and joined in with what was happening. I gradually became aware of other things, like you sweeping the floor, and I joined in with that. At each step there was this kind of attitude of letting go and joining in with what was there. This doesn't explain anything, just describes one's subjective feelings.

Q. I find so often with people, very painfully, that I'm an object in front of another object and there is no communication. I want to communicate, but I don't know how to be able to join in with feeling.

A.G.E.B. I want to remind you of something I was discussing last night. Wholeness is something primary. It is something there; it is a higher world, (in the jargon it belongs to 'world 6'). Out of this condition appear individuals, minds, and eventually personalities. Many layers of conditioning come in and produce our typical, fragmentary experience. It is very helpful to cultivate the attitude that what matters is not me in front of that person, or me in front of that job, but the wholeness into which this job, this person, and myself fit. One is no longer concerned with solving a personal problem. Whenever I'm able to do that, then it comes out right. If I try to correct something, I get it wrong, because the correcting is bound up with the same laws from which the 'error' came.

In the education of children, Gurdjieff recommended us 'to begin from afar'. We can help ourselves by educating our attitudes.

Q. During a break this morning I tried to visualize what would be happening in another part of the building. I used my memories to get a picture and expand into the whole. Is there any value in this?

A.G.E.B.   The short answer is yes. There is much benefit. It has to do with a certain mode of expansion of the present moment that has a spatial aspect to it. We know that when we're in a bad way, so to speak, attention focuses down to a couple of square inches and it's a tiny sort of space we live in. The more we are able to use the power of creating mental images in a constructive way, the better it is for us. Doing this, I myself have found a transition from 'making a picture' of the different places and rooms, to somehow or other 'being in them'. It is like being in the same space or place as the kitchen or bathroom, although the physical body is in the meditation room or in the dining room.

Time Out of Time

MAN IN TIME

We have been building up a picture of our experience which includes more than what is actualized. What is actualized belongs to time. What is not actualized is different: we cannot be aware of it through our senses, and since all our knowledge comes from operations linked to the senses, we cannot know it. We cannot point to the non-actual and say, "Look, there it is," because it *does not happen*. But this does not mean that it is somewhere far away or separate from us. Quite the reverse!

We have grown used to an awareness which is full of things happening, that is, actualization. This awareness is not even full of the material world; it is full of the *actualizations* of the material world. In science what is not actual is represented by a set of concepts which enable us to do convenient calculations. In ordinary life the non-actual is regarded as the subjective shadow of the 'real' world. When you can begin to see this, you can understand how it is that our ordinary awareness is chaotic and artificial and makes communication very difficult.

The attitude in which only the actual is real is inculcated in us as children. Our access to the full world is steadily diminished, until one day we cannot stand the emptiness in our feelings and go chasing after some esoteric or spiritual method to make us approximately human again. We try to make sense of the unknown part of our experience. In doing this we usually end up exchanging one kind of actualization for another and believe this to be significant change. Not until we have become fairly disillusioned with this chasing round of the actual, can we face it that nothing can be changed in the actual world. What we suffer from is not materialism, but actualism. The non-actual is as material as the actual.

We *do* experience the non-actual, the 'time out of time'. We *are able* to notice this kind of experience. The question then is, "Why don't we notice it as a matter of course?" Something spoils the awareness in us as soon as it arises. In our present state of existence there is a conflict between the awareness full of actualization and the awareness of time out of time.

This morning I asked you to look for experience of three kinds of time: the time that is passing, the time in which we 'have time', and the time which 'does not pass'. From the observations you made it is clear that the conflict I mentioned operates both ways. We can get into our *own state*. This is where we locate our experience or where we feel located. When this happens, we, so to say, disengage from what is going on. The result is on the one hand a dream — the mind in a particular state — and on the other, an activity — the behavior of the body. Something gets out of gear and we fail to control the situation. We become occupied with imaginary events. Somehow we have not reached the genuine state.

Some of you reported going into the condition of 'having time' and how it began to feel incomplete. It became like a dream; you felt it like a dream, albeit, a strong one. What is daydreaming anyway? We don't see where it comes from, and we do not see *what it is*. When I speak now about dreams and dreaming, I am speaking of something that is there.

What is missing is something to do with 'presence'. We lose contact with where we are. There is something that determines our ableness to be in our own place. In the daydream we have a kind of eternity, but it is not present. In the going-on of things we have actualization, but it is empty and 'we' are not there. Presence does not come by actualization or non-actualization. We can say that presence comes through the contact of the inner and the outer and then both are real. The whole situation becomes concrete and part of this is that one has presence.

Yesterday I talked about the inner in terms of 'sameness'. To go inward is to go towards one's own pattern and being, to increase one's sameness. But in time there is a movement towards 'otherness', loss of what one is and confusion. Every part of us actualizes — thinking, feeling, and moving parts. What is it to bring together the disintegrative power of time with the integrative power of eternity? This is the important thing we are after. We know that we are not pure spirits waiting to drop the veils from our pristine wholeness. And neither are we assemblages of traces of the world process which have happened to glue themselves together. What *is* is what is present.

The fusion of inner and outer is in a third kind of time, that which Mr. Bennett gave the name of *hyparxis* meaning ableness-to-be. It is terribly important to grasp that this is something more than eternity. It is the difference between 'being there' and just 'being in potential'. What we call our minds is the inner sameness of our lives, and we know how tenuously it is connected to the course of actual events. Within the mind is the pattern of what we are, or a pattern on many different levels, but it can remain the pattern of a dream. To develop the pattern something has to be *done* but people rarely stop and ask themselves what kind of action is involved.

Presence. It has something to do with being here; one feels it is a spatial kind of something. But what is behind it? All that can be derived from the spatial condition is a place in relation to other places. This kind of place has nothing of strength or weaknesses in it, nothing of 'being in the right place' which was so important to ancient understanding. Yet these things of strength and rightness we all know and feel. They correspond to a direction, a meaning of life which we do not know how to move along. What our lives come to may depend very much on how far we go along this way. Indirectly and directly you all know what it is to *come into presence*.

These general psychological considerations are only the prelude to understanding something important. Eivor gave me the clue. I shall have to talk around it for a while in the hope that you will see what it is without my defining it. It is to do with our connection with moments of insight. There is a moment, for example, in which you really see that there is no need to be negative and you have a complete reorientation on what experience is for. But you know, (if you have had some experience of self-observation), that the next moment you will not have it. There is no guarantee that it will continue or that you will have it again. How does one remember an insight?

I remember very keenly when it most strongly came to me. It was in a moment when I was plunged in deep despair about the impossibility of communication with people in the world, constructed as it is. It was such a shock to me that my whole psyche disintegrated in front of it. Then something renewed in me and gave me wonderful sparks of hope and faith. I remember then that I was crying and saying, "How can I remember this? I know that tomorrow I will forget." What is this, this cry to remember? What is one trying to remember?

What exists in the future of the moment is just traces that have to be interpreted to produce the secondary experience of memory. It is not direct enough. The direct thing has to do with making a new connection between time and eternity, the actual and the potential. Take the example of the moment of having a new attitude towards negativity, an attitude that has power. Within us there is a capacity to see how things are. It is there in the inner. But it is not there all the time — which is the ordinary way of thinking about eternity — it is usually there none of the time. Then a situation comes, a moment that is concrete and specific, and the dream or the theory becomes real. Really to see it has to come in the moment of actualization, then *it is there*. But we pass away from it through further actualization, carrying the echoes in our memories. Then we may come across another moment of seeing and say to ourselves, "Here it is again. The same, but different." And the two moments are closer than anything else we know.

It is really the same for anything at all we recognize, but there is a scale of significance. What we can begin to approach is the level at which we can say "I remember myself." Most of you have heard this cryptic phrase of Gurdjieff's. Perhaps some of you have come to the point of seeing that there is no self or memory involved in any ordinary sense. It is a condition of being here that ordinarily we forget, because we are disordered by time and tempted by the dreams out of eternity.

In any moment of insight one comes nearer to how one ought to be. It is unbecoming in three-brained creatures to manifest as they ordinarily do, with self-love, vanity, subjectivity, and so on, which are even cultivated so that people can have some sense of existence. When you see the right way for a human being to live, it is concrete, that is, effective. This seeing is not thinking or imagining or emotion, it is a realization; it is 'hyparchic'.

What is this talk of a right way? You see, when we go in the direction of eternity, it is not simply like reaching into the potential energy of a simple material system like a pendulum. The content is more and more qualitative. It merges into the realm of values and becomes the source of 'ought'. Yet none of this has any significance unless it is brought into contact with actualization and made manifest. As Mr. Bennett used to say, "Goodness is meaningless without the action of temptation."

When there is a realization of the pattern, we become more like we ought to be. This is what the Button-Molder explains to Peer Gynt, (in the play by Ibsen), and he says that without this realization through the temptations of life there is nothing there; there is no presence, only certain ingredients which can be recycled.

What really matters to us, what we have to come to, is 'to be more than what we are'. This 'one-ness' of ourselves is not simply something factual like being so many feet tall or having such and such a rating on an intelligence scale, it has to do with the qualities of being human, how man has a role in the cosmos, how we individually manifest what humanity is. What appears to us to happen is puzzling. Presence seems to come and go in an erratic fashion. Insights come and then utterly disappear. When they disappear, we feel threatened or disappointed. When they re-appear, we see they have remained whole and that the new moment of insight is the brother of the one we experienced before, or that the previous moment of insight lives again in us.

All of this has to do with the dimension of *hyparxis*. There is something that is fully ours which is connected with this dimension, and this is *understanding*. I think Rodney Collin expressed it very well when he said that if you understand, you do not repeat a mistake and do the same old thing again. If we truly understand, we can be effective; we can accomplish something that really makes a difference. This is not so easy. There is a lot of activity in the world and very little that accomplishes anything.

As I have said many times before, the ordinary view of understanding as a mental property is such an utter bastardization of what it could mean. There is a similar problem with eternity, but not quite so severe. You see, eternity corresponds to that in us which is given the name of *consciousness*. The one sure thing for me about consciousnes, as I want to use the word, is that it has to do with the feeling of depth in our experience, rather than with any different content. We can notice too that as the depth increases, the usual distinction we have between ourselves and the world, or between mind and body, dissolves into something else. In depth there are levels which do not correspond in their nature with the distinctions that operate in the world of bodies. But I want to add that consciousness is not single valued or all of a kind, so that we can have more or less of it, or more intense or less intense forms of it. In the theosophical tradition that Gurdjieff picked up and used in his early days of teaching, there is the concept of finer and coarser gradations of matters in which the finer is able to interpenetrate the coarser. The concept does give one's brain something to bite on, but it is misleading, because you tend to assume that there is some kind of continuum or gradation, and then you miss the possibility that there are radically different modes of consciousness. You can certainly have more of a certain kind of consciousness, but this does not get one beyond a certain level.

Gurdjieff tells many tales about 'the kind of consciousness people now have'. This is the same as the 'ego consciousness' of psychoanalysis, and Jung and Gurdjieff totally agree in calling this 'personality consciousness'. Gurdjieff also says many times that what man calls his unconsciousness is his 'true consciousness'. The kind of consciousness man believes he has is one in which *he cannot be what he is*. I puzzled about this for years until I saw that Gurdjieff was saying it as simply and accurately as it could possibly be said. There is another kind of consciousness in which we can be what we are. A long time in trouble and confusion is spent in learning how to recognize the signs and nature of this second kind of consciousness.

According to Mr. Bennett and other people, there are for us men and women four important kinds of consciousness, and of these all our ordinary waking and dreaming make up only one.[1] This gives us some feeling about the depth of eternity. Along hyparxis we have our understanding, ever new, always the same, which reaches towards Gurdjieff's 'objective reason'.[2]

The ideas of the work are permeated with extraordinary insights into the three kinds of time. We can add something here about the time of actualization. The different parts of ourselves actualize semi-independently and sometimes quite independently. It is this which enables us to know about time. There is a line of actualization to do with each of our centers, thinking, feeling, and moving. It really was to this that Gurdjieff referred when he said that man had three independent personalities in him. A personality is a line of actualization in us. It isn't until there is a coalescence, which is given the name 'I', that the three can enter into a common time or, if you like, manifest as a whole.

Once at Coombe Springs Mr. Bennett said that the theme of Gurdjieff's Third Series was time. If you read that book again now, you will perhaps see what was meant. We are creatures trying to remember what we are trying to do!

A DIGRESSION ON THE ROSE

What is the equivalent of a moment of insight for a rose? Can we look at this without eliciting silly anthropomorphisms? When we contemplate a plant like the rose, or a species of animal like the cheetah, the lion, or the stork, we can see that they have their own pattern, and we can feel that they have, or 'are', a value in their own right. We can't put our finger on what it is, but if we neglect it, we get into a wrong relationship with living beings and they are turned into things. In the case of the rose, we can see it more easily because in horticulture we try to help the rose be what it can. The true fashioner of roses is an intelligence that is able to communicate with what the rose is. This is true whether or not there are also a multitude of gardeners hell-bent on treating roses like circus animals trained to do ridiculous acts for human amusement.

Within the plant is its eternity. The eternity of the rose is so much more than either the image of the 'ideal form' or the structure of the genetic code. We must remember that it is no good looking at eternity as either an endless perpetuation of what is actualized or a static ideal that has no material base. To remember this we have to keep in touch with our own 'withinness' and what it is to be the same as ourselves. It is really very simple and almost easy once you have accepted the reality of the non-actual.

It is tempting to say that the genetic code is the carrier of the pattern of the plant. But we have then to understand what it means to be a carrier. Scientists tell us that the properties of a plant, its shape, color, size, fruit, cycles, etc., are encoded in special micro-elements like little computer programs to direct the organic factories of the cells. If a part of the genetic molecules is damaged or altered, the plant cannot grow in a proper way.

A certain analogy can be found with our human speech. Language is a pattern of communication, an aspect of which can be known as vocabulary and grammar. In ancient tradition language was looked at as the genetic code of human intelligence. Animals do not need words and neither do the angels. It is only Adam who speaks and names. If there is a defect in language, something goes wrong in human life. Children brought up by wolves do not *lose* their human potential; they are unable to *manifest* it. As we imply when we say such things as "words fail me," we know very well that language enables us to manifest in certain very important ways. It is unnecessary to consider whether there are non-verbal forms of communication, telepathy or anything else of the kind. It remains that language is a genetic code which enables a certain aspect of the human pattern to be made manifest. Very probably it is in connection with this that Mr. Bennett laid so much stress on the fact that only modern creative man, *homo sapiens sapiens*, who appeared ca. 40,000 B.C., had the power of speech.

To say that language itself speaks is as wrong as saying that the genetic code grows the plant. The genetic code is obviously terribly important to the actual life of the plant. It is itself a product of the evolution of the plant and of myriads of living forms, one of the staggering achievements of the biological evolution on this planet. But the genetic code is not 'the thing that does it'. It is the outer side of the powers of manifestation of the plant, and these powers are within.

Very probably as the child learns to speak, the species of plant learns how to grow and integrate itself with the activities of the biosphere. We do not easily accommodate the endless depth and variety of the real worlds of human beings and living beings, of planets, stars, and galaxies. We are incessantly reducing the complexity, freedom, and uniqueness of reality to repetitive models. The plant species has to find its way in life as the child finds its way. It is just that for the plant 'we look' at just the living organic side, and for the human 'we look' at the psychic and more than organic side.

The recent book *The Secret Life of Plants* shows the dilemma here. To begin to talk about the inner side of plants, we seem bound to use language that suggests human psychic properties. We need a more neutral frame of reference. I think that this can be found in the idea of eternity.

When our inner perceptions open up, we begin to be aware of the 'withinness' of things. Men like Goethe were able to see what they called the *idea* of the plant. Perhaps Goethe inspired Rudolf Steiner to take the possibility of super-sensible perception seriously, and Steiner himself contributed greatly to our understanding of what life is. The only drawback is that when such men talk about what they see, they often forget that the image they have has been formed in their own consciousness. That marvellous man Ogilvie, known as 'Roc' at Findhorn, described this very accurately when he spoke about his meetings with nature spirits and the god Pan. There was something there, but the image that formed acquired its shape from the accumulated experience of human imagination. It remains that Pan *is* beautiful and noble and has horns and the rest of it; I would not want to offend him.

As I have often said, our experience is such that it always involves actualization. Anything that we can be aware of must actualize in our own presence. This is done through the centers of thinking, feeling, and moving, giving the variety of modes of perception that are our natural inheritance, but hardly recognized in this barbaric age.

We can say that there is the idea of the plant, and there are the images of this idea both in our imagination and in the actual plants which grow before our eyes. 'Image' and 'idea' are names for something to do with the eternal nature. For this rose to be here its chemistry must be able to correspond to the idea of the rose: there must be an indwelling image. The image is able to speak through the language of the genes. It speaks to us in the luster and scent of petals, with an allure it also favors the insects of pollination.

This image is not a picture on a screen which we can think of as entirely outward. It is a sensitive presence. It is life. The secret life of plants is really just *life*. Life is a balance of time and eternity, and this is also the nature of all sensitivity. Test this out by being sensitive: you will see that there is always the feeling of the potential, of what might be, and the awareness of the passing. It is like a bow brought under tension, the shock of time taken up so that our attention can be directed.

For us sensitivity is alertness, the ability to notice, to discriminate, and to organize our activities. When it is right, it is regulative. It does not determine what shall be, but enables us to be 'normal'. In the plant the sensitivity is also regulative. Mr. Bennett spoke of this in connection with a special term of his, the *hyparchic regulator*. This is a rather dry term for something rather precious and wonderful. It might even be better to call this factor the *spirit* of the plant. Then it is easier to understand why I introduced the notion of the indwelling image and spoke of how this can manifest to us as a substantial presence according to our disposition.

You will possibly see now why I also talked about the 'idea' of the plant. This 'idea' is the pattern transmitted through the image, just as there is an idea of a painting which we tune into through contemplation of the canvas. The pattern is not a single thing and not a thing at all. It is not isolated so that *here* is the rose pattern, *there* the cabbage pattern, at least not in the kind of space we have discussed. There is some principle like this: pattern comes from pattern as actualization comes from actualization. Just as there is a real basis for causality, there is a real basis for the wholeness and integrality of the beings of the world.

The pattern of the rose is within the pattern of the biosphere. In great steps from order to family to phylum to genus to species, the pattern is adjusted. Goethe spoke of the relationship of patterns in terms of metamorphosis, because we see only the evidence of pattern on the outside, in spatial form. But he obviously had an intuition of the great work of the articulation of living forms out of eternity.

We almost have to speak of a 'movement in eternity'. That is why it is useful to think of eternity as a kind of time, even though it can accommodate no motion that we can picture. In ourselves we speak of the pattern of our fate, of our destiny, of the pattern of humanity, and of the great potential soul of man. How do these patterns arise? The curious thing is that they have no beginning in time. Yet it is wrong to presume that they were there for all time, from the foundation of the world. This puzzle is only resolved when you begin to see that there is not just one life, but a compresence of many in the same time, and for that we have to go much further than Ouspensky and the Tibetans. Perhaps we will get there!

So here is the rose, a particle of the life of the whole biosphere. It is wholly a rose. The spirit of it is remembering that it is a rose. If the spirits did not 'remember', there could not be the individuality of life, its wonderful variety and autonomy. How would the biochemicals know they belonged to a rose if the spirit did not inform them?

It seems we are bound to talk in this poetic way; if I put it more coldly, then you will start thinking of some mechanism and turn it into a causal process. As long as our feelings are a little disturbed by the notion of the hyparchic spirit of the rose, we can steer our way between the twin follies of mechanism and anthropomorphism. What we are after is the common element in all that exists, of which man is a very tiny part and materiality only a very small aspect.

In material systems the hyparchic spirit is very dull. Our old favorite, the simple pendulum, just repeats itself. It is through this repetition that there come about properties of the world such as the 'conservation of energy'.

We can even get rid of the existential properties of things like pendulums altogether, so that there is nothing there to swing and no masses to set up a gravitational field. Then we get to what *inertia* is like, and we can feel how very extraordinary it is. When we go further still — into the absence — we are left with properties of identity such as we use in counting objects. Being able to say one plus one plus one plus, etc., is also hyparchic.

All of you can come to see these things. Everyone has some specialized experience which can be used. What is fundamental is *how we see our own experience*. This is equally accessible to everyone. This is the touchstone of what Gurdjieff called 'objective science'. 'Subjective science' is science without 'self-remembering'.

THE INNER DOMAIN

I am going to put up a diagram of the four dimensions of our experience and arrange it in a certain way.

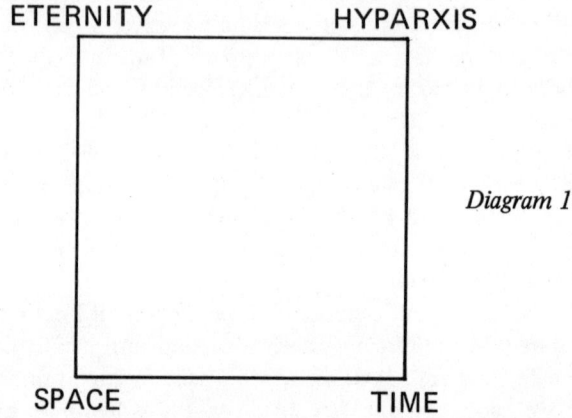

Diagram 1

This diagram contains all I am going to say. But all I am going to say is in the inner side of it, and at this moment you are puzzling over the outer side. If you see what this means, you can understand the nature of *symbols* and why we need them — because they can do things that words cannot do.

What I call our ordinary personality-experience belongs to the bottom line. It is the world we fall into when our attention is taken up with the surface of events. It is the world we can associate with determinism and causality. For the moment I am not going into any deep examination of what we mean by causality.

The lower line, space-time, represents the surface of reality that we know through our senses. In it is what we are up to, what is going on, where we are. Now what about the rest of our possible experience and existence? I am going to deal with it by looking at the connections between the dimensions taken in pairs. This is a severe limitation, because when we come to human experience, the four kinds of conditions or dimensions interpenetrate and blend; we really should take the four of them into account at once. But this is impossible for us. It is hardly possible for us to grasp three independent elements in one mental grasp. Since even the triad is difficult, we are forced to use the artifice of dealing with the four dimensions in pairs.

The first linkage I am going to look at is the one combining *time* and *eternity*. I spoke about it last night. It is the linkage that gives us the feeling of going on being ourselves, a very strange thing. What is this continuity? What is continuing?

We must realize that the feeling of continuity does not come simply from carrying traces along with us. The traces are the material of memory. It is certainly true that our minds are identified with memories as they are also with expectations, and we think of ourselves in terms of memories and anticipations rather than in terms of what is present. This mental identification is in the line of time and really it is taking us away from ourselves. The linkage with eternity brings in something quite different from the mental activity which is based on the traces in us. It is right to call it a feeling and useful to remember that Gurdjieff once said — to a group of dull Englishmen! — "What you can get hold of is that thinking is personality and feeling is essence."

Essence is not far away. Is is more profound than you think to say that feelings have to do with essence. There is the inner perception of something invariant. It is *not* the common factor of our memories and anticipations; it is what we are. It is the sameness within the different thoughts, the different moods, the different actions, meeting different people, going to different places, eating, looking, touching, and so on. If you try to pin down what this is, you cannot find it. It cannot be contained in the actual

As we are it is unusual for us to look in the direction of eternity. Mr. Bennett once wrote a book based on the idea of 'eternity blindness'.[3] It is unusual but not impossible. We can even to some degree acquire the ability to look in an eternal way. What is needed is to give up the looking-at kind of attention we are used to and tune in to a dwelling-in kind of attention. How to do this is available to us in the intelligence of the feeling center.

Our feelings are able to bring us into contact with our own pattern. That is how at times we are able to recognize when a certain life possibility corresponds to our pattern and when it is just an accidental thought of no substance. But there is a big difference between having certain feelings from our pattern and really seeing what it is. It is quite absurd to expect to be able one day to have a look at our patterns and say, "Oh, yes, now we see what we are." The absurdity is in expecting an affair of our heart to be treated like an external object we can look at and think about.

The heart is the link between eternity and time. Once you see this, you see how critical it is to be able to 'know through the heart'. Our heart is analagous to the image of the rose.

It is so rich in potential; we do not see how it is that the affairs of our lives are influenced from within us. Where does this life of ours come from, our loves, our searchings, our emptinesses, our hopes, our longings, our faith, our despair . . . ? The eternity within is not a sterile blueprint. It encompasses a million lives in its possibilities. In one moment we can die and be born again a thousand times.

Eternity is manifold and time is singular. Eternity has layer upon layer which we crudely try to describe in terms of different 'energies' or 'levels', or for human beings, 'selves'. It is the counterpart in existence of the qualitative infinity of being. It is restricted, not unconditioned. The idea of 'fate' and 'character' acknowledges this fact.

The feeling we have of being ourselves can lead us into all sorts of illusions. It gives us the illusion that we are something, but the eternal compound is only potential. We put words to the feelings and start talking about 'I'; it is not 'I'.

Now let us look at the vertical line between *hyparxis* and *time*. Here we come to something very interesting for understanding the whole theme of the seminar. Let us look at hyparxis and time confronting one another. So far we have spoken about time in terms of actualizing, selecting what will become actual and rejecting the rest. I have said that there is something to see beyond this. To be quite honest we have hardly come near in our own study and observation to see this something. It means *seeing what time does to us*.

Bennett put it in a very original way when he said that 'time is disorder entering our present moment'. We can connect this idea with the exercise I suggested to you this morning about 'having time'. What makes us *not* 'have time'? To 'have time' means to have a capacity for being in a state of order and of maintaining and even making order. There is something that erodes this capacity. Someone made observations about being subject to this erosion: she found herself trying to decide what to do and being out of phase with what was going on. This kind of experience is a direct contact with the nature of time.

In the face of time there is the capacity for creating order, or bringing order in: *hyparxis*. The arising of disorder is time and the arising of order is hyparxis. Out of this comes all sorts of phenomena.

In the plant there is *self-renewal* where a state of order is able to restore itself. There are other cycles of ascent and decline, intensity and weakness. These cycles play a big part in our lives and in the behavior of the whole world.

In the middle region of the hyparxis-time connection, we live out our lives in the ebb and flow, coming and going, waking up and falling asleep. We 'get it together' and we 'fall apart'. Through this we learn about the nature of ourselves and of the world. Hyparxis is the way of understanding and is connected with our capacity *to do*.

It is the thinking center that is most closely aligned to hyparxis-time. The reason for saying this is that the true nature of the thinking center is *to see*. In the ordinary state thinking is entirely caught in the disorder of time. People like

Krishnamurti even say that thinking *is* time. But the thinking center is also the organ of contemplation through which we are able to see what we experience to be the truth — to see through time to the creation of how things are.

Hyparxis is the way in which we *recognize* elements of our experience. You see, for this to be possible there must be the 'same in the different'! This is true for recognizing a material object which we see at different times from different points of view. It is obvious when we think of what it is to 'get to know somebody'. Here I am bringing in the other dimension of eternity to say that hyparxis can be looked at as the reconciliation of time and eternity, of actualization and pattern. But it is an independent dimension. There is nothing in eternity which allows for repetition and therefore, nothing that permits the act of recognition. Hyparxis is the dimension along which we return to the same insight. It is the direction of 'self-remembering'.

At any moment in any state, there is an ableness to 'remember oneself'. In this sense there is always 'I', but this 'I' is not great, holy, complete, or anything like that. It is simply our capacity to return to what we are in the midst of actualization. This is the very same property as recognition on any level. Through this we are able to contemplate.

You will probably be puzzling over something here. If I have connected eternity with our pattern, with what do I connect hyparxis? There is neither actualization nor potential. If you look at this, you may see that it is only through hyparxis that every moment can have its own character. It is what makes or renders experience important, life important. Life and experience are something. They belong to a world of complexity and infinitely subtle interactions within which everything is trying to be what it is and to find its own place.

On the level of human experience the selective actualization we associated with time is not a single, determined thing. Hyparxis introduces a fuzziness in actualization which allows for a connection between different 'versions' of an event in the same moment. Try to get hold of your experience in listening to this. See that your moods are occupied with just a picture of yourself as an absurd kind of thing, an object which you are bound to think of as fixed and definitely something. We are not definitely something. This is the really wonderful but necessary property of our experience and of existence as a whole. Without this we would be stuck, unable to act, to achieve, to come to be anything. You have to hold yourself before the fact that you *cannot* get hold of yourself. 'Self-remembering' is not like finding the right answer to the puzzle of one's existence. When you come to lift the lid, you will say, "It is not what I expected!"

How can there be the unexpected? How is the world so constructed that we can find ourselves in surprise, wonder, and joy? Our experience tells us that we make transitions from the more conditioned to the less conditioned state of existence. This transition cannot be in time.

For Mr. Bennett a central idea for understanding the world was *hazard*. The ordinary associations of the word are rather negative, i.e., forms of danger and ways in which we fail to reach our goal. These negative associations accurately reflect the fear in which we live. But hazard also has to do with forms of help, ways in which we come to something of lasting value in spite of our blindness and stupidity. Hazard is the unexpected that makes a difference to what we are. It is the source of both fear and hope.

Through hyparxis different possibilities are present in the same moment. We feel this particularly in what we call a 'moment of choice'. We also feel that it has to do with recognizing an opportunity, giving ourselves to the opening that appears to us. And if we can look at all objectively at our experience, we know that we can neither see nor act in the moment according to any rule or formula – if we are to 'get at it'.

But we have to be realistic. On the one hand, morality is not stupid. Embodied in what Gurdjieff called 'objective morality' is great wisdom, such as the principle that freedom cannot be got by acquisition, but requires sacrifice. This is totally different from any notion about suppressing one's desires and fighting the flesh. True sacrifice is without struggle and does not increase one's egoism as struggle can. We all know the self-inflation of martyrdom. To understand the place of morality, we would have to see into the world of energies and of eternity. I can quite honestly say that morality is part of man's accumulated knowledge of eternity and how to move in it. Movement in eternity requires a fulcrum, and this is given by *temptation*. Temptation is only a part of it. There are equivalent things in art and science, and of course, the Greek dramatists knew a great deal about it and incorporated real knowledge into the structure of their plays.

Another point is that everyone of us here is constantly trying to explain to ourselves why things happen as they do. It is very difficult not to do this. In some respects the more sensitive we are, the more we get caught into it. Everyone has their 'philosophy of life' which amounts to a rhetorical version of the explanation they fill themselves with. All of that is a cover-up of our lack of perception in the direction of hyparxis. One of the most powerful things in life is being open to the impact of unexpected events. It is this that does a great deal towards opening the inner perceptions we need. Gurdjieff in *Beelzebub's Tales* even describes this as the way in which objective reason can be awakened in us. To get beyond spurious explanations is a monumental task, and that is why Gurdjieff's achievement is overwhelming, especially in the Third Series, *Life is*

Real, Only Then When "I Am". Most people calmly chuck away morality and waffle about eternal bliss or happiness. What really matters to us is *how to live*.

Our human situation in many ways is very terrifying. Our ordinary minds are constantly seeking for answers and for explanations, which can only take us away from the concrete events which are really there. It is this that makes us unable to participate in real events and to take our place in the creating world. But to abandon the explaining, which Gurdjieff attacks as 'self-calming', is agonizing. Something has to happen in our feelings; we have to be able to bear our feelings as they are.

The ordinary images of the higher worlds in terms of eternity alone are paltry! Who cares if God is in His heaven above or if I have a spiritual self in the seventh kingdom? Where do 'I' come into it? Where am 'I' in the various worlds?

I am digressing a lot by talking about hyparxis. It is a shame that there is not a popular word for this dimension. Because it is a relatively unknown word, people imagine they do no not know what it is. Whereas, because the word 'time' is known by everybody, it is assumed to be obvious (even by St. Augustine).

How do I remember? By returning to the same point. Do we really believe that we are travelling in time on some journey to get to heaven or somewhere? Our bodies are not like the number 7 bus. The goal is not along the line of time, but the connection between hyparxis and time says something very important, exactly expressed by T.S. Eliot, "Only through time, time is conquered."

Now let us look at the other vertical line between *eternity* and *space*. I deliberately arranged the diagram so that eternity and space were on the left and hyparxis and time on the right, because these do, in a certain sense, act in parallel with each other. There's some level of correspondence between eternity and space which people like Rudolf Steiner have tried to represent through devices such as projective geometry. Space is a matter of arrangements, configurations, shapes, and so on. Eternity is a matter of wholeness, pattern, and potential. The simplest example of the space-eternity coupling is in an energy field such as magnetism. A more complex example is in a painting.

It would not be right simply to say: the pattern of eternity is reflected in the spatial arrangement. There is a tension, a distinction, between the spatial and the eternal. It has engaged human interest over the millenia and people today are groping for its secrets through such things as 'sacred geometry'. You see, what makes a geometry sacred is when it is brought into correspondence with a pattern. This is what the painter does. To a certain extent the perception of this correspondence can be formulated in words, but not very well. Gurdjieff spoke of some extraordinary examples such as the room in Persia that moves everyone to tears. There is the suggestion in the Chinese system of 'feng-shui' of a vast ancient work of sculpting the landscape to set up a correspondence with hidden patterns.

I want to call all the linkages between space and eternity *communication*. The reason for this will emerge as we go along. It is important to draw back from the esoteric fascination of sacred geometry and look again at our ordinary common experience.

I look at this room and I see it. What could be simpler? But it has puzzled every scientific mind for thousands of years. Let us take a realistic view of perception and assume we see what is there. Really the whole puzzle is to find out what this can possibly mean. There are all these things out there, your bodies, the floor, the ceiling, the windows, the pillars, and so on. How on earth do they get *in here*? We just take it for granted. But if we happen to be neuro-psychologists or such, we try to track down the journeys of impulses into our brains and see how they all get put together into a picture. We stick needles in here and there, cut nerves, analyze the chemistry of the retina, chop out bits of brain, put prisms in front of the eyes, administer drugs, and all sorts of cunning things. By the time we have chased all the impulses round we have convinced ourselves that they are a chaos of fragments and that the brain must be a super computer able to build an integrated world model out of them. Then comes the crunch of understanding how even a computer-generated model actually becomes an *experience*. We come to the same basic connection of space and eternity when considering the brain and the mind. The brain corresponds to space, the outer, and the mind to eternity, the inner. You cannot derive one from the other. They are not absolutes either: brain, entirely space, and mind, entirely eternity. The popular phrase 'inner space' is an intuition of this relativity of mind inherent in the connection between space and eternity.

The brain itself has obviously centers of sensitivity with special properties. It is a highly evolved linkage of space and eternity. Our whole body with its various organs is a structure that has a pattern in the inner side.

If I had to choose another word than communication for the left hand side of the quaternary, it would be *structure*. The structure of a building, a tree, a poem, a society is that which enables there to be a correspondence and a communication between different levels. The structure of the brain allows ideas to come to manifestation in external form. The painter produces a structure which enables us to enter into an idea. We may think of structure entirely in spatial terms, only if we reject our feelings of there being different levels.

Two years ago when I was here at Claymont, we had the theme of 'home' for one week. I found it a very interesting theme. Home is definitely a place, but what makes it a home is in eternity, in its connection with eternal values. There is a spirit of home. A home is the place of a family, with all that it means in human life. So we can see that very simple things which have a great significance in our lives have to do with the linkage between space and eternity.

Those who work in theatre will be able to understand how a space can be more than an outer relationship of things. The actors have to dwell in a space different from the ordinary one, which is flat in comparison, where only material energies are taken into account as in physics and technology. The stage is sometimes described as the landscape of a dream. Of course, most theatrical designers, producers, and writers are just concerned with surface titillation and have no understanding of the eternity of space. Rudolf Steiner's book *Speech and Drama* is very remarkable in unveiling some of the secrets of the theatrical space.

We can also look at living things. Many biologists at the beginning of this century tried to describe an intuition of a formative power in the spatial unfolding of the embryo; that is, how the cells divide, and then one bit is destined to become a heart, another an eye, and so on. It is amazing to look at it even in pictures. How is it that different places in the emergent embryo assume their different destinies?

Then there is the whole landscape of the earth: sea, rivers, mountains, trees, each with its special feeling. It is not a subjective projection, the feeling of the romantic; it is perception of eternity through space. And this is what we enter when we use a symbol or spatial arrangement to enlarge our vision.

The world of symbols is not entirely a world of human artifacts which have gathered strong associations. In divination and astrology we use the spatial arrangements of nature to enable us to feel the pattern of events. The heap of yarrow stalks, the arrangement of the heavens, the entrails of a sheep, or the clouds in the sky are all symbols of the pattern of the moment. What we find through divination is an image of the pattern. Because there are many levels involved, the reading depends on the sensitivity of the reader and his or her depth of perception.

I have not attempted to go much further than the plain fact of communication inherent in the linkage of space and eternity. But I will add these few points. The ancient philosophers such as Aristotle took it for granted that there was a meaning to the phrase "Everything seeks its own place," and they understood that this is the source of all motion. In Gurdjieff's language it is the 'law of falling'. It is a simple and extraordinary idea. Why am I here in this building with these people? Is there something in my pattern which makes me belong here? Do people really 'belong together'? Sometimes when I 'wake up' I feel this kind of question very much. I am often surprised to see where I am. But in this surprise there is often a feeling of rightness, that I have fallen to this particular concentration because it corresponds to something in my inner world.

It is almost to be expected that experiences of journeys and transitions into other worlds are related to a different sense of space. I have seen this when I have fainted and also in very special experiences of being taken out of ordinary space into another kind in order to be able to see something. Reports from the dead are full of this kind of thing. Our negative, subjective life inverts the truth of things. What is near to us becomes very important and what is far from us unimportant. When a transition is made into the natural, positive world, (world 24 in the Gurdjieff-Bennett language), we no longer feel ourselves to be the center of the universe. Being at the center in a unique place is the ego-feeling of the personality, and this makes our lives individually and collectively quite mad. When you begin to understand that there are different laws governing the different worlds, you will see that the character of space must change according to the world we are in. This is a reflection of the convergence or divergence of space and eternity.

The structure of the world is such that the form of everything reveals something of its pattern. It is this that makes science possible. We cannot see into eternity, but we can feel how things are, by their visible structure and by models we create in our minds. Rutherford was able to make tremendous strides in atomic physics by imagining the atom to be a miniature solar system with the electrons revolving around the nucleus. Like all such models it is eventually superseded by a more sophisticated one, but this does not invalidate the intuition. Nearly all physics is a matter of supposition about the 'inner space' of things. If it is taken literally, it is nonsense. In particle physics we are reaching dimensions where any notion of extension begins to break down, and so it is barely possible even to talk about different bits in different places.

But we must move on. There is the linkage of *hyparxis* and *space* which we have discussed before. These are the inner and outer faces of being here, of presence. The inner side is not space-extended, nor does it give rise to the different qualities of different directions which come from eternity.

Why does presence have to be somewhere? We have an idea here that presence is not occupancy of space; space is the condition for presence to manifest. If you remember our discussion in the second talk, you will see that space is essentially the absence that makes presence possible. Space is the property of excluding other things. Hyparxis is the property of including oneself.

Space, so to say, by itself is just emptiness. But it is never experienced by itself. The hyparchic component always gives a special power to *here*. It also gives the possibility of 'coupling' so that there can be a material presence. This happens in what is called electron-sharing by which atoms form larger wholes called molecules. Certain electrons are 'here' for more than one atom. It may be important in sex, but on a level we do not experience directly.[4] In the wholeness of our bodies, it is a certainty.

We are in the habit of naming things and then, because of the names we have applied, thinking of things as always separate and having to be connected from the outside. When we talk about a symbiotic relationship in nature, it seems very special and strange that there should be such cooperation. But if we look at this as a phenomenon of being in the same place, we see it in a new light. Hyparxis is the condition of *sharing*.

Finally the top line, *eternity-hyparxis*. As we had causality on the bottom line, we have something quite different from causality at the top. What could it possibly be? To get at this I am going to talk a little more about the middle area between the bottom and the top. In this area we have the linkages that we have called communication, presence, remembering, and continuity. Here is the world of such things as intention, attention, being in contact, awareness, discrimination, seeing, and so on. When we enter into the experience of the middle realm we have perceptions which belong in the world within the world of bodies and things. This world is called the *spirit world*, and we enter it through sensitivity. Later on John is going to talk about the various energies and describe the nature of 'sensitive energy'. There is another energy to take into account which is described as 'conscious'. Through this energy we are connected with the world beyond the upper line.

Once we have got out of the shape given to experience by actualization in space, then we enter into what is usually for us a fuzzy region. We do not have developed perceptions belonging to life and the spirit world, and so we ourselves are fuzzy there. We try to develop in ourselves attention, presence, etc. The middle region needs to be articulated for us in our experience. Some people look to spirit guides, others to various inner disciplines. The point often missed is that we can only work with the material of our own inner world, and we have to find our way through that. Anything that keeps us thinking it is like another version of space-time is bound to hold us back. In practice this means that we have to be very careful with the images that come to us of the inner world.

The articulation of the middle region where space, time, eternity, and hyparxis begin to converge is the condition for there to be purpose in our lives. Otherwise, there is just causality and muddle. You can, if you like, associate purpose with the top line, as long as you understand that it is connected with a universal property of all existence. There is nothing without purpose. In the material world purpose is divorced from causality, because there is no inner experience. In life they begin to meet. In men they can begin to interpenetrate, and this makes what we call *decision* possible.

We are again bordering on vast subjects. I have to bring in here something about the material world. This world is very limited, largely causal, subject to the disordering of time, but it is not and cannot be entirely divorced from the whole of existence. This means that it is not entirely, absolutely just a mechanism which has no rhyme or reason. The purposefulness and wholeness of existence is manifest in the material world. We say in our human world that the machines we have are instruments for some purpose. This does not alter their mechanical character, but it does mean that we cannot understand them without the context of purpose. The word 'context' here is very vague.

People like Aristotle and Rudolf Steiner have had an intuition into this question. They say that precious stones and crystals 'grow' from the influence of the stars. Steiner's description has very much to do with seeing into eternity. He is not talking about rays coming out of the sky which do things, but of the structure of existence in which there is a connection with a pattern. In other words the linkage of eternity to space.

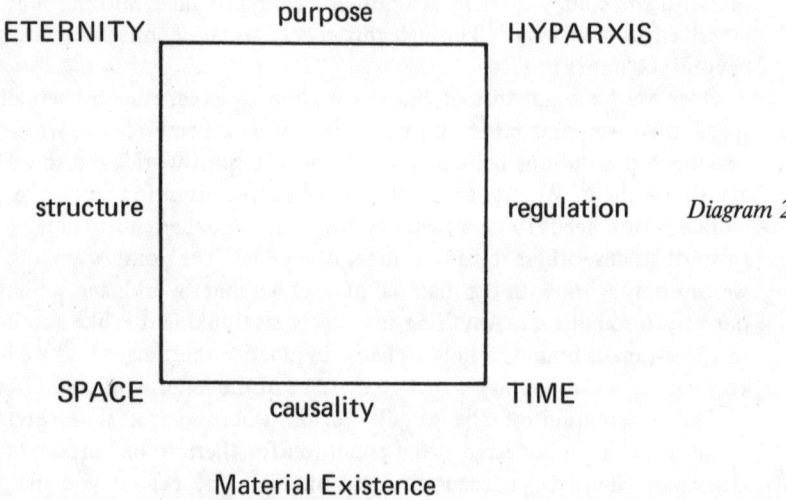

Diagram 2

If I made a diagram like this, I mean to draw attention to the emptiness of the middle region. It is very tenuous in there, insubstantial. Material things have little being.

Time Out of Time 73

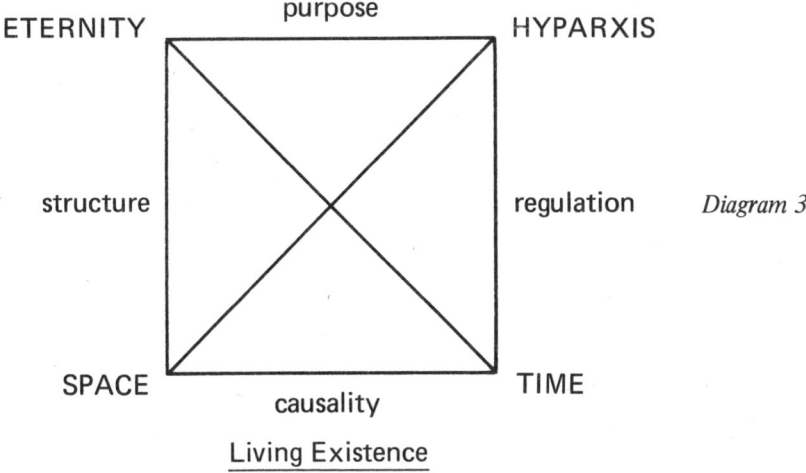

Diagram 3

Living Existence

In a living existence there is some correspondence between the four conditions. It has its *own image*. This image is what is in the middle region.

The next step must turn the whole thing inside out, and we have cosmic existence. We have no idea what this can mean, but man is between the cosmic and the living in his nature.

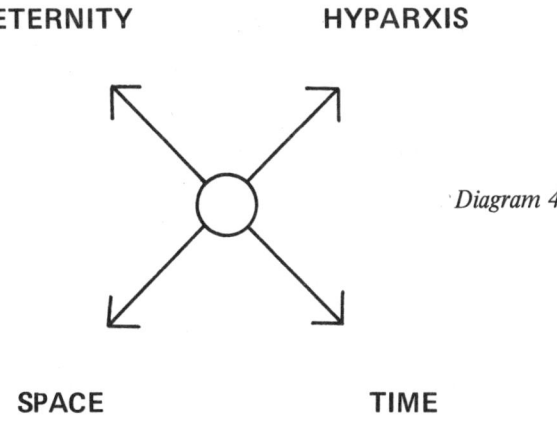

Diagram 4

Cosmic Existence

Between eternity and hyparxis nothing is happening, and we can even say that there is nothing. What this strictly means is nothing is happening — there is not time, there is not space, nothing is there. This is the region in which 'time shall be no longer'. Maybe this is the *Kingdom of Heaven* which has the peculiar character of being within us all, but yet to be realized on this earth.

What is the character of this linkage of eternity and hyparxis? I have spoken a little about purpose. This does not mean having an idea today about doing something tomorrow, or having a design here which is going to be executed there. It is what we come to when we say, "This is to be done because it is to be done." It is *creative*.

I don't think we realize how conditioned we are in the way we look at events. Our world experience is like this. On the one hand, anything that happens is because of something that has happened. This is not only the world of natural science, you must understand, it is also the world of our enslaved emotions. When we 'blame someone', what we are doing is believing that our own negative state is *caused* by what they have done. Time and again we condemn ourselves to the terrible world in which everything comes out of the past. Freedom is quite incompatible with this attitude. All the basic 'work psychology' is directed toward awakening the intelligence in our feeling center so that it can see the lie of our mechanical life. Justifying, blaming, negative emotions, and all of that is slavery to the line of causality.

Now, on the other hand, there is the kind of 'because' which we feel in terms of what we *want*. I am acting like this because I want so and so. There is an image in me of the future that I want. Anything that gets in the way is evil, an enemy. All of us are living on the childish level of feeling. To have really strong, coherent feelings is so precious! It goes beyond *happiness*. In the customary state of wanting all we do is condemn ourselves to causality. Because of this image of what we want, we try to make causes to make it happen. It is composing poetry by computer. Stupidity!

We have this word 'because'. In our experience it is a mixture of past and future. Maybe there is something *within* our feelings and images that is drawing us on, as the rose is drawn to produce a flower in due season. Maybe man and woman are drawn together in spite of themselves to produce a means for a child to be born. But what is the world of the child or of the beauty of the rose? These are not artifacts or fabrications of the material world. The child and the rose are infinitely precious realities longing to enter into the visible world. They are part of the love and compassion that aches to give itself to the 'poor in spirit'. Being aches to give itself to existence, to find a way to bring some substance to the 'apartness' of the separated, disordered, world of space and time.

Every man and woman of heart has striven in their lives, in their thoughts, in their words, in their deeds, and in their dreams to give themselves to the significance of the world 'from which birth originates'. Of course, it is the angelic realm in the old language, the realm of the Annunaki. Now in this time we begin to learn that the angels and the men and the women and the animals and the plants, though different, need each other to play the game of existence, to find delight in each other.

If we look at one rose or one child and ask about the 'because' of it, the whole thing is clear. Bennett used the word 'fore-ordainment'. You have to take the word into your heart, or abandon it and all words. Look at the one child sleeping in its cot, playing in the garden, beginning to speak. Why do we want then the miracles which amount to conjuring tricks? I use words like eternity and hyparxis, and you think them to be clever ideas which make your heads tense. I wish I could cut out my tongue when I think about that. These children, these flowers, are evidence of the truth of existence which is beyond causality. They teach us directly about the world, which is not because of something else, but because of itself. Why do you live? Why is the miracle of spirit and flesh walking about on this planet? These are miracles according to law. They teach us that the worlds beyond any kind of existence must be so strong and overwhelming that we could not bear to be their witness while in the flesh.

I must leave this topic in your hearts. There is the true nature of the stars and how this world is made. It is not at the other end of telescopes. But thank God for telescopes and computers! All these wonderful instruments of detection and measurement can help us to awaken our hearts. Our images of holiness and meditation make us blind to the significance and wonder of the world. Until we can learn to see the nature of the leaf, of the flower, of the rabbit, of the bird, of the child, of the feelings, we cannot come home to this earth. What are we going to be doing here? Do we want to go on living in a dream of mind and causality?

If we neglect the information given to us by science, we are stupid animals. If we neglect the delight of the heart, we are worse.

Eternity-hyparxis is the symbol of the purpose of existence. It is saying that this existence is created and renewed in every moment. It is saying that we can look at our own experience and all that others teach us and come to see this for ourselves.

It is no good looking at this as a nice idea, because it is a nice idea to believe in. Belief is nowhere. Interesting states are nowhere. There is the serious business of building the earth even as God has built it. We do not know God. But if we have in our hearts the sense of the value of this earth, then God can be born in us. God is what we see that is beyond belief.[6]

A Note on Space

The three time-like linkages with space give the three 'feelings' of being somewhere. For a human being time is emotion; whereas, for a thing, time is motion. There are, therefore, three kinds of motion in parallel with the three kinds of feeling. A cosmic reality is the same whether experienced mechanically, chemically, or consciously.

Space-time is the linkage which can be expressed as "I am here because I am not anywhere else." It is the feeling of accidental place, of drifting under constraint. There is no *inherent* direction in the situation. It corresponds to 'inertial motion' as defined by Isaac Newton, motion continuing in its way until acted on by an external force.

Space-eternity is, as we have said before, the 'law of falling'. It is this linkage that gives one direction a significance above all other directions. The feeling here is of moving towards one's place, nostalgia, coming home, being gathered into the bosom of the Fathers, going to meet one's woman, looking towards the rising of the sun as at Stonehenge, a moment of noticing something that is *there* independent of us. In the world of things this linkage is simple 'acceleration' and corresponds to the action of force-fields.

The third linkage space-hyparxis is, from the side of space, being in one's own place. It is the space within the home, within the embrace. In the person, it is *attention*. In things, it is the recurrence of the same place, sometimes described as 'rotation'. Hence, this feeling of entering into one's own place is often associated with the vortex and spinning. It is how different qualities of energy can enter the same location, and different qualities of events can involve the 'very same' actors and scenery.

'Higher Space' in ordinary language is simply eternity. The subtleties of space itself are more interesting. The qualities of our ordinary experience are so immensely rich with information about the dynamics of the dimension of *all existence* that we are drowned in them. What can we ourselves win out of this nexus that we call life and, even stupidly, call 'our lives'? What will we bring to harvest out of our extraordinary sojourn 'on earth'?

We cannot bring mercy back to God who is All-Merciful. We cannot even bring intelligence, because He has angels with intelligent bodies. What we can bring is the fruit of being here, our realization of what is possible in practice for a human being. You see, no one knows in advance what is possible.

Dreams

This morning I asked you to record as soon as you awoke any dreams that you had last night. Can we speak about this?

Q. From the time the bell rang and I woke up, I was very disturbed because I did not remember any of my dreams, and I normally have a fairly good recall. I don't know whether I woke up in fits and starts from then till breakfast or whether this was in a dream. But I remember being very disturbed for the next period of time desperately trying to recall my dreams. One dream took place here in Claymont. I was with a group of people in a room somewhat like the lounge. I was standing and waiting, and each of us would take a turn to lie down on a couch at which time we would go into a death-like slumber; all this while some leader exorcised something located in each of our chests and put something back in its place. Then we could rise from this kind of death, and the thing that we had to be able to do was to give up our fear. That was all I can remember.

A.G.E.B. You mentioned the house and said it was like Claymont. One has dreams like that about places that one knows. When you woke up could you, so to speak, enter into that place? How did you see that place, did you see it as *somewhere*?

Q. Can you rephrase the question before I answer?

A.G.E.B. All right. You talked about being at a place. One can remember something like this as a record that one went somewhere. You have it as a kind of mental note. Were you able when you awoke to get the feel of being at that place and what it was like? Was it really somewhere for you, even when you were awake?

Q. Yes it was. I remembered that I had color in my dream. There were some other dreams that I only could remember pieces of, but I do remember a dress that was green. I remember that it was a lovely, lovely color green. But that was another dream that I had.

Q. I had the same sensation of waking up and being disturbed, because I lost contact with the dream. I didn't have contact with the dream. When I tried to go back, there was a key something that gave me contact with the dream.

A.G.E.B. A key something?

Q. A key something: gears, car gears. When I remembered car gears the whole dream started to come back, and at this time this feeling of the dream was more real to me than how it was not real in the dream. The specific thing that I remembered was that I'd taken my car to be worked on, and the man who worked on it mentioned incidentally that I had three or four extra gears with which I could drive my car. I was incredibly frustrated, because I had been driving my car all this time and not knowing that I had extra gears to work with. The next part of the dream I was in a room and the sensation I had was that I'd gotten drunk and passed out, but when I woke up, a snow drift had piled up into the room. I was lying on the top of the snow drift, and a man was also there. He started to tell me a story that one time he had been to a strange land. In this strange land that he spoke of in the dream, I made contact with another dream that I had had. It was the same strange place, and he told me that he had tried to dig deeper and deeper into the snow, and when he finally got to the bottom, he found buried bodies. When I woke up out of my sleep in the snow drift, or even sooner, I asked the man, "Do I remember right? Are you the one who told me the story?" And he said, "Yes, I am."

A.G.E.B. We're not concerned with interpreting the dreams. The dream comes to you for yourself as part of yourself. But what we are after is this: when you wake up and you try to remember the dream, how do you enter again into the dream? How do you make contact with it?

This morning I woke up and found I had no contact at all with my dreams; I didn't even know if I'd dreamt or not. But then something came. When I look back on it, it's very difficult to say whether I was walking around the room remembering the dream or if I was entering the dream, dreaming again. It was that kind of feeling. How I got there I don't know. At the moment of awakening there was nothing at all. Then I contacted it again.

Q. I remember that when I woke up I was very disappointed. Usually I do remember my dreams, but I was real disappointed that I didn't remember this dream. I remember thinking that, "Oh, but I didn't dream anything." Then I had an urgency about making a contact, but this urgency to make a contact didn't seem to be itself coming from the dream.

A.G.E.B. One of the things to look at is this very definite sense of being at a place. You have it in a double way: here is a place and there is some knowledge, some idea coming to you about a special place as well, because you have 'caught on' to something. When I finally did remember the place in which I'd been, I found it very difficult to get out of it. Even now when I've begun to talk about it, it's as if I'm half there and half here. I couldn't say my presence is totally here; it is also in this other place.

In our language we have to speak in terms of going to a place — as if it were separated from the place we are in — and what happened in a dream as taking place in the past. All the depth of our inner life has got to be expressed as if it were part of a linear process in ordinary time. Truly, our form of speech is a 'procrustean bed': what is too long is cut down to size and what is too short is stretched to fit. With our minds, therefore, we try to live always along time and space; whereas, the sources of life within us do not work like that at all. The problem is that the mind has to be delicately educated so that it would no longer impress its own restrictions on all our experiences. If we try to throw out the mind or thinking altogether, we get caught up into *hal* or states and are unable to integrate them with our daily lives. That is, in part, why the Sufis say we need the combination of state, *hal*, with knowledge, *ilm*.

The dream is past only when we have lost contact with it. When we have some contact, it is no longer like that, but seems to exist in a sort of *limbo* — perhaps waiting to find its meaning. It is almost like a thought; and for quite a lot of people their dreams fulfill the role of thinking about themselves which others can perform in a 'waking state'. It is even possible to say that dreams *are* thinking in that we are drawn into possibilities to do with our entanglements in space and time. In waking life our 'thinking' is often as ineffective as our dreams. We do not notice this. We do not see what an immense amount of energy goes into thinking and imagination which bears no fruit at all and perpetuates itself to no purpose.

Our thinking produces nothing of significance in the external world and nothing of significance in the inner world. The situation is truly absurd. Because every now and then some result is obtained and all the wastage is swept under the carpet and forgotten. Or, we invent the idea of 'creative thinking' as something special when it is really *normal* for a man. People fail to see the terrible uselessness of our ordinary thinking which is constantly preoccupied with 'ourselves'. And what is that? This 'ourselves' is nothing but the feeling attached to our personalities and probably is nothing but an apparatus to deal with life in space and time.

Just now I used the word 'limbo' with an idea in mind. If we can bring ourselves to entertain the notion that we *are* really in our dreams as well as in our 'waking state', how much or little doesn't matter, then we have direct evidence of parallel states in us, or of living in different worlds. The dreams are not before or after, they are partially rotated out of space and time, though we remain attached to external forms in them. To put it bluntly, our dreams have all the characteristics of what we think of as the 'life hereafter', the 'next life', and 'life after death'.

One of the objectives of our work is to establish normal thinking and to gain a perspective on ourselves that is beyond dreaming. There are at least two regions of work: one is in our contact with the material world and our ability to be 'active' and not 'passive' towards its working, and the other is in our contact with ourselves and our ability to go from 'dreaming ourselves' to the realm in which *conscience* can enter our experience. Conscience is the enemy of dreams. But while we remain dreaming, at least we can try to *understand* what dreams *are*.

Would anybody else like to say something? It's just exploratory; we're not concerned with interpreting the dreams, these have their own way.

Q. I remember that I had some dreams. When I woke up, I looked at my watch; it was forty-five minutes before the bell was to ring, so I decided that I wouldn't write them down, I'd just go back to sleep. I woke up about three times before the bell rang. I also had a dream when I decided it was time to get up, but it was very vague, and I remember just two little fragments.

A.G.E.B. One of the reasons I suggested this exploration, this experiment, was that we all have this transition from being asleep in our beds to being able to walk around and do things in the ordinary sense which we call the 'waking state'. This is material available to all of us. What do we notice about this transition? Is there something which can be communicated across the barrier of awakening and sleeping? In going to sleep I know some communication is possible. I was once interested in this; I tried the experiment of dozing and then coming to and writing it down. Once I got the revelation: "This regatta postage stamp welcomes Sibelius." It's very good, marvelous; it is perhaps better than William James's "A smell of ether pervades."

Just for a moment I will be somewhat technical. We begin to see that dreams *can* give us some insights into our situation, but they tend to be obscure, indirect, and paradoxical. Dreams do not provide the wherewithal to produce effective change in us. Something else has to operate.

I would say that dreams are a manifestation of a movement in eternity, but they are not a movement in hyparxis. Hence, they can enrich our communication with different levels in ourselves, but they cannot give us the power *to do*. It is different when we have very deep experiences which transcend altogether the dimension of waking and dreaming, because we pass totally into another *kind* of consciousness and not merely another version or state of our ordinary consciousness. In such a deeper experience there can be an hyparchic change, and we are able to do things we could not do before — at least for a time.

What happens in a dream is like having the same life but seen from a different perspective. To some extent we can reason and feel about what is going on, but there is a far more intimate connection between what we reason and feel and the events that take place than appear to be the case in waking states. This is a tremendous clue to the nature of displacements in eternity: you do not get anything different, but 'the same seen differently'. A shift in eternity probably has to be discontinuous. An in-between state would appear to be quite unstable. Or, we could say, the in-betweens of levels in eternity would correspond to the real irrational, it may even be the place through which creative action can enter.

Already we see that there is something interesting and significant in the question of how we integrate waking and dreaming and pass from one to the other. As soon as we *set ourselves* to do something about the transition from one to the other, or to remember, the scene shifts and what happens is different. I want to suggest that this can help us in our lives when we realize that while 'awake', we are still immersed in dreams.

Q. I almost never remember my dreams. The funny thing was yesterday morning I woke up remembering my dreams very vividly. I thought, "Oh, how interesting; I never remember my dreams. I wonder why?" And later on in the evening you mentioned remembering our dreams the next morning. Of course, this morning I didn't remember a thing.

Q. I had a similar experience in that I didn't know that you had asked people to recall their dreams, but lately they've been washed away in getting up three times a night with the kids or something like that. I had one dream just as the morning broke. I was really surprised that I had such a clear and vivid dream. It was about this woman that I lived with when I was going to college, and whose life parallels mine in an amazing number of ways. We'd have the same ideas at the same time and read the same books. She recently wrote to me and said that she'd become involved in this work. I had mostly strong visual images of her. One image of her is with an uncharacteristic bouffant hairdo, something that she'd never wear, some very straight-looking clothing, and she is there with her husband, and they are standing in the doorway. I had the sense that I was in their home and I had been invited there, but I'm not welcome at all. I really shouldn't be there. It was somehow connected with the work too. Somehow their teacher didn't want me to be there. I can't remember any details about the plot, just this image of them standing there trying to smile, looking so different from the way they usually looked, and their disapproval of wishing that I weren't there.

A.G.E.B. There's nothing to say at this moment, except as I said before, there are two kinds of states, when we're awake and we're occupied with *activity*, and when we're asleep and we're occupied with *images*. We can also see there's some kind of barrier between the two states. We have a certain degree of freedom to pass from one into the other. Whenever anyone tries to make this transition intentionally, it's always interesting, because it must tell us something, give some clues about what it means to make a transition from our ordinary state into a clearer state. One thing which is important for me is this thing about place. You have an image of somebody or a place where an action takes place, and you begin to get the taste that an image and a place *are the same* in the world we contact in dreaming; whereas, ordinarily we take an image to be some kind of subjective response to our chemistry or to the environment around us or to a memory. It only happens, so to speak, in our heads. There is some other kind of substantial image in which we can exist. It has properties very close to those we know of space and time, but in some sense it is different. I can say no more than that, because we know we can project all kinds of fantastical interpretations on our dreams. There is some problem of communication between the two states. If one goes anywhere in a dream, it is into an image. But this image has, and sometimes very strongly, the sense of a place much as a place we can be in when awake. This is also a clue to understanding the nature of space and time, not as something out there in which our bodies are, but arising out of dwelling in an image. This gives you a different perspective on space and time and events.

It is particularly interesting for understanding historical events. Events are not just what happened; this is a common fallacy of fact-hungry historians. Events are also *what people dreamt*. We ourselves are dreaming this seminar, and the dreams give shape to the feelings we are in.

I am trying to avoid the two extremes: one in which we assume that dreams are only a subjective 'mish mash', and the other in which they are taken uncritically. It is probably true that a lot of our dreaming comes out of the automatic regulation of our psychic energies, which requires a periodic discharge or using up of potential which we are not able to do during the day because we don't live intentionally enough. Without this discharge we would become more and more cluttered and confused with the residue of succeeding days of experience. This has been partially demonstrated by experiments in dream deprivation and by computer simulations. There are deeper things to do with the layers of anxiety and negative attitudes which produce internal disorder. This is intimately connected with very primitive needs to make sense of our experience, to feel all right, which in the waking state manifests as justifying, for example. There is always a residual anxiety and doubt, because we fail to confront what is actually there in us. Dreams help to reconcile conflicts, they warn and show us different ways out, and they compensate for our lack of wholeness. All this was explored by the psychoanalysts, and their work should not be sneered at.

But there is a side of dreaming which is not merely the residue of interaction with the world and the working out of disorders. Dreams are quite substantial. They arise when the ordinary flow of actualization is suspended. Gurdjieff said that in sleep the centers are, so to say, uncoupled and work in isolation to recharge their energies. Dreams arise when there is a partial leakage, so that one has a partial actualization that gives an in-between kind of experience. With the partial suspension of actualization, other kinds of time are more prominent. So there is still a kind of space and time, but it has a *different order* to it. Then we have a kind of experience which gives us a taste of the 'laws of the inner world', laws which do not entail actualization as we ordinarily know it: succession in single-valued time and separateness and exclusion in space.

The inner world is also known as the *spirit world, the ālam-i-arvāh*. An historical event is also an event in the world of spirits. When there is a 'strong dream', the event has the power of an organizing image which is able to shape the experience of men and women. It is not nothing. And because the spirit world is not subject to the laws of the world of bodies, it allows for transformations to take place that are not causal – to do with the coherence and pattern of the present moment and the direction of the future.

J.W. When I was studying judo very hard and deeply, I read in one of the books that the judo master said that you couldn't be a good fighter unless you won in your dreams. I was always getting beaten in my dreams, and I remember very clearly the first time I won in my dreams. From then on the dreams became much more malleable, and if I didn't like a dream I could run it back to a convenient place and start again. One could actually work directly on them.

A.G.E.B. Now that you've raised this point, I'd like to add that what one does to make a dream malleable is done through one's creative imagination. What you said reminded me of the time when I was trying to learn some complicated Morris dances. The way I learned them was to imagine myself doing it. When it worked in my imagination, it was like it was happening and I was doing the dance. Then I was quite confident that I could actually do it physically. I went out and did it physically, and it was easy. It's often the same with the movements: when they really become alive and they move in your mind, then you have them.

J.W. This was found in skill training in athletics and sporting activities, particularly in golf where you've got to perfect the swing, what they call the 'all important swing'. Professionals who had to travel a lot couldn't actually practice. If they used the power of active imagination, it was almost as good as physically practicing, and sometimes better, because when you practice physically, unless you have somebody watching you, you tend to develop bad habits, not good habits. But when you're using your active imagination, you tend to be concentrating on the perfect movement.

Q. Can I ask a question? You seem to be touching on the idea that a dream is an image that you can enter into, and what we're living in now is an image that we also enter into.

A.G.E.B. That was suggested, I didn't say it.

Q. You didn't want to go further?

A.G.E.B. I want to say this about your remark: they are not the same. If you really accomplish something in this way, it is quite different from daydreaming; thinking about something or picturing it doesn't work at all, it's just flat. There is another kind of imagination which does it, but which we get somehow or other to a certain degree in dreaming and in some strange way for free. All the depth to it is not what we find in the same way in our waking state where it's more of a flat experience. Let me illustrate this a bit by the exercise we did of seeing the third dimension. Now for me, ordinarily, my perception is very two-dimensional, flat, and 'cardboardy'. You exercise the third dimension, and the depth somehow or other *brings you to it*, brings you into the world and you have that feeling. Feelings get evoked in you, and this is akin to what happens in a powerful dream where you come into a place. But you notice that one also gets different feelings about time and space when it's like that in this waking state. Really the ordinary flat world is the world in which *we think about* space and time, and it corresponds to a more conditioned state. Something is set free in the dreams which ordinarily we don't know how to handle. We do certain exercises intentionally which help to attune us to this less conditioned state while we're walking around.

Q. Mr. Bennett said that this is a dream world in which we live. Is it a dream world that has certain different kinds of properties than the dreams that you've been describing? One thing that comes to me is that it all comes back pretty much the same: if I go to sleep in Claymont, I wake up in Claymont.

A.G.E.B. This is a difficult question. What I see about this is what John put in a practical way when he talked about a malleability. When some kind of intention is brought into the dream, it's different, but the substance of it is the same. A crude analogy of this is giving everybody a box of paints. Very few people can paint beautiful pictures. What is the difference? Is it different somehow or other when something we call intention is brought into this realm? What is this realm?

There is movement for all of us in this realm. The majority only feel it in their dreams. But the common and utterly mistaken view is that there is an 'I' which dreams or does not dream. In reality there is a kind of broken up, fragmented movement which we are pleased to call 'my inner life'. The inner realm is the same for sleeping man or enlightened man. We can say that all organized dreams are souls. Souls are made out of the same substance that makes dreams possible.

I do not wish to belittle the insights that are given us by people such as Jungian psychologists or mediums. There is a very complex action in the inner space. Our dreams are one way in which we come to terms with it. Mediumistic communications are more efficient forms of dreaming. But what we are called upon to accomplish, in our heart, in our conscience, is to wake up from dreaming altogether. After all, what is dreaming? It is translating the substance and potential of the inner world into a similitude of the outer world. This we can persist in doing even when we die. *The Tibetan Book of the Dead* is an accurate commentary on this. It portrays people under the spell of images that they themselves create. Doesn't this sound familiar? Isn't this a description of how we are in this life and why we never accomplish anything?

It seems easy to accept that we are under the influence of images in our own minds, but these minds are not our own. What is 'mine' in them is the contamination, the subjectivity. This kind of subjectivity can be precisely defined in terms of our attachment to what we know; that is, dependence on our instruments of sense and our immersion in repetition, in the future that is like the past. We need to be purged of reflecting the inner world into the outer. Without this, we cannot be free.

There's already in us a working in the inner realm. The problem is that it is incoherent and blind, *because it cannot communicate with the personality which works in the outer world.* It is not another personality, as in popular images of schizophrenia; it is a working.

What 'we' are is the composite between personality and the inner working. As long as these are not integrated, we are not much at all. How are they integrated? In part by seeing, in part by doing.

Then dreams give way to the active meditation in the midst of life: the ability to see what is needed without recourse to techniques, then it is direct. Experience is simply a medium of exchange. This is the domain of will, of 'I', when reality is not identified with existence.

Q. Once I had a dream that I was in a school, and I was working on a puzzle. There were esoteric symbols which I worked with and did something. I went out of that dream, and later I said, "I did it. I saw something in this dream, I had a wonderful thing happen and what is it?" And a person said, "No, no, it's not right for you to remember that. This contradicts the reality that you are ordinarily in." Now that I'm thinking about it, I see an image of understanding. I'm plagued with this desire to . . . I know that when I had the dream I understood, and I never in an ordinary state ever understand like that. The fact that I'm questioning even in this state that I'm in now, shows I don't understand; whereas, in the dream I remember I didn't question – I understood. Do you know what I mean?

A.G.E.B. Yes, it is spontaneous.

Q. It really gave me a very strong sense of what understanding is.

J.W. You never had that other than in a dream?

Q. In a way, yes, I suppose I've had what understanding is, but there's something always added afterwards. What I'm trying to say is that in the dream there was no need to understand what I understood; whereas, now it seems that I always try to understand understanding, somehow with the rational mind.

A.G.E.B. I just want to say this is a marvelous description of going from world twenty-four to forty-eight. Trying to understand your understanding is adding on another twenty-four laws.

J.W. ... like when you try hard to relax.

A.G.E.B. You know it's still there, but you've got this additional burden that you described. It's a remarkable description. In that state you're in before, it is direct. There is a problem of integration between the various parts of ourselves and the right balance in ourselves. This is the whole problem. *Where are we?* I remember a time when I had a couple of dreams, one of which was a dream about a triad of all things, about the affirmative force in the triad, which really taught me something. I remembered it clearly afterwards, and it greatly influenced me. My favorite one was when I was reading *All and Everything* in a dream. I was reading a passage on objective science, and in the dream I was exclaiming, "There really is objective science, here it is." Then I saw something to do with Plato and Aristotle. Of course, when I woke up, I had no idea what I had read on the page and was very frustrated. But what I've found is that this is for me a source: if I don't mess about with it, it's there, and this does something for me. If I'm in this other state and I'm not in contact with it, that is all right, because *it is still there;* it hasn't gone away.

Q. Is it true that if all your energies are really put into working on yourself, you dream less?

A.G.E.B. Here's the expert on energies. What happens when you put all your energies into working on yourself, John? Tell me.

J.W. You die. You're all laughing, but ... what's so funny?

PART TWO

THE ORDER BEYOND TIME

A Chance Moment in Time

Time and Energies

Ask yourselves: what is an energy? Are there different kinds or types of energy?

We talk a lot about energies and hardly ever pause to see what we mean. We say something about energy in the phrase, "I can't do that," and in the phrase, "I have too much energy."

In scientific books energy is described as the power to do work, but this does not tell us enough. What else do we need to know? We know there are different kinds of apparatuses or engines requiring different fuels or energies to run them. We can't run a car on water. Our own organism relies on food and can't work on a diet of rocks, sun, air, and water. Every apparatus needs a specific form of energy.

Then there is the factor of intensity. The control of intensities of energy is very important to us. We won't get very far if we try to boil an egg with a candle, and if we put it in a furnace, it will be burned to a cinder.

If there is something we want to do, we know that it will require a certain quantity of energy of a particular form and at a certain intensity. This is true for things working in ourselves as it is for things working in factories.

We have mentioned the need of food for the organism and of gas for the car. Food and gas are different forms of energy, but what is essential about their difference?

There is something in food which is of a different quality than the energy in gas. This factor of quality is not really mysterious. There are different octanes of gas to suit different kinds of gas engines. So even within one form of energy there are gradations of quality. Then there are big differences such as that between heat and mechanical energy. Heat doesn't have any directedness about it, so it can't be used to push things along; it has to be converted first into another quality of energy that does have direction.

If we look at everything that can possibly happen, it is possible to sort out energies and grade them according to quality. What we get is an enormously simplified picture. It ignores quantity and intensity and all the variations within any given level. It also assumes that there are pure energies, something that we can never find in practice, because they are usually mixed and work by combining together and changing into each other in a variety of ways.

The grading of energies according to quality rests on the fact that we can distinguish between things that require very highly organized energies and other things that require only minimally organized energies. It must take a high quality of energy to transform a human being and an even higher energy to regulate the whole universe in a way that allows for independent intelligence. Only very coarse energies are needed to move things around and hold material objects together.

J.G. Bennett formed the energies into twelve different levels. He put the twelve levels into three groups of four as in this figure:

E 1	Transcendent		
E 2	Unitive		
E 3	Creative		Cosmic Energies
E 4	Conscious		
E 5	Sensitive	Human Energies	
E 6	Automatic		
E 7	Vital		Life Energies
E 8	Constructive		
E 9	Plastic		
E 10	Cohesive		
E 11	Directed		Material Energies
E 12	Dispersed	*Diagram 5*	

From E 12 to E 1 the energies become more coherently organized. E 12, the lowest energy, is exemplified by heat which has no structure of its own. Everything has heat in it. E 11, the directed energies, have no form besides that of direction. A magnetic field is directional. The cohesive energies, E 10, are the energies that bind and hold things together and give them shape from atoms to the visible things around us. The earth is bound together by them; they are in this chair, in this floor, and in our bodies. E 9, the plastic energies, enable things to change their shape without falling apart. Through them things can adapt to external pressures and forces. Through the plastic energies we are able to mold things. E 12 to E 9 represent the material of mechanical energies.

The first class of living energies is called the constructive energies, E 8, and produces DNA and enyzmes. They act as catalysts in the construction of molecules for life, but in themselves they do not change. E 7 are the vital

Time and Energies

energies which give every living thing its urges of growth, reproduction, and survival. With these energies we come near to what we human beings can experience in ourselves, so we know when we are 'lacking in vitality'.

E 6, the automatic energies, keep things going without any act of attention or anything that requires us to be directly aware of anything. We partially exist as an automatism. When we get into the realm of the sensitive energies, E 5, the organization is much greater and there is what we call 'awareness'. There is very little awareness in the automatic range, even though information can be taken in and dealt with in an efficient way. With sensitivity we can feel aware that we exist and that we are alive.

Then we cross the divide into the higher energies, first with the conscious energy E 4. We have to draw consciousness down into us in some way. Creativity, E 3, enters of itself — that is why it is associated with spontaneity. As we are we do not even have control over the conscious energy.

We will not speak about the higher energies.

Another factor that has to be grasped is that one energy by itself cannot function very well — it needs a higher form of energy to help it along, as it were, from the back. When we become sensitized, a degree of conscious energy starts to come in. It is the force behind the experience, but our experience is not conscious. In other words we can say that all these energies permeate downwards in some form or other; but, as with the worlds, in the lower levels there is less organization and more fixation.

How can we relate this to time? Do you remember what Tony was saying just now about the different worlds? The thing that is not grasped is that when we go from world 24 to world 48, there are twenty-four more laws to which we are subject. That is an awful lot. One or two extra laws would be one thing; twenty-four laws means there is a totally different world, a totally different realm that we are experiencing. When there is a shift in our state of consciousness, we do go into an entirely different world. These energies operate in the same way. The impingement of a higher world on a lower one is, in a sense, a miraculous event. Our ability to transform relies on this miraculousness of the higher energies permeating into the lower ones.

When we are in the automatic state, what is time to us? What sort of time do you think we exist under in the automatic state?

Q. It would seem that we're totally unaware of time, the passage of time.
J.W. So what sort of time would it be?
Q. We don't have any. It's not ours.
J.W. But there is time passing, even in the automatic state.
Q. Causal time, causality?
Q. Clock time.

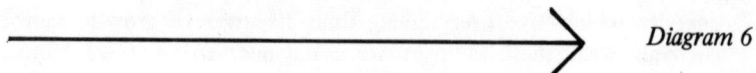

Diagram 6

J.W. Clock time is to be what I call 'under time'. This is time of a fairly simple nature. Perhaps it is just a linear direction; it goes along blindly, and we are just taken along. When we move from that sort of time and we go into sensitivity, what sort of time could we say we come into?

Q. Towards eternity?

J.W. How do you mean towards eternity?

Q. According to the graph that Tony had the other night, where we become aware of our nature, our pattern.

J.W. When you're sensitive?

Q. Well, true. We go towards that when we're sensitive.

J.W. So there is more *depth* in it than in the automatic state.

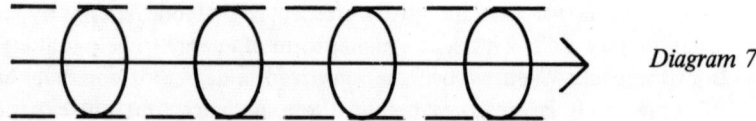

Diagram 7

Sensitive (E 5); awareness of self and depth, "in time".

At least we are in the present moment when we are sensitive; we have more depth. We are going from a simple line, as it were, towards something with depth, something where time and eternity start to join in the present moment. There is a present moment each time that I am sensitive. There is a place on the line which is no longer without any breaks. There are significant moments.

Try to become aware of this with your own bodies now, and see what happens when you lose sensitivity and collapse back into automatic time. You become absorbed in the automatic time and lose the ability to have present moments, to have a greater awareness of the now. In the automatic state there is no self, there is just an automatism. In the sensitive state there are the beginnings of self and selfhood.

Now when I go up a stage higher, I have this problem: when consciousness descends, I see that 'I' am nothing. The problem here is that the sensitivity finds this very difficult to accept, because it has established a selfhood. It finds great difficulty in accepting nothingness, so it tends to retreat back.

A.G.E.B. In the sensitive state there is something fixed. It is like one is at the center of the world. The experience one is having in a sensitive state is the world, but when consciousness comes, it reveals that the present moment is in fact open all around. Before, you were inside a region, really there. Now

Time and Energies 93

suddenly, the place where you are has no walls around it. There is wholeness. You have to leave the center of the stage and realize that there is a stage, there is a world, there is a wholeness, and it does not belong to you. Your sensitive attachments have to be surrendered if you are to enter into conscious experience. People talk about a reversal: when I become conscious I get the sense of 'being looked at'. I exist in this seeing. It is a very hard jump to cross the gap between the sensitive and the conscious.

J.W. Now I'd like you to speak about any experiences you've had that you think are one or the other, the sensitive or the conscious experience, particularly the jump from one to the other. Is this something you recognize? If so, what sort of experience have you had in that situation?

Q. Are you saying from sensitive to conscious? Wouldn't that be where understanding comes? I think I see the kind of a jump you mean. The moment of understanding brings in some kind of contact with consciousness.

J.W. Can you give some sort of experience of it? What actually happens?

Q. It's like a hammer that hits me over the head. I don't have an example. I might think of one. I think we've all had them.

Q. There's a time when I need an answer to a problem and there is no one to go to. I get into a space where I can write and I have to start off by being there and by starting to write something from myself, something I know. And then what happens is that it just goes on writing. I don't know what's going to be written next; I have no control. I control, but I'm allowing it to write itself out. When I get done, there's a message there. I don't think I've been really able to catch the point of transition. All of a sudden something will just continue itself.

Q. John, I had an experience yesterday morning while I was working at the chicken house. I was scraping down the filth-covered walls. To scrape that you have to have the roost propped up on a post. I did that, and I was trying to connect with what was happening here in the barn, keeping my attention on my breathing. Then I heard a sound, a small creaking sound. At that moment it seemed that I had a picture of a sequence of events, it seemed like a very long time space where a reel was played over. A chicken jumped onto the roost causing it to move which dislodged the trough which was about to fall and hit my head. That all took place in a . . . it was like seconds. But I saw that happening and was able to put down my shovel, get out of the roost, and catch it before it fell. It seemed like there were three things happening.

J.W. Sounds good. That is what we can write up here, 'having time'. When there is consciousness, you have time. Somehow time expands.

When you are sensitive, you are very subject to time. It is a very limited state, even though it has depth. In the automatic state there is no time at all, because you are not aware of it. When you are in time, you feel it is precious; but once you get into the conscious energy, then time expands and you have plenty of time.

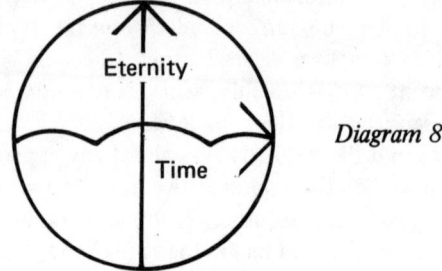

Diagram 8

Conscious (E 4); awareness of nothingness, "having time".

Q. Something happened to me today during the reading. I was falling asleep, but I had been trying to listen to what Tony was reading. I couldn't follow it, and finally I just realized I was in a very negative state. I was going to try to find some good will in myself, and I looked out the window and had a contact with the nature out there. When I looked back in the room, I wasn't actually listening to the sound of the reading. It was like there was an awareness of being in the barn and being here rather than being at a reading. I don't know how to explain it any more definitely than that, but it was almost as if I had been encapsulated in this thing of trying to listen, trying and trying and trying, and all of a sudden it just exploded out. It went out literally as far as the trees which are on the horizon and all through the air and a little bit back. The funny thing was that after that I was really able to follow what Tony was reading. I wasn't sure whether it was just more interesting at the end, but it did make a complete difference in my concentration. That moment went fairly quickly. It didn't last in terms of time, that is, clock time. I would not even have thought of it in terms of time.

J.W. In the reading I decided I would do a silent zikr with words, knowing this would cause problems. Every so often I could set the zikr; the words would go on, and I could also listen and be upright and be aware and so on. I had plenty of time to do it all, nothing got in the way of anything. In the other state there was a struggle, struggle with this or struggle with that. There is a difference in this ability or capacity to take in what is necessary at the moment.

Q. Consciousness has such an integrality to it that I feel very subject to time. There's always a sense of urgency, of wanting to strive after something and yet, not being able to have it.

Q. I think I experienced something in the movements. Time just slowed down; there was enough time for me to make the movement, to place myself.

J.W.   You can be aware that time is short, but at that moment you are not subject to time. You have time to see there is no time, so to speak. There might be a tremendous sense of urgency, but you are not subject to time in that moment.

I was saying that we talk in theory as though the energies were all separate, but they are not. What happens depends on the mixture. To cross the threshold you need a higher octane fuel. If you don't get it, you might be going faster than a sensitive car, but not as fast as a conscious car. So you are stuck in a twilight zone where it is neither one thing nor the other. As soon as you go into the other side, there is this expansion and you can see things as a whole. It is what I would call a moment in eternity, when time is suspended.

A.G.E.B.   Let me say some practical words here: that consciousness doesn't worry.

Q.   I was going to say that I've had this kind of transition in athletics. I remember particularly one time playing basketball. I was very aware and sensitive of my position, the ball, and two people in front of me. I had to get to the other side, and all of a sudden I was about thirty feet beyond them, having done some moves that I don't even know how I did. I wasn't the center of the whole thing, the whole court; the whole area was in my awareness. I was thinking there is a funny expression in basketball when somebody's in the kind of state that they can't miss when they shoot, 'they're unconscious'!

J.W.   In many things it's amazing how you can bend time. In some states you can do some impossible things.

Q.   I remember having seen something, done something, and in looking back had seen that I had done it, but I don't remember having done it. It didn't take any thought, but I was able to find the time to do this thing so quickly. How can I explain it? I saw my son going into a door. There was no way I could have gotten to that door. The next thing I knew my hand was there. Somehow I had found the time to do this, but there was no consciousness that I can remember. I was amazed that it happened, and yet I had made the time for it. Somehow I think that's instinct, but I was able to make time.

J.W.   Sometimes you get up into the region of the creative. Now the creative energy comes into our life usually through sex. When creative energy comes in, it performs miracles. Because whatever you do must have the right fuel to do it with, and in a state of shock, or some form of heightened awareness, we are then opened to other energies which flow through. What we're concerned with in the transformation of energies is that we learn to do it intentionally, or learn to participate more intentionally. That in itself is a contradiction in terms, but this can and does happen to us accidentally, all the time. We are not conscious and yet *something is conscious*, something has changed the moment from one level to another. It takes part in anything where there is a super-heightened awareness. Normally we think of sexual energy in terms of sexual intercourse and so on, and this is a very limited way of looking at sex energy. It will enter into anything. It is said that any true spiritual experience has sex energy involved in it. A fanatic is a man who has sex energy. You can see sex energy working in this barn during the term in forms of greed and malice. Various habits become stronger than normal; you've seen how it's happened. People don't just drink, they *really* drink, they *really* smoke, and so on. This is the sexual energy coming in, it is so powerful. It happens because there are certain conditions of repression. You are not allowed to go out, you are held in a sort of sausage machine. This will create conditions for this other something to happen.

How to obviate the destructive effects of sexual energy in places like this? I feel it is something we do not understand very much and must learn something about. We must be able to transform something really creative. Something that concerns me and a number of other people at the moment is seeing if there's any way round this. Does this have to be released in crude destructive ways? It is fairly obvious when our normal behavior becomes more than normal, becomes hyper-normal, that sexual energy is usually involved in one form or another. That is the most obvious manifestation of creative energy that comes into us. Look at the power of it when it comes into the automatic region and when it is in the sensitive region of like and dislike.

A.G.E.B. You haven't brought up the point about the energies working in different centers. People have said very clearly that when the higher energies go into the moving center, as in athletics, "You find it has happened." The thinking center tries to find out what has happened, but the moving center is extremely fast. Its working can't be recognized by the thinking center. When the thinking center has consciousness in it, it is like understanding. Suddenly you see the problem, or whatever, as a whole. With the feeling center it's different again. It is when you really are able to see yourself as you are, and it means both to accept and to see.

J.W. I was avoiding any reference to the centers; we think of them too superficially. But there is one striking example of what you are talking about connected with the emotional center. In tennis matches or anything like that, the strange thing called 'initiative' changes. One person is winning but suddenly starts to lose. It is more than sensitivity, it has this other quality. Suddenly one person can do no wrong, and then it will switch back again. I've seen this dominate in competitions. I will never forget that when I went in for my black belt, I was very thin and fairly light. There were no weight categories, and that night I had seven competitions. I drew one match, then I could do no wrong. I remember going against my friend who was better than me and smashing him down very quickly. I just couldn't lose, and yet he was better than me; it was the wrong night for him. It has to do in a very strange way with the feeling center.

A.G.E.B. It is true that 'better' or 'worse' is a matter of skill and belongs to the sensitive level.

J.W. There are people who seem to tap in, and they can win in spite of their disabilities.

Included in what we were taught about energies was: "The higher blends with the lower to actualize the middle." It was a theory for a long time with me; now it is a real practicality. How this happens, how we use this in our work, has to change and develop. You start by using your head to work on your limbs, so that your feeling starts to develop. This is a basic form. Some people stay there all their lives, doing that to that to that. But one day it has got to shift.

Q. What are the things that we do? Is it work on ourselves that causes the transition from being subject to time to having time? What are the things that we can do?

J.W. The question was asked this afternoon. In fact, there's always this dilemma that we can do nothing, and yet, we've got to do something. There's nothing we can do to get creativity for ourselves, or even to make ourselves conscious, and yet there's something on the sensitive level that we can do, but it doesn't guarantee a result. Bennett used to say that if you work as well as you can with what is in front of you, you draw consciousness down. But the consciousness won't enter a place in which it isn't wanted or respected. We can, in a sense, encourage it or prepare a place for it, but we have no control over it as such. The other point is that the sensitive energy doesn't wake up, unless there's a certain amount of consciousness anyway. So we must be very careful not to separate them out.

When it is awakened, what do I do then? We say that waking up is an act of grace, but what do I do then? This will determine whether anything else can happen. If I do something then, even though it's not obvious, something has accrued, something is stored till there is a sufficient amount. Remember that we are made up of various engines which need specific energies. Organs of perception are engines; if the right energy is not there, they cannot function.

Q. What do you mean, "What can I do now?" It seems to me that we have to accept and go about our business. It seems to me that if we try to do something, that in itself loses it.

J.W. Why, you just said, "Go about your business."

Q. Yes.

J.W. As you did before?

Q. No, no, not as you did before, but on this level you go about your business.

J.W. Well, maybe that's a form of doing. Don't always think of doing as imposing something artificially. Doing might be doing exactly as I did before, but in a totally different state, with a totally different quality. The mistake we make about doing is to think that it is arbitrary. There is this funny thing about the word doing, as if it has to mean imposition. It is much more like seeing what is necessary and then getting on with it. It might be going on with my business, but how then am I, when I go about my business? Will I fall asleep again just as quickly or is something kept going a bit longer? Perhaps I am not caught so easily. In that situation do I just fall asleep again or do I, having become aware of being awakened, make some further step to pass the threshold? Then we enter this other world, and there's no question it's a different world, a world with half as many laws.

This is the extraordinary thing about man: he is between two worlds. This is his dilemma. He has a visible and an invisible world. Somehow he has to find his place in the middle and develop the capacity to withstand the demands of both worlds and serve them adequately: one which he can't see and the other which tends to ensnare him with material rewards. This is our fundamental dilemma. If we can start to understand something about the energies which are in this world, then perhaps we can act more intelligently in relation to our experiences. But we must at the same time always realize that it's more complicated than we think. Tony's reading tonight was to show us that it's even more complicated than that. When we look at the combinations we can have of the blending of various energies, it is mind-blowing.

Q. Is there more that you wanted to say about the creative level being beyond the mind? All I can recall is about sex energy causing various compulsions, but I couldn't relate that to time.

J.W. The creative level is not subject to time. It is not even subject to eternity; it brings in a new dimension. You read stories of geniuses — how they worked and worked and worked — one moment they got it in a flash.

Q. What about heroes, war heroes, people who are forced into war situations and do heroic acts? Is that not a form of creative energy, possibly necessary for that time?

J.W. Creative energy pouring into the sensitive world through some shock, without participation of consciousness, manifests as hate or some extreme reaction. Usually people whose friends have been shot get very angry. Some of them are very stupid people; they literally haven't any fear. Do you know the saying, (which is for me a marvelous saying, because I am a coward), of Gurdjieff's, "Cowardice shows the presence of will"?

Q. What I just described and you said was creative energy was not an intelligent act; it had nothing to do with intelligence.

J.W. Even beyond intelligence, it has to enter our intelligence. Do you have anything else to say about it, Tony, being a creative sort of bloke?

A.G.E.B. Only when I'm beyond time! I'll say something to do with the idea of 'room to maneuver'. All the things that will happen on the automatic level have already happened; there is repetition and you don't get anywhere. In the realm of sensitivity you have contact with the moment, but it is not big enough because it's locked in a certain perspective, a certain point of view. Consciousness gives a greater wholeness, but still it is, so to speak, a wholeness with regard to what is there.

Now, creativity is concerned with what is not there. And where's that going to come in? One answer to it which we will be looking at tomorrow is that the only place it can come from is the future. You can understand this best in sport or in war, where there is something to accomplish in a very uncertain situation. Here is extraordinarily great complexity, and something is opened up in the situation which has to do with what will happen, not to do with what has happened. People were asking, "What do we do? How can we produce this?" This puts us back in the stream of time of trying to push something, when all the time we are being carried along by the very thing which prevents us from achieving anything. I say: get out of this stream. But what is the only way to do it? To effect something in this stream you have to get ahead of yourself and come backwards to where you are. How can you introduce a new cause into the state of affairs? It can't be in the past, because the past is past. The present is too small. So the only space you've got is the future. A creative action in us is always ahead of us, and we're trying to catch up with it. It is the situation of our lives, trying to live a life that catches up with our creative self, but being too slow. We have the old word in the Bible, 'quick' — in the phrase, "the quick and the dead." The stupid modern translation speaks of the "living and the dead." Quick is such an incredible word. Being quick is not like making an effort. Learning the right relationship with the creative stream is the quickening. Unless we are quickened, we do not have a chance.

J.W. You see this in lives like Napoleon, for instance. Napoleon in his earlier days knew exactly what was going to happen before the battle had even been started. He knew what was going to happen.

A.G.E.B. And then he would make it happen, because he knew.

J.W. It only lasted until he started to believe in himself.

A.G.E.B. Yes, this believing in oneself is like shutting if off.

Q. Is sexual energy a creative energy or a conscious energy?

J.W. Creative.

A.G.E.B. The energies are neutral. The power of creativity is such that it can destroy. This is very astonishing, and something that is, for example, in very extreme forms of crime, violence, and so on. There is something behind people like the Manson killers. They talk about the 'fourth state' in much the same way as those bizarre Australian girls who murdered one of their parents. I do not understand why it is, but it is something very deep that is operating there. Enormous destruction can come out of this creative energy. It can create in the ordinary sense of being constructive and producing works of art, or it can destroy. There is a puzzle connected with this in interpreting events in modern history or any period of history. Take this century: the world wars, the phenomenon of Hitler, the atomic bomb, and the release of very powerful ideas which lead to incredible destruction, material destruction, and destruction of life. How does one look at these events? How does one deal with them? It may be that they are enabling something to happen, and it has to be in that way. Something has to break down. It is only something very strong that can make it break down.

J.W. It is said that something on one level cannot change unless something from a higher level enters, something from outside. Christ had to come from beyond to bring the unitive energy down from beyond the creative energy, to change something that may have gone wrong up there. Because it is higher, because it is less conditioned, it is more miraculous. The creative energy can be really constructive or something highly destructive. In itself it is neither one nor the other. And this is why it is so interesting that religions and all the paths tend to turn us towards the blessednesses, the virtues, etc. People say how 'yucky' that is, but in fact it is very important and practical, because, if we are going to be able to be open to these things, and maybe one day we will be vehicles such that they will come through us, we want to be able to serve the future, not destroy the present. I will never forget when we were doing exercises of the positive and negative sides of things. One day Bennett said, "That's enough, we won't do that anymore. We'll cut the negative out; we will only concentrate on the positive." The negativity is easily fed, it can easily take us, so we have to point ourselves towards the virtue, towards the blessedness, in order that eventually the vehicle that we become is pure enough to help the future. This is the difference between black and white magic. They use the same forces. The difference is in how they are used and what sort of vehicle we want to become, or wish to become. We turn ourselves towards our aims.

Q. So destructive energy falls in the same place as creative energy only it's the . . . negative side.

J.W. Depending on how it's used. Used lower down, it's highly destructive. The higher up you go, the bigger the destruction, because it impinges on lower worlds.

Q. Does it all come from the same place?

J.W. The place is here.

Hazard

I would like to introduce the notion of *hazard*, because it will become increasingly important to us in our studies over the next few days. As many of you know, this notion was introduced in a special way by Mr. Bennett, especially from the period of about ten years ago when he saw in it a new and deeper significance.

Ordinarily we think of hazard as a danger. The basic notion is that it is something unexpected. It is because we cannot know the hazard in advance that a danger is possible. Can you also see that the nature of danger is that the outcome is not predictable either? We may find ourselves in a region where there is a threat to life, but if our death is certain there is no hazard. We can say that being alive makes it certain that we die, but unless we are concerned with different possibilities that can come out of life, hazard is lacking.

We feel that danger releases energy in us. That is because it is associated with a high potential. It is both physical and psychological. We often say that in moments of danger we confront ourselves: many people seek danger in voyages, expeditions, and war, because they can make contact with the significance of life through doing so. It is probable that this kind of lust for danger has a sexual origin, and hazard is of great importance for a creative life.

Usually, we take hazard to be something destructive, but if we look more closely we can see that hazard, even in its material form, is a sign of reality. *We know that we are actually in the world, because things happen which we don't expect.*

This is the first kind of contribution that hazard makes to our lives: it enables us to re-establish contact with the world. Contact is something concrete, real, and significant, but we can reject it. I myself try to practice entering into the potential of contact that is released when a part of the material world comes up and hits me — when I drop something on my toe or hit my head. I know how terribly often I reject the contact with a curse; although in my mind I well understand that I can be shown things at such a moment. For example, nearly always when I get a painful blow, I can see that my thinking was in a wrong way just at that moment. This is partly connected with the release of energy through sensation and feeling. Maybe there is also a true *'acausal* connection': a connection that is nothing to do with causality.[1] There are many clues in this area having to do with understanding the parallelism of events in different worlds.

Even in such a seemingly simple and trivial thing as stubbing one's toe, there are involved different worlds. There is the world of material events and the world of my experience. If you like, you can say a world of bodies and a world of energies, or even a world of movement and a world of feeling. As I have often said, *feeling is the key*. Without the release of feeling, there can be no contact. This goes all the way. Let me explain.

Ouspensky in talking about 'self-remembering' used to say that all we can do is to pretend to do it, to do it only in our minds. This prepares us for moments in life, some crisis or other in which *a sufficient intensity of emotional energy is released* which makes real self-remembering possible. As we are we have no control over the release of emotional energy, and we have to gear in our intentional efforts to the possibility of impacts which we cannot forsee or engineer.

A world without hazard would be like a perpetual motion machine feeding back into itself, every piece fitting exactly, turning smoothly, completely, isolated, and utterly meaningless. Though it is this sort of picture people turn to when they think of the universe, it is nonsensical in terms of our actual experience. Such a smooth running whole would really have no parts to it. The very character of separation that our world has is the source of interaction from which hazard comes. You see, even in physical science there are unpredictables once we get beyond an interaction of two things. There is the three-body problem in which three gravitational masses affect one another. The actual motions cannot be predicted, because we can only deal with them in pairs.

Separation is critically important for our experience of ourselves. This is where we begin, and why the passage from childish essence to adult personality is not just a disaster. We have got to be separated out in order for there to be an action towards unity. This is so blatantly obvious, yet utterly neglected. Unless we were made apart, fragmented, what would be the point of all this work and effort and searching? It is facile to say, as many gurus do: just forget about all that, just be whole and ignore the illusion of separation. It is true that within us is the Truth, God, the Self. But it has to be *attained*, and perhaps it is through the muddle of the striving that we really contribute to the ecology of this planet!

It is pretty clear to see that if there were only a perpetual mobile, that nothing could change and there could be no intelligence, no will, and no choice — in fact there would not even be a future as we experience it. I know that when I get into a closed state the future vanishes; or there is no future except death. What opens the closed system to life is an 'interruption', or something that we first crudely experience as an interruption, which is hazard.

The idea of contact is immense. You know the Sufi story of the man who waits for hundreds of years for the door of heaven to open and then falls asleep at the critical moment? This portrays the other side of hazard: unexpected events have the power to wake us up, but we must be awake in order to take advantage of the opportunity. It is these two sides together that make hazard the key to the realization of freedom.

Hazard is a 'shaking between worlds'. Whereas mind is possible because the worlds merge, hazard is possible because the barriers between the worlds are unstable. Nothing can keep strictly to its own nature! Within ourselves the very instability of our psyche is the necessary condition in which we can be awakened to the need to search.

I say again that our thinking, whether it is called 'scientific' or 'religious', is nearly always stale, fixed, and inadequate. We think something is definitely something because we give it a name. Of course, there are definite characteristics or essences, but these are not of the kind we pin our attention on in the visible world.

Heisenberg's principle of uncertainty is valuable in opening us to the possibility of a basic instability, or at least fluctuation, in existence that arises from the concreteness of interaction in a world that is 'partially in parts'. It is connected in principle with the three-body problem. What it leaves totally out of the picture is what makes hazard significant. The way in which it is expressed is in a statistical form that smoothes out the unique character of a particular observation event.

How can we live a life that takes into account the reality of hazard? The way to begin is with *aim*. Ordinarily if we aim for something in the future, we imagine that what we want is something that we can picture to ourselves and define exactly. But in practice, if we are to achieve exactly the result we want, we have to spend vast amounts of energy to keep things on the rails. In doing this, we will produce side results with unforeseen consequences. It is like the Heisenberg principle: the more exactly we achieve the result we want, the more we have to apply connections which have unforeseeable ramifications.

It has become a virtue in business and technology to be able to achieve exact results, but there is always the unease that having got what we wanted, we may find it inappropriate or inadequate. It is a commonplace that pursuit is more satisfying than possession; the culminating embrace is liable to be a letdown.

But if we abandon the aim, what is left? Only the statistical averaging out of accidents which amounts to nothing of significance. In this we can gain nothing for ourselves. The reason is mainly that we cease to expose ourselves to *temptation*. Temptation comes in when we have an aim, but can compromise with it at a point of hazard.

We can see that the *whole* situation is one in which there is aim and also all the consequences of action. The complexity of the whole cannot be contained in our thinking, picturing, and emotional responses. But there is something else. The whole is not simply a collection of bits of action and intention in an environment; it is primarily a whole, because it has an 'inherent pattern'. An artist will often incorporate 'accidents' into his work without at all compromising his aim: he is able to come closer to the pattern that is there to be realized. As I suggested in the talk on 'time out of time', the work of a painter is closer to divination than one realizes. Fundamental to both painting and divination is communication with a pattern.

Here we come close to the difference between imposing a plan on life and working to realize a pattern in life. In the former the content of hazard is swept under the carpet where it is liable to fester. In the latter the content of hazard is the very lifeblood of making progress.

When we have a living aim, we must have inherent in the aim an understanding of the world in which it is to be realized. It was useless to aim for the moon before there had emerged a world of liquid propellants, versatile alloys, and computers, but at a certain point, having that aim was a major factor in *creating* such a world.

Perhaps we can picture it simply as an impulse coming from the present seeking union with an impulse coming from the future. Then it is hazard which enables these two to come into harmony — however uncomfortable it might feel at the time. But a better way of looking at it is as an impulse coming from the whole, the pattern. Time is only one aspect of this uncertain liaison. Then we can begin to appreciate that living aim is an act of synergy, or cooperation, between different levels.

This relates very much to our situation. As separated personalities with our own conditioning and biases, we seek for self development and come across the idea of the Fourth Way. But the Fourth Way is not Gurdjieff's system or any other system, formula, philosophy, ritual, or method. It is an action in the *whole* of humanity, a pattern of work that is right and effective.

The failures of our naive ideals are inevitable, but also useful; they can help us to see in a quite unexpected way. If I say to you: "Each one of you must have your own personal aim in this seminar, but you must realize that the sign of achievement will be the realization that in what you wanted, you were utterly mistaken," it sounds a bit severe. But it is the truth. If I do not come to the point of realizing that before this seminar I had missed the significance of the question of time, I will not have done my job.

Of course, what we have to lose is the conditioning, the restrictions, the biases that we bring into the situation. We do not have to lose the essential aim.

In what I said a moment ago I defined an essential aim, but you must grasp the point that such an aim has the impossible in it and is not something I can go out and do just because I have thought it. An essential aim creates a need in oneself. It draws on the shadow, in psychological terms, and on the darkness that is where the whole is 'waiting to be realized'.

We can realize something together. Already we have material enough to understand that new ideas are not concepts, but actions. What is significant comes from a direction that we cannot work out in advance, however clever we become after the event.

Gurdjieff's cosmology is founded on an understanding of the unlimited significance of hazard – though it took J.G. Bennett to help us realize this. What does it mean that the fundamental laws were altered when the world was created? The 'law of seven' was altered to incorporate points of uncertainty, stress, and unexpectedness. Nothing in this world can be achieved in a straight line. Achievement comes by a cooperation between different levels that cannot be determined in advance. That is why free intelligence is a reality. The real world is the world that is created, and we can enter it only by participation in creation.

If we ask, "What is it we have to do?" it is quite impossible to answer. *The way has to be discovered in action.*

Doing is really different from how we picture it. What is required of us is simple, much simpler than we believe. The clue is that in our ordinary state there is a combination of activity and images. To put it crudely, we are actualizing in a certain way, which we call 'doing something', and we are having thoughts about what is going on and what it is for. As long as it is like this, we are dreaming, we are asleep.

Then, in common experience, something happens, an external thing that makes us stumble, the appearance of what seems like an opportunity, a new insight. The rock that stubs our toe reminds us of the reality of the world. We get angry and distressed. An energy has been released. Here is material of the inner world.

When the fixed ideas or images we have of what is happening and what it is for become broken, there is an opportunity. The rock that stubs our toe represents all the kinds of incidents that shatter our composure or self-calming: an eruption in a relationship, a failure of what we hoped for, the tool breaking, things taking an unexpected course. In all of them there is a 'flash of light', pain, shock, surprise. Can we enter into the light? What is the light? It is fleeting. The power of the flash is that it is a destroyer of images.

The flash can for a moment burn out the image. It is then possible for us to come into a true aim, not one made out of cardboard, but one that works effectively in the inner world. Such aim is connected with the way in which things can be done. This is creative. It is the law of the unique.

Gurdjieff spoke of the greatest satisfaction of a man: realizing his aim in accordance with conscience. Conscience is the test of aim. Conscience is the nature of the light flash in the hazard. Remember that a direct experience of conscience would render us totally unconscious. In our lives conscience has to operate fleetingly or in an indirect way. The world helps us.

Untitled

What Makes the Future?

"What Makes the Future?" is the title of one of three books that Mr. Bennett proposed to write before he died. All he left behind was a synopsis of what he intended to write. I'd like to do what I can to say something of the possible content of the unwritten book; but, of course, not to do it in the way in which he structured it and he pictured it, but to do it from the point of view of the direction we've been following up until now.

Usually there are two kinds of answers to the question, "What makes the future?" sometimes separately considered and sometimes combined. Firstly, that the future is made entirely from the past or by the past. This is the motif of causality typified by Laplace, the French astronomer and mathematician, who said that if he knew all of the positions and velocities of all the particles in the universe, he could tell the future history of everything. Even if we say that there are a lot of problems in knowing the position and velocities of all the particles in the universe, (and therefore, this is only a theoretical possibility); still, it leads us to a certain view, namely, that the future is nothing but the passive recipient of the shape of the past. The second point of view is that there are beings – minds, people, powers – who can choose their future: that there are uncaused causes in the stream of life which make a future that cannot be foreseen in terms of the past. Like most ordinary pictures of things, there is something sensible and reasonable behind both these viewpoints, but we can only see it if we take them deeper than how they are ordinarily approached.

Let us start with the point of view of causality. Clearly there is something to it; we can trace back from what is happening now to things that have happened before. We know, even if we postulate the presence of an absolute free will in ourselves, that we will act in terms of what has happened. Why? Because what has happened gives us *what we know*, our knowledge, and from this knowledge we construct a possible image of what we can do. Therefore, in some sense the future will always carry in it something of the imprint of the past, even if we adopt the unlikely view of there being some kind of absolute free will in human beings. To reiterate: we look towards the future and we imagine ourselves completely free; but, what do we think of doing? What material can we draw upon to think about the future? Only the material that we know: but what we

What Makes the Future?

know is from the past, an ordering of what has actualized in our experience. No matter how we are picturing the world, there must always be something, some truth, in the effect of the past. Different people at different times and for different reasons have spoken about this from different points of view.

There is, of course, the material causality of the physicist, really of the nineteenth century physicist; today's physicist is very unlikely to talk about causality in a strict sense because of his current problems. But it is nineteenth century science that dominates the man in the street, because the ideas of science take one or two hundred years to filter down to him. He sees machines constructed in such a way that they go on behaving in a predictable pattern. If you swing a pendulum, it will oscillate with the same frequency, even if it is subject to air resistance; and it is upon this, of course, that we base our whole ordinary measurement of time. This is the time in which the past is repeated in the future.

We can find this time in our experience, because it corresponds to what John, yesterday, was calling the automatic energy, which is for us associated, psychologically, with habits and the materiality of memory. When we live automatically, we simply repeat what has been, and we live in a state in which our future is exactly the same as our past. It is very interesting to wake up from this state and to realize that nothing on this level can lead to anything. There is, in fact, no change possible. This then corresponds to the view I started to express about this causal picture, that the future becomes the same as the past, and it's all indifferent whether there is past or future. There are mutual constraints of one thing upon another. When our attention gets caught by a small detail of it, we believe that something is changing. Rather like if you visualize a circle, and going around that circle a little spot of light: that little spot of light is our kind of attention. When we are in that state, then the flow which occurs will seem like getting somewhere or it will seem that things are changing, and we won't notice that we are returning to a repetition of the previous behavior.

There is the traditional idea of 'karma', that we reap according to what we sow: if we do bad, we receive bad; if we do good, we receive good. As Gurdjieff said, "If you hurt even a worm, one day you will pay." This attitude about karma leads into theories about reincarnation. It isn't really quite the same as mechanistic causality. We can picture it in a simple way: we cannot get out of the world of action and reaction. We do something, therefore something is done to us; it doesn't matter whether we can pin it down to that moment or to a later or earlier moment. We incur upon ourselves a future corresponding to the reactions of the world according to what we have done. This is an interesting variation on the causal view; when you look at it, it's rather like saying that the future is coming out of the present, because it is in the present that things are done. You must understand that in the ordinary, causal, mechanistic perspective there isn't really a present at all. It's all a space-time configuration subject to certain laws. I've said past and future are not really distinguishable; they are only distinguishable when there is a present *now*, and the present is distinguishable by some power of action.

So we have these slightly different perspectives: one where everything comes out of the past and therefore is fixed; and another where it comes out of the present, which means that what we do now has consequences. But they share very much. The idea of something having consequences is the bare idea of causality in general — one billiard ball striking another leads to the motion of the second billiard ball. But there is a range between the completely mechanistic causality, which leads us to a completely static space-time continuum in which everything is completely part of a configuration, right through to the more qualitative "How you sow, so shall you reap," and some idea of there being a present, a possibility of present time. Along this continuum you get all the shades through which we look at our lives and our experience. The ordinary world we think of in terms of doing things, changing things, altering things, is in that band between karma and mechanical causality.

We tend to think this way even though some of the things that impinge upon our experience are quite outside it. I'll mention two things in connection with this. Firstly, there is in the material world itself, (that is, in the visible kind of existence such as we have on the surface of the earth), something 'acausal'. This does not violate any of the laws which correspond to this stream from past to future; this creates a puzzle for our minds. I'm talking about what Bennett derived from Gurdjieff, called the 'elementals': material forces that impinge themselves in our lives. There is what is called the 'perversity' of inanimate material objects. There is something willful in the material world associated with such major forces as war, famine, and pestilence. In ancient Anglo Saxon poetry you find this referred to by the word 'weird', and it is from this we get the contemporary degenerate form of that word when we say anything strange is weird. This strangeness in the material world is a reality, and it doesn't correspond at all to this causal stream, neither does it violate it. At this point I will not say anything more in detail about it.

Secondly, I want to refer to our perception. As I mentioned yesterday, if you say perception is *realistic* it means that there is some kind of action connecting material events with experiential events. Perception is an action in which nothing happens, because all the happening is in what we see!

I will just remind you of the diagram we had yesterday because I will be using it today. Space-time is at the bottom of the square and eternity-hyparxis at the top.

What Makes the Future?

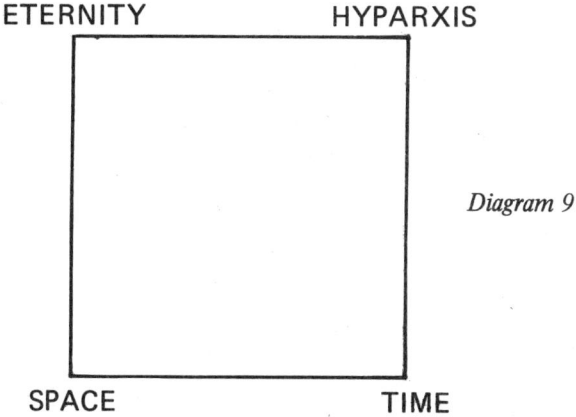

Diagram 9

For the line on the left, eternity-space, I gave the name 'communication' and used the example of perception. I deliberately used the word communication in this unusual way in order to highlight that real communication, even between people, is not back and forth; it's in a different direction altogether. When it is back and forth, it is a sure guarantee there is no communication, because people, and what is communicated to the presence of people, is not in the nature of billiard balls. In the act of perception the content is a going on, but the action of perception itself is not a going on. This shows that there are modes of connection which are, so to speak, rotated out of the stream of causality, out of this direction of causality which is along the bottom line. The world of our feelings and our thoughts, our psychological world, has a sort of coincidence, or communication, with events in the material world. I believe that our feelings which touch upon fear, awe, and these kinds of things do tell us something that is really there about the material world. And fear, even fear of the dark, tells us things which our ordinary intellectual apparatus and the things that have been worked out to deal with the line of causality cannot cope with. But remember we will project onto our sensitive experiences our thought forms of the causal world. So we talk about spirits *doing* things to us as they are pictured in fairy tales: leprechauns, gnomes, elves, pixies, and so on; whereas, you see that in our human experience where they enter is in a moment of communication in which a certain meaning emerges. For men who lived before the modern epoch this was given the name of gods or spirits. We can give it the name *energies*; it is the same. The language we use and perhaps even the form of attention which we have changes. Maybe there are even different ways in which this arises for men and women. It is difficult to say. I brought these things in mainly to remind you of the content of that square. There are some kinds of connectivity or some structures of connectivity which are not causal, which are not from the past to the future. These connectivities only become apparent to us in certain kinds of sensitive experience. Sensitivity is a threshold. If we are not sensitive, then we are locked in the squirrel's cage. Sensitivity in the way John talked about it, where there is some kind of evocation of it from the consciousness, begins to enable us to see into these other kinds of connectivities.

When people say, for example, that there are presences in the room, it is not to do with anything happening. When we try to put this into the stream of past and future and ask why these presences are here, it all gets silly, it all becomes misunderstood. One has to accept that kind of experience as a communication. There must be something very important to learn about how we can be open to useful forms of communication and closed to others which may be damaging. This is not done by doing things in time.

Now let us think of people doing things, people with free will. There is an utter contradiction here. On the one hand we've got everything fixed from the past, so that if anything happens it will have had antecedents behind it. Then we can have the sense, so to speak, laterally, that maybe there is something different which is not a happening. All right, but when we say we want to make something different happen, then how does one do this? What can it possibly mean? Can it possibly mean, for example, that there is this Mr. X who does something that bears no relation to anything that happened anywhere before? You say, "But this would be absurd!" Suddenly in the middle of the universe something comes out of nowhere which doesn't fit in. It has no place. Either the laws of the universe have got to be suspended for a moment or the whole thing will blow apart.

The Sufis talk about this when saying, "God himself cannot act in this world," (that is, the world of 'nâsût' — in conditioned man immersed in the material world), because this world is too dense, there are too many laws, not enough room to maneuver, to do anything. Therefore, certain kinds of special apparatuses are needed, some of which are called human beings, in order to enable an instrument to evolve so God can act in this world. That is their way of talking about it. One has to grasp how everything in existence, if it does exist, must be linked to everything else. I sit on this chair, the chair supports me, but my sitting is also to do with the whole gravitational field of this earth. My whole possibility of sitting on this solid body has to do with all kinds of complex and long processes in the formation of the solar system. Take this speech which I am using. If I started speaking in some yet undiscovered tongue, what use would it be? What meaning could it possibly have? I wouldn't know the meaning, you wouldn't know the meaning, not even God Himself would know. If something new is going to come into the world, it has to come through what is there. Now this makes a puzzle, you see. Either we've got to give up altogether the idea of there being freedom, or we've got to find a way for it to come in which is different from what we ordinarily think. Because, and this is very important, it has to do with the future, the creation of the future in which we can participate actively.

Our bodies work according to causal streams: certain parts of ourselves bear the consequences of our actions; we operate through memory traces. All of that simply 'goes on'. 'We ourselves' are some kind of possibility of making the future different from the past. This is one kind of definition of *real aim*, that my future shall not be the same as my past. Where is there really sufficient maneuverability? The past is already formed, is already actualized. You may say that actualization is the fixing agent.

What about the present? What can be done in the present? We can choose in the present, and we can choose between various potentialities that are present in us. If they are not present, we cannot choose. Potentialities belong to eternity. Making them present belongs to hyparxis. In a moment we'll see the significance of this for understanding what corresponds to the direction of hyparxis in man. I think it is clear enough that it is no good having in general all sorts of potentialities unless they are present in this moment. One knows that one's capacity of seeing potential in the moment is limited. It diminishes and increases. At one time there are no potentialities except the one that's being actualized, and therefore, you're stuck; and this is the state of identification with no degree of freedom whatsoever. In order for there to be a degree of freedom there must be more than one potential present in our experience. In terms of what John said about the energies, this becomes possible when there is a separation between sensitivity and consciousness. Left to itself, the consciousness will become attracted to the automatic and will become fixed. Think of the *moment of choice*. This is not how it's talked about in management books on decision making where you have alternatives which you can discuss, enumerate, quantify, argue about, think about, and weigh; it's quite different from this. The moment of choice which I'm trying to talk about is where the potentialities are concretely present, not simply thought about or known about. The thinking about or the knowing about can be automatic, but the real presence is to do with something that involves consciousness. Really, this moment of choice involves something more than the mere factual potentialities, because these carry value with them. Thus we can say that when we come into the moment of choice, we become moved by values. We begin to experience in terms of why and should, and we can make an act of the kind, "I shall do this, because it is right."

Something emerges which becomes independent of the causal stream of the past. This is why out of moments of choice one comes to fresh experience and new insights which are the spin-offs of being in a different world and therefore, subject to different laws. When you can accept and enter into the moment of choice, you come into what is represented by the square and begin to move in it and achieve something in it. This does, of course, release one, not in the form of escape, but by addition, by establishing a different substantial something on another level from the causal. It is itself not utterly free. The region in the square also has a kind of form. It is not the form which is that of the past, a space-time form, or as we sometimes say, material form, or as in the reading I gave yesterday, a form corresponding to the world of the four elements. It is another kind of form. In the Sufi terminology it is the 'mithāl' world, the world of similarity or analogy to the divine attributes.

I'll pause for a moment here to talk about all these different terminologies. Aristotle, for example, talks about this region as 'soul', and he calls it the form of the body: that which gives meaning to its acts, which organizes the body and is the source of initiative in the body. It is quite a sensible way of talking: there is something which is a source of initiative with respect to the body, which is its 'form'. Then there are other people who say, "Well, really, there's something here which is a sort of subtler version of what we see visibly." This must be so too, because there is no strict dichotomy. This similarity has to do again with the left hand side of the diagram representing eternity and space. There is a correspondence between a form in space and a pattern in eternity; but in the middle region of the square, one, so to speak, turns inside out, and what is an external arrangement becomes an internal pattern. This makes for a paradox.

We'll proceed to another language and perspective with such things as astrology and divination. When they are worked rightly, they have to do with the middle region which psychologically is the consciousness-sensitivity separation. When, for example, the divinatory procedure of the *I Ching* is done correctly, it involves the discipline or sorting the yarrow stalks which takes a long time. It is very tedious if one is impatient, and it has all to do with what is called quieting the mind. What is quieting the mind? It is reducing the disorganizing effect of the sensitivity which John talked about yesterday, the sensitivity that gets disturbed. When this disturbance becomes reduced, then this corresponds to a separation of consciousness and sensitivity, and one comes to a different state. It is through this that the translation operates between a pattern and a spatial arrangement.

If you take the diagonals into account and look at the middle region, you see how eternity-space comes together there and then goes out into time and hyparxis. People ask about astrology, "Does it mean that one's life is predetermined?" The answer is, "No, one's life is not predetermined by the astrological pattern — in the sense that it is caused in the same way as certain things happen because of what has happened; it is altogether unlike that." What it says is that a certain kind of pattern is fixed, and from this pattern there comes the shape of our experience. The shape of our experience is given names such as 'character', our kind of nature, and in Gurdjieff's language, 'essence', which is what we have from birth. What is it about? It is about the kind of relationships into which we can enter. This is also a very important clue, because one can look at our relationships with people and say there is something here which cannot ever be quantified. If you count your status by the number of friends you have or something similar and believe that if you have more friends, you are in a better state or a better person, this is the world of madness. Essentially it's something qualitative and subtle, and what this relationship consists of is unseen in spatial-temporal terms. It is a patterning of significance. The stuff of it one is not aware of, one lives so much in it. Rudolf Steiner once said a magnificent thing, that one thing for sure enters into the life hereafter, and that is the relationships we have built up in this life, not our bodies, not our concepts, not our emotionality, but these relationships. And so it is not surprising that one can look at a relationship between planets and the earth and human relationships as coupled in some way. They are coupled so that these relationships for an individual have an archetype.

But how the life is lived is not wholly contained in this, because it is *yet to be lived*. What this means, this 'yet to be lived', has to do with hyparxis and time; it has to do with the confrontation, the struggle between the creation of order in hyparxis and the disordering of time.

The planetary influences of character and fate meet with the act of choice. We are able to choose when we come to presence and become aware of recurrence. Out of these meetings something is formed that has an independence from space and time.

Yesterday John was talking about energies. The transformation of energies is not visible in time and space. We do not see it happen, because it does not happen. I was realizing it myself at lunch time during the exercise to do with conscious breathing. Only at times does one do it for real; the rest of the time one thinks about it or pretends to do it. Suddenly this totally different thing was there, and it had a 'thereness'. I know if I say, "It was really myself that was there," this is nonsense: it is simply another kind of thereness. But how did it come? If I start saying it was because I breathed in a certain way, it's not true. If I say I put my attention there, putting attention is not an action in time. I will leave you to describe the act of attention in terms of the diagram.

This something which can be built up does not wholly escape the past. Why should this, though, be a problem? It is a problem only if we look for a condition in which we can return or come to the same place as our *origin*. By action in the present we remain in the world which has a shape not of our own choosing — we call that *fate*. On a lower level it is called karma. We have to accept the consequences of what we do even if it is through a moment of choice. And we see time and again how the moment of choice, which has a degree of freedom in it, produces consequences which can condition us.

The dominant image for thinking about my life and about time has been like this. Here I am in the middle of a stage, speaking certain lines, dimly aware that I have a certain role incumbent upon me, and around me there are other actors, and there is scenery portraying a place. (In this picture one isn't sure what the audience is.) And you ask, "Well, who wrote the script?" I can say that the language in which the script is to be written was prefigured for us in terms of events in the solar system. The actual lines that we speak, though, can be automatic or conscious. We can pick up lines allotted to us by other people, or we can speak our own lines. Still, we have not created the language. "But who is writing this play?" I am not writing it; I am just coming into it and beginning to improvise a little every now and then. Something was already in progress to which I am somewhat awakened. But I can not, as I am, get back to the beginning of the action which was set in motion by my birth and will cease with my death. How am I going to do anything like that? How is it possible? This is the same image as Mr. Bennett had many years ago in Istanbul, which he was very fond of describing: seeing a sphere expanding, which, as it expanded, left behind the dead past. On the surface of the sphere there were beings who were living; these were ordinary people. There were other beings who could fly in and out of the surface of this sphere; these were the free ones — the *quick*. In Gurdjieff's account of human life there is "objective evolution," but it is slow; and there is subjective evolution by the way of accelerated transformation. This has to do with attaining the state of those free beings who can go in and out of the start of life when they wish, which means that they can become masters of their lives. What we can do is to come into what is already in progress, that is, belong to the present moment of humanity. This is possible for us, but how that present moment is being created is totally different.

Does this coming into the origin have any relevance for us at all? It probably does. This coming into the origin is the same as creation or creativity. Today, especially in this country, any scribble, smear, or twitch is called creative. Any dead repetition in countless hundreds of papers is called creative. Try to use this word in an intentional way, as an origination, something coming into being which is new. This is a real puzzle, because it has to do with *beginning;* that is why it is interesting. Why do most astrological charts deal with the moment of birth and not with the moment of conception? (I know some do, but mostly they deal with the moment of birth.) It is right there in front of us. The moment of conception is to do with the origin, the source. How does this miracle of human possibility enter into time? This is the question that confronts us every time we ask ourselves whether we can be free in the strong sense of being free, because this means to create a beginning.

I take the question, "What began this seminar?" It was scheduled to begin at five o'clock last Thursday. Was that the beginning? There were people here already, people were thinking about it already. Or was it when I first came to Claymont – because Pierre had phoned me and tried to entice me over here by saying, "Wouldn't you like to do a seminar on time?" And then I'd think back and remember last year, that for some reason I thought of doing a seminar on time in America, which was relatively unexpected to me. Where would we stop in this tracking back?

Perhaps we're tracing in the wrong direction, and the clue is in this phrase I just used, in the unexpected. This indicates directly something to do with the creative energy. Why? Because we cannot make ourselves creative. People constantly say time and time again that the creative step is non-doing. Yet, at the same time, we have to do something about it; but any sense of doing something creatively is nonsense. There is the creative act which enters. Whenever it comes, there is a sense of the unexpected. As Rumi says, "When you lift the lid, it is not what you expected." This is a clue, another clue to do with the future.

If there is the future that I can easily visualize and look at, then what is it but carrying my past along with me and going on in the same way so that nothing changes? If I can really anticipate the future, then it's determined, it is fixed. Maybe we can speak as much as we like about how we shouldn't be fixed in this way, but it's a real temptation for all of us, because we know the kind of panic and emptiness one feels in front of a future which is blank. We say, "I wish to God I knew what I would be doing next year, or where I shall be, or what I should do next." So there is something in our nature like this which tries to achieve security by fixing. This is part of our nature and we have to accept that.

When we actually get there, if it was what we anticipated, it's flat, it has no value in it, it's the same old thing. Gurdjieff expressed it as 'self-calming'. He talked about an absolute calm as the end of everything living. This state of calm is what is desired by all highly paid planners. They wish to produce this calm amongst themselves and amongst other people. Life is much more untidy and constantly, thank God, wrecks the planners plans.

Now we begin to get a different aspect. If we really enter into something or we are touched by something, we begin to say such things as, "Is there a purpose in this?" or even, "Are there higher powers at work in this?" And all this kind of language we use half ashamedly; sometimes we joke about it, sometimes we get fantasies about it. We start projecting about how the higher powers are with us and everything's right with the world. But behind it, is there something authentic? Can we hope or look towards something authentic? I want to put aside any idea of the higher or lower powers whatever they are, and just look at the kinds of time, kinds of future. Something comes which strikes you because it is so totally unexpected. Once it has happened you see that it does not violate any causal laws and it can be traced back. Picture two men separately going on a journey, and every step they make is perfectly rational. Then they meet and suddenly discover that each has something that the other needs just at that time. Now, no part of it is against causality or karma or anything like that; but the significance of the meeting introduces something quite new, because something enters at that point. Try to hold this image, we shall come back to it tomorrow. We look towards the past, but what is entering from the future? The unexpected is the mark of something entering an event which is not from the past, which is not from the present, but is from the future. *The only region which the truly unexpected can come from is the future.*

There is a reality to do with a future which is influencing now. We tend to think it comes from above. The Russians sent up Sputnik and said, "Look, we went up, and there wasn't anything there." How right this is. It's very good they did that. The only direction left to look into is the future; but clearly this is not the future which has got a causal imprint on it. It is another kind of future altogether. It's also not the future of our pattern, because our pattern is a shape for our whole life and is always with us.

This other kind of future is the realm of our 'destiny'. Our destiny comes from the future; our fate comes from the present. Those of you who heard the reading I gave from Rodney Collin, will remember the picture he gives of the moment of death shooting back to the moment of conception. It had, I said, a certain limitation in it, because it brings it down into linear time. Try to see that the act of conception, of origination, comes from the future — and leave it at that. Then you can approach a pure taste. Now you will start thinking, "Look at ourselves, our origination came from the future." You will turn it round and look towards the past. That inversion 'down' is typical in every creative act. The act comes from the future; it enters into the mind which looks in terms of the past. The purpose, in this sense of destiny that I was talking about, is from the future; but immediately as it enters the lower mind, it goes into sorting out the past, and we lose awareness, we lose contact. Mr. Bennett used to say there is the lightning flash, but what we are aware of is the after-image of the lightning flash in our retina which has a duration. We do not see the electronic action, so to speak, but only its after-image in us, in our apparatus. So we come to the possibility then of this creative act belonging to us human beings, but in a way which means that nearly all the time we miss its significance.

What Makes the Future?

Last September it came to me unexpectedly to do a seminar on time. I don't mean that one day I sat down and suddenly, as in the comics, a little bulb of light lit up . . . ah! It was just a reorientation which I noticed. Now say (for the sake, at least, of my feelings) that this seminar on time has some use; it belongs to something which is of service. Then make a mental jump and look at things such as science, and you see people coming to the same kind of realizations at the same time even though they are separate. I remember the powerful image that Koestler gave the astronomers in the middle of the seventeenth century: Tycho de Brahe, Galileo, Kepler, the 'sleepwalkers'. But these sleepwalkers had strange dreams involving an unexpected reorientation of attitude in the mind.

In a change of epoch, what happens? Men begin to have a different attitude towards the world. It is an unexpected reorientation. We're seeing it now. Somehow or other peoples' attitudes are changing, being reoriented. Where is this coming from? What region is it coming from? I am saying it's coming from the future, because only the future can bring the unexpected. Only this kind of future can itself be a region that is not formed or conditioned by the structures and patterns belonging to the other regions, those of fate and causality. This region has to be free. It gives itself through the power of the creative energy. The image we have of it is that of making an image, but it doesn't have to be a picture, it doesn't have to be a thought, it is an orientation. We see only the sensitive image, and we lose contact with the significance of what has happened. We become blind servants of the new element which has entered. But what more powerful thing could there be than changing peoples' attitudes? When we personally enter into this, we have the situation of stepping into a world in which we are moved by something in the future to create the future, to bring it about. Something enters from the creative realm, from the future realm, to set us going, to give this orientation that leads into action, to realize and bring to fruition the same future.

This is a whole here which we can only grasp through consciousness, consciousness in the sense John was talking about yesterday. It's only the consciousness that can see wholes, only the consciousness that can genuinely see beyond this mixing up of lines of causality, see beyond the ordinary way of doing things. Consciousness is then the gateway for an understanding of how change is really brought about. It is through this same gate that our own 'I' can act. Where is the master? Where is he? "Is he in heaven, is he in hell? that damned elusive Pimpernel." No, he is in the future. It makes sense to say that one's own 'I' acts in a way to produce unexpectedness which releases possibilities for choice out of which come modes of action corresponding to conditions in which this same 'I' can be realized in this life. "I am seeking to improve myself." It's very difficult to form any realistic image of this. It's the same for those of you who have done the 'decision exercise'. The act of decision comes from the future and you enter into it. There is in any spiritual event a combination of two quite seemingly separate realities: the unseen reality, which is the object of our faith, and the visible reality, which is the place of our existence and action.

The world is not only created as an object which then goes on. It is created in every moment. This does not mean it was created yesterday, today, and will be tomorrow, because that is crazy and mixed up in time. The act of creation doesn't work in time at all. People grappling with the problem of the big bang of the universe have the same problem. If only they would turn it around and look at the universe as being created from the future. Instead, they try to look for the origin in terms of some origination prior to the primal heat ball, the primal sun. It's quite possible to look at all the current problems to do with cosmological theory and relate them to the different kinds of time. The steady state universe corresponds to fate. The big bang theory is a muddle between the future, creative time and causal time.

It is almost impossible to represent to ourselves the existence of anything without making it equal to God. Only a sense of the power of the unknowable future can help us awake from unconscious blasphemy.

To summarize what we have been talking about, here is a table of the kinds of futures, their origin and character:

PREDETERMINED FUTURE	**CAUSALITY**	**PAST ORIGIN**
CONSEQUENTIAL FUTURE	**KARMA**	
SHAPED FUTURE	**FATE**	**PRESENT ORIGIN**
OPEN FUTURE	**CHOICE**	**FUTURE ORIGIN**
UNEXPECTED FUTURE	**DESTINY**	

Table 1

The things I plan to talk about now go beyond what can strictly be talked about in terms of eternity, hyparxis, space, and time. The reason for this is that eternity, hyparxis, space, and time are what Mr. Bennett tried to make, as far as possible, factual elements. We should now begin to introduce a larger tetrad dealing with the depth of our experience, not restricting it to what we can know and to some degree quantify and find repetitions in.

Eternity extends into the realm of value. If you contemplate a painting, you see the beauty being present there has an eternal character. The realm of hyparxis extends into will, and it is this direction through which freedom enters the present moment. The characteristic of space extends towards *separateness*. Space means that there are outer relationships. Separateness is stronger — it means the possibility of being alone. The extension of time is disintegration, or disorder, which is exemplified in us by the threat of death. As we enter into the regions of experience which don't belong to knowledge, we come into the worlds of 'being' and 'will'.

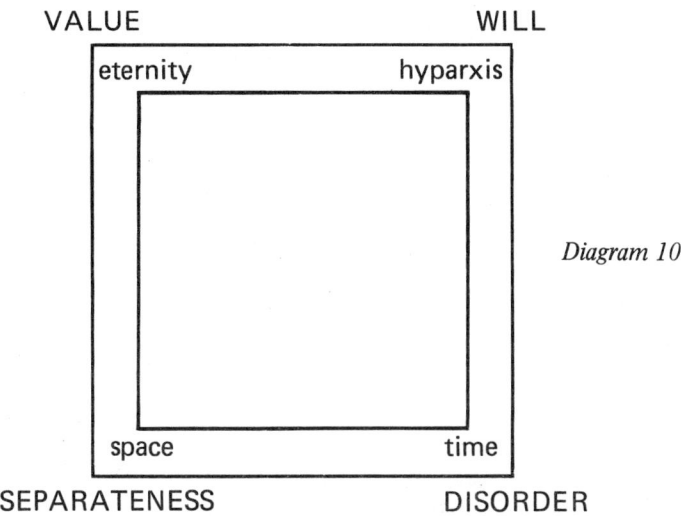

Diagram 10

I want to represent the structure of experience that is the meaning of a painting. I'll talk about it in a way which I hope will be meaningful to you, but the way I express it may only be appropriate to myself. What we see visibly in the painting is a form; we can all agree to that. There is something in front of our eyes. When ordinary people like ourselves paint, most of the time we produce what is obviously just a combination of paint on a piece of paper. But if we are in front of a genuine painting, we feel it has something of its own and it is something in its own right. This quality I wish to give the name 'pattern'. The painting has its own inherent pattern. If it doesn't have its own pattern, it will not have its own life. Very strong images such as those mentioned by Rodney Collin, the series of Rembrandt self-portraits, continue to become a source of experience for people for hundreds of years, and it's even possible to talk about communication with such a painting, a two-way communication. Now what is inherent? What is it that enables one to be in front of a collection of paints and shapes on a piece of canvas and also in communication with a pattern? I'm simply going to call this *seeing*. This idea struck me more and more deeply in looking at the work of the impressionists. The focus of the communication combining form and pattern is a way of seeing the world. What is *represented* in the painting is not simply the form, it is the seeing. Seeing is the focus of significance, whether the painting is realistic or abstract. If the painter hasn't seen, if a seeing is not in the painting, there is nothing and it all amounts to nothing of significance.

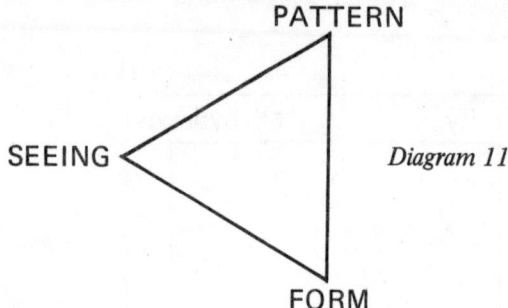

Diagram 11

All this is within the orbit of the painting. But a painting is a cosmos, and every cosmos is a region of meeting between other cosmoses. *Below* the form of painting is the world of 'separation'. There is something important in the action, whereby materials, which in the existing physical world are in a state of separation, have to be intentionally combined and prepared. This is not insignificant. It is the whole technology of painting. Materials from soil, vegetation, ash, and so on have to be brought into a state in which they can be used. What draws them together and refines them is service of the seeing eye.

Beyond the pattern of painting is the world of *values*. We say, "It is beautiful." We mean beauty has been incarnated. It is not something pasted over the top or added to the mixture; it is an act of realization — something is offered up. As we enter into the beautiful, we submit to something unconditioned. We do not know values; and nobody can describe beauty. Beauty can only be realized, and then it is seen.

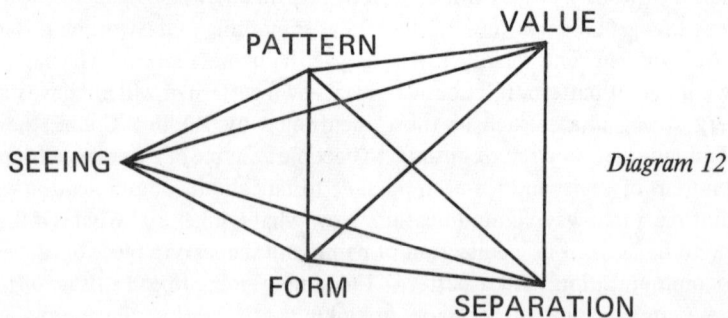

Diagram 12

What Makes the Future?

The significance of a painting has a five-fold structure. In terms of the tetrad we can equate form with space, pattern with eternity, and seeing with the central part of the square.

A painting is like a 'static' moment which is 'right'. A painting has to do with eternity. In contrast, I want to look at the realm of action and return to the moment of choice. Something is *done* that is significant. There is some *action*. This corresponds to the *form* of the painting. When we say that this action is meaningful, we are saying that it has a *purpose* — which is equivalent to a pattern in the painting. I am going to say that there is a realm of purpose, which is not the same as people wanting to do things, but purposeful, because it's connected with the future.

But what kind of connection with the future? It is the connection in which the future is the originator of action, in which the future is made by the future itself. In ordinary language, this is creativity, but people do not understand the meaning of the word.

What is the act in the action? I want to use the word that Mr. Bennett often used, even though, again, in contemporary life it has become almost completely useless. It is the word 'judgment'. This word really means to be able to enter into and see what is there. It is the power to *taste* the potential of the moment; it is not analytical. The assessment of a situation is both 'what is' and 'what can be done'. It brings us into the moment of choice.

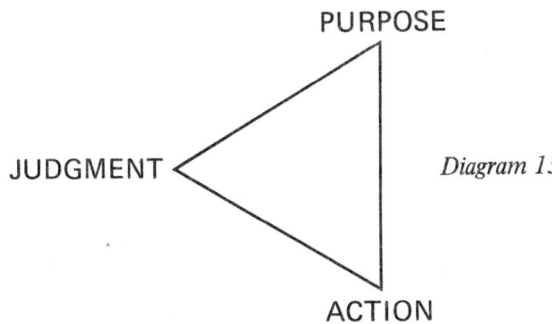

Diagram 13

Meaningful action will tend to restore order and even create it. But what has to be achieved is not possible without the contribution of *disintegration*. It is disintegration that releases the possibility of choice. The complexity of the world of space and time with its innumerable interactions is the condition for opportunities to arise. But these have to be *recognized*, and that is the power of true judgment. What is failure and setback according to our expectations of 'getting somewhere', may prove to be the necessary condition for a subtler and profounder change.

Judgment is the servant of *will*. What acts is always will. But will requires an instrument and mediation. It is mediated by the future and made effective by an act of judgment. This is putting it in a very cold, abstract way. The evidence for it is in the Qu'ran and the injunction: in making a vow, first say, "If God so wills" — insh' allah!

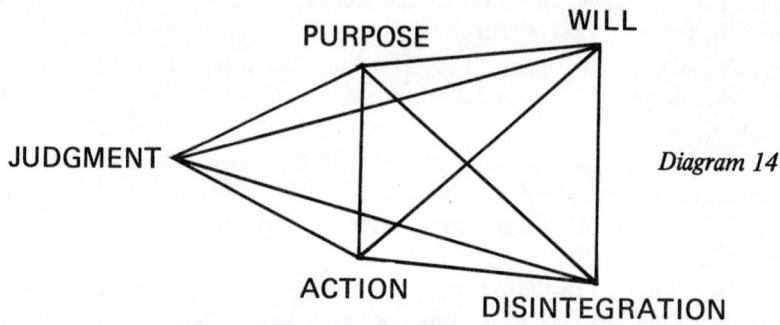

Diagram 14

Incidentally, this pentad expresses very well the role of man on earth as a conscious being. He is destined to realize the kingdom of heaven here on earth. Real man is ahead of his time!

The Pentad of Time

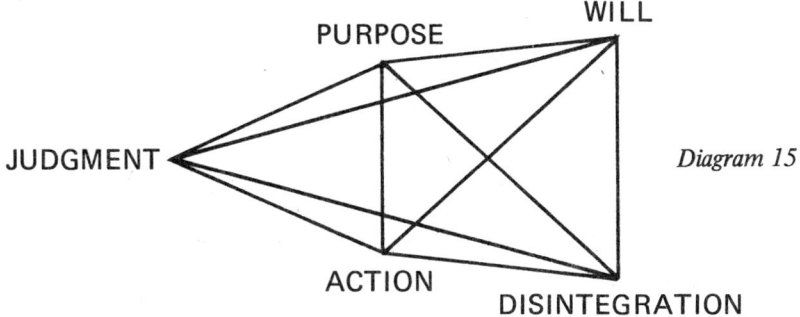

Diagram 15

Yesterday, I talked to you about the pentad, or five-term system, that represents significant action. This morning, I want to relate it to the cosmological scheme derived by Bennett from Gurdjieff's teaching.

Will. This is will in the cosmic sense, the will that redeems us from our own actions. Yesterday I said that whatever we do, it will have karmic consequences. This implies that without redemption, there could be no way out of our situation: whatever we achieve we undo. It is not an easy thing to see that the totality of action resulting from ourselves cancels itself out, so that we never get anywhere — far from easy! Unless this is seen, it is impossible to understand what is meant by the 'Mercy of God'. Gurdjieff's aphorism, "There are two things without limit: the Mercy of God and the stupidity of man," sums up the deeper significance of this pentad. The 'redemptive act' is realized whenever we accept in our judgment that we are inherently limited and we allow ourselves to participate in the acts of will that come from what is called the 'cosmic individuality'. Such moments come if we forgive and 'make peace', (as described in the Sermon on the Mount). The 'cosmic individuality' is the essence of what we mean by will; as an energy, it is love. All existence is involved in the need for redemption.

The realm of *purpose* is that of will working in existence, which is what is meant by 'higher intelligence' or the 'demiurge'. This realm includes the potential to attain a present moment measurable in terms of thousands of years. Here are the great times associated with planets and the working out of solar destiny. In Sufi doctrine the angels are the higher faculties of man. Why? Because man can attain this quality of purpose. Remember, purpose is not the same as wanting or thinking; it is the ability to enter into directly the action of the future. The relevant energy is creative.

Judgment depends on the separation of consciousness from sensitivity. It occurs in a self involved in an existential situation. We can come to the domain of *awakened* men and women and three-brained beings in general.

The realm of action involves the instruments that we have as living beings. All these instruments and capacities refer to that kind of existence which we call *animal*. Our physical existence on this planet amongst other life is that of an animal. Finally, we come down to disintegration, which is associated with the dismembered strivings which are in every part of ourselves. Every part has its own urge, almost every cell, every thing in us strives in its own way. This enters into our psyche as many 'I's'. Without this there is no hope, because this whole disturbing, disintegrating, activating thing makes our freedom possible. In *The Dramatic Universe* this is given the name, 'germ', meaning that of a sexual cell.

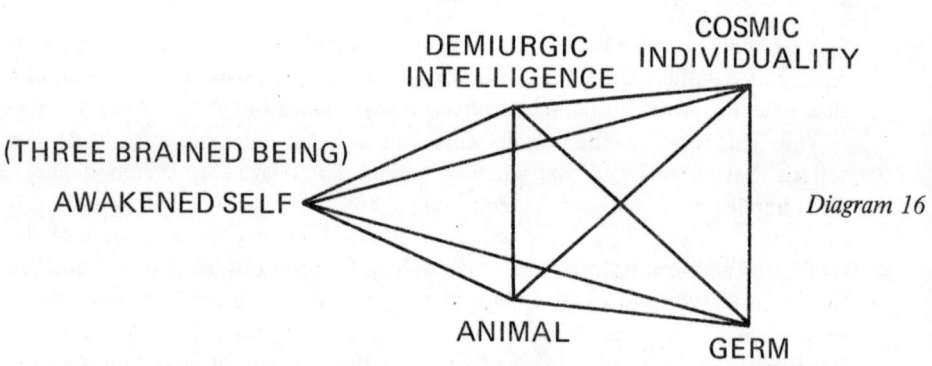

Diagram 16

What we have, then, is the essential structure of a three-brained being. Ordinarily this is described as part of the whole system of essence classes in terms of eating and being eaten. But what I wanted to put in front of you, for those of you who have looked at the essence classes and tried to think about them, is how they emerge naturally once we can enter into the structure of experience which is available to us directly. The abstract presentation of 'this eats that and is eaten by that' is very difficult to follow. But if we look at it in terms of the mutual participation of different degrees of freedom, then it becomes clearer. In fact, the essence class of man only really arises when there is a moment in which the capacity for choice enters, or something equivalent to that. When there is not such a moment, there is not a man; there is not the essence of a man.

Let us look back to our study of the four dimensions and their extensions.

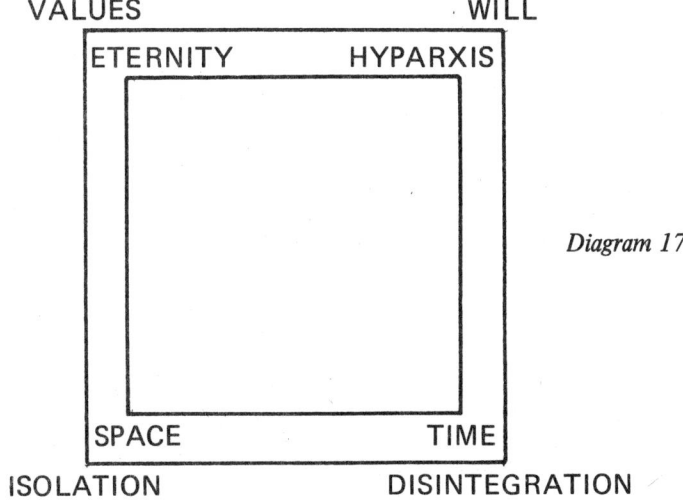

Diagram 17

The essence of a man becomes significant when the central part of the square is something in its own right.

The line of eternity-hyparxis represents the way in which we can communicate with higher intelligence.

The space-time line represents the domain in which we exercise our animal nature.

Disintegration, as I have said, is not something negative; it makes our lives possible.

Will is the source of our redemption. It is the source of the impossible.

But there is a problem with these ideas; especially as they came to be presented in *The Dramatic Universe*. It all seems so perfectly worked out. You see beautiful diagrams, and everything is tabulated and codified. It is not at all like that — really not at all. When I was working with Mr. Bennett on his *Dramatic Universe*, I saw that the minute he had a new insight he would change things. He would sometimes look at his own material and be surprised, "Did I write that, was it really like that?" When you only read about all the different distinctions being made, it is hard to get into how they were arrived at.

You have to find your own starting point and follow it up. Eventually, you must take into account what has been expressed by other people, but you need your own starting point. For this seminar I had to find my own starting point. Even if it is much worse than anybody else's, it was still mine. Each of us has got to come into his or her own starting point in order to participate in this seminar. By participating first of all from your own starting point, there can be something concrete and something which can belong to all of us.

We have these vague terms such as 'being aware', but we don't know how to be aware or make ourselves aware *now*. But it is true that we have some capacity for entering into the wholeness of the event. Through this we find our place. We can, with confidence, look to the whole with hope, with optimism, because there is something right about this seminar. I don't know what it is; but there is something right. I have the confidence that we are not entirely playing and amusing ourselves to pass the time.

Q.   When you started out this morning you mentioned something about disintegration and related it to the idea of many 'I's'. I felt I had some experience of that. Then when you related it to the essence class of the germ, I felt I didn't have any contact with it at all. Is there anything you can say that might help me to see something about it?

A.G.E.B.   There is a very good image, you know: there are many thousands of spermatozoa and every one is swimming like crazy, and perhaps one will make it. You can see in photographs, especially of any kind of unicellular life, an incredible activity and striving, which doesn't seem to be striving to anywhere in particular. This is talked about in terms of the 'germ', because within the germ it is most concentrated. It is related to what John was saying, the other night, about the sexual energy. I say it's a strange thing. It is said that man has creative power, and we can form some sensible picture of this. But when the flower is fertilized, this is also a creative event. However we think about what sort of experience a flower does have, we get nowhere. It wouldn't be experience such as we know experience. What we see of the creative energy is how it enters the mind region. We have intensity, emotional excitement, sensation, and so on because of our nature. The creative energy is more universal than that and can enter into the whole working of nature. The idea of the germ is extraordinary in that it is to do especially with the sexual parts of all living things. We come to the idea of the grain, the seed, which is such an important food for man. The first outward sign of the essence food is heavily biased towards the reproductive parts. All of these things have a certain concentration in them. We cannot easily picture what it is; but clearly there is a certain kind of concentration which comes from the creative working. This is the source of striving.

Any micro-organism would take over the whole world if it had its way. Everything is held in balance, and on this level it is the competition and the mutual destruction going on all the time which keeps things in balance. That's why there's a correspondence when we look at history. Mr. Bennett associated the germinal essence with politics, because politics has to do with the allocation of power, and everything that has power wants to be all power. Soon you get other people who want power, and they fight it out.

The idea of many 'I's', striving, politics — it's all the same characteristic of a region made of atoms, so to speak, which have energy and power. How can we come to the right attitude towards them, because they're not negative? They are an engine of life working in us. We are involved in them. John was saying that you can't get anywhere without passion. When you're 'eating' the germ, you get this passion. There is no escape route into higher being. The germinal essence relates to what Gurdjieff was trying to get across to people about time, the 'Merciless Heropass'. We cannot escape the lawful commands of the merciless heropass which is the diminishing of possibilities. There is this disordering of our experience. But when we take it in, absorb it, it enters into something else, it plays a part in something else which itself is free. You can say that there is something almost like the *eating of time*.

The Qualities of Time

Q. There's something that I wanted to ask about which has to do with the moment, more or less, when you feel free of time just by not being aware of it anymore. Again and again I notice that I cringe when it's announced that we're going to do something for a certain amount of time. For me it never seems to be any good. I really feel threatened by: "Well, let's do this for an hour and a half; let's do that for two hours." Somehow just setting the limit makes me feel really closed. If I can get into working on something, then it will go away. A lot of times there comes a point where I've got outside of it, and then I'm surprised that the time went as fast as it did. But the initial feeling of it, and the longer I'm aware of it, the harder things are.

A.G.E.B. I'm sure there's something very important here. What can we see about this? Somebody says, "All right, let's do this" — for example, the extreme exercises we had of drawing a line for an hour and a half or digging in the garden for a straight three hours; and it seems a threat. It seems that something is being put upon you, encaging you. You do have the attitude of being subject to a restriction, but later there is a different attitude. It may be that this first attitude comes through being at that moment in a world which has the belief that when time is just passing, the future is open. And this is associated with the feeling that there is always plenty of time to do something, because if we don't do it now, we can do it tomorrow. It's intimately connected with what Gurdjieff called "the disease of tomorrow," that is to say, living in a time when we are not present. Using our own language, we're in the state where we do not have any time; we are just in the midst of time. When we are flowing like that, we believe that there is always more to come as though it were a space. If things are not right now, they can be put right tomorrow. It appears that the flow of time is really open; whereas, it is probable that this flow of time, which is related to the automatic state, in fact, is closed, because it is entirely repeating the past. It is not getting anywhere at all and it cannot get anywhere at all.

It is interesting that when something is put in front of you — to work at something within certain constraints — you feel it as a threat. You get this upside down perception of what is there. For me the core of this upside down

The Qualities of Time 131

perception is the belief we have got that in our ordinary automatic state we have time. For example, we have the notion about our time expressed by the phrase, "Why are you wasting my time?" Someone makes a demand on me, and I say, "Why should I go into his world? This is taking away my time, the time of my life. If I go away with him, I cease to exist."

What does this point to? It points to what we call in our psychology, 'identification'. When one is in a state of identification one believes that one has something, is something, is free, and all the rest of it; whereas, in fact, one is inside a very tiny box which one doesn't notice — because one is the box. There is a good test of identification; and I saw it in myself time and time again, when I had this reaction of feeling my time being taken away from me by other people. When I wanted to think about something and other people wanted me to go and do something or talk about something, I would resent it. I believe I have my own time by rejecting the demands of the world. But we only have time when we have time, when we are something, when there is 'is-ness'.

Now, when you are involved in a task and you accept it, there is something very interesting that can happen because of the constraint put there which specifies a beginning and an end. A potential is possible which ordinarily wouldn't be possible. When an action is restricted 'between then and then', it is quite unlike the indifferent, amorphous spread of time in which you believe yourself to be. 'Between then and then' is making a container. When you have your attention towards a fixed duration, it is like a container. What it contains is difficult to say: it contains experience in a way that the amorphous kind of state does not. Because it is contained in that way, it is obviously not a container made of metal or stone or anything like that, or even strictly our own bodies; it is a container in our minds. Something can be built up, something can be concentrated, something can come to presence.

While one is inside it, it is extraordinarily dynamic like the exercise we were doing. John said that we needed two more hours to do something with this, keeping at this one particular action for all that period of time. You try it in one way, one state, and you get tired or bored or sleepy; then you separate from it. You go through all kinds of maneuvers around a fixed approach which eventually peters out, and a moment comes when it can be different. All of this is possible, only because there is a containment. What we have here in fixing a duration is the visible part of what is necessary for there to be an *event*. An event is where something can be concentrated, something of our experience. We can say further that *significance can be concentrated* so that we can come to see something and accomplish something different from what we have done before. Everybody knows the power of a deadline. When you have a deadline and you come up against it, you can say it increases your energy. What is that famous saying? "There's nothing that concentrates the mind like the prospect of being hanged."

Q.   I find that when I'm doing almost anything like washing the dishes, I'm rushing to get through it to get to something else. Then I get to that something else, and the same process goes on; I'm not there at all. There's a kind of emotional energy to finish what I'm doing, because this isn't it; there's something else that's going to happen, that's going to be it. This keeps carrying on like that and would always carry on, if work or life didn't enter into it at some point. When there's a fixed duration, it seems to me to increase this emtional tension a lot more. When John said that we needed at least two more hours, I felt an immediate horror inside, knowing what it would be like sitting there two more hours to have to do that. Sometimes in meditation, after there's a certain period when that happens, I go beyond it — when a kind of rustling inside happens.

A.G.E.B.   You used a very interesting phrase when you said that ordinarily this is not it, it's something else; because I find in exercises like the one John showed us today, that one of the key turning points is entering into 'this is it'. This is realizing that *this* is the only thing I can do in *this time*; and there's nothing else to consider but doing this in this time. It's really extraordinary. I don't know how to express it; previously I had been playing, pretending, not really doing *it* at all, but doing it in terms of something else; and then there is only this, and you enter into it in a different way.

J.W.   Something that's been around for a long time in me is the phenomenon of what you called 'containers'. What is a container? What does it do? It seems in a sense to create a vortex rather than a steady flow. Something can build up within that. Why is it that we have four walls around us, and for certain work it's easier inside than out? At Coombe Springs we tried many different experiments to work outside, and they were tremendous failures. There seems to be something reflected off the container.

There is another thing Jack brought out, and that's this upside down view we have of freedom. Because there is a discipline laid on one, one thinks that that is restricting one's freedom, and one's freedom is this concept of a miasmic time which goes on forever, where nothing really happens, but you feel free. Somebody who was really in a desperate situation or at least thought he was, once asked me, "John, I'm in prison; how do I get out?" I said, "Let me turn it round; you're in prison, and you'll never get out. Now, what are you going to do? " This is the same in a sense with a container, when you reach this point: "This is all I've got."

A.G.E.B.   I know how frustrating it is, and I remember one time at Sherborne I shall never forget. I was on child care, and for me child care was hell. It would drain my attention, and I had this complete incapacity to do it. I had four hours with these children in this cold room, and I said, "I will be present, I will be present, I will be present." I kept saying to myself, "This is my only existence, it's here." I kept looking at that clock; my eyes wouldn't go away from it, and it was one of the most torturous experiences in my life. It was amazing — trying to will that clock hand to go around and reach lunch time.

It can touch very deep things in ourselves, this reluctance. I knew the principle that in a fraction of a second I could enter into that moment; but there was something, some barrier against coming into that present moment. It isn't simply a matter of failure or success. This sort of barrier is important: because there's a barrier, something can be built up. My way of expressing it is as if this barrier is a sort of inner container. There is the visible container of the walls in space and a duration in time which we know. Then we see another kind of containment, such as a containment of oneself, a containment of one's psyche or of the inner world which we can't get at directly, because we can't know it, we can't pin it down in ostensible terms. Associated with that containment is something much subtler, much stronger, and also much deeper. In these circumstances of rejecting what is in front of us, there is something to do with our own nature coming into play here, maybe a very deep kind of rejection. Possibly there are different levels to it.

It is also very interesting what John said about the four walls. You see there is a spatial element here as well as the temporal element. You have to do something within four walls and within a certain time.

I'd like to ask people about something which has just come to my mind in connection with this. When you people have gone out from this place during this week, have you felt disconnected from the event? Can anybody speak about this. For example, S——, you had gone out to the races yesterday, did you feel that you'd left?

S.   I was just going to ask this question which has been with me for a lot of years: how is it possible that anything goes on when I'm not there?

Q.   Isn't that called egocentrism?

A.G.E.B.   Not entirely.

S.   It has something to do with time; for example, yesterday in Susan's class when John and I were here and we were being a bit loud; that was making part of the event happen. If John and I weren't there, it would have happened a whole different way. Does that have something to do with this potential of actualities? Do you get a taste of what I'm saying? When I'm present an event happens somehow; and if I weren't there, it also happens, but I don't have any contact, though I know it's going on. When I was sick for a day and the events went on, I was not there, but they still went on.

A.G.E.B.   That's such an amazing question.

J.W.   . . . there's this shock. I'd left school to get another job, and as I left, I got this tremendous sense of shock that, in fact, I will not be missed, it will all carry on . . .

Q. So yet, when we came back last night, I felt we came back with a freshness. I'm not quite clear on that. I knew while I was out at the race track that I was getting caught in this, and this, and this; afterwards I could see this even more clearly, but we came back with a certain freshness, or I felt that I did anyway.

A.G.E.B. Did you feel disconnected while you were there?

A. Yes and no. There was something that wasn't disconnected, but most of me was getting caught up in the races, the excitement, the betting, the drinking, the horses, and the freshness of the impressions.

Q. There was a certain solid connection in that there were almost seven or eight of us there. Everyone was coming back for the meditation; there was just not any doubt about that.

A.G.E.B. That's very interesting; that is the containment.

J.W. There's a difference between letting go and letting go. You let go and you blow it, or you let go and enjoy it and come back.

S. That's what happened.

J.W. You see so much of this; people don't get the hang of this, of letting go and . . .

Q. I saw this same thing, I felt I was connected to this seminar.

J.W. That's very good.

Q. I had a lot of trouble, it seemed like a movie. I had a lot of trouble making any reality out of the race track. There were the seven of us, and then there was this flat show . . .

Q. The people were so strange, like they were caricatures; it was just . . .

Q. It was awful, about five people bet on the same horse, and we all lost.

A.G.E.B. If we go back to the same building at another time, we feel, "Well, it happened yesterday." Or, we can be at another place at the same time, so we're not there. All of this is in space and time, to do with the properties of our poor physical body which can only be in one place at one time. Now, how do we deal with this, how do we make sense of other regions of our experience? You don't want to say that there's some kind of magical, astral substance which is floating around everywhere connecting us together; it's not like that. But there is something like that, there is something to which that idea crudely approximates, and it is to do with the sort of thing that I was trying to get at when we did the experiment with dreams. I said then that you go to a place, and that sometimes this place can be very real. It's a very real kind of place, but it's not a place in space and time in the ordinary sense; and it's rather like saying you are where your heart is. There's this marvelous interpretation of that line of Antony's in Shakespeare's *Antony and Cleopatra*: "In the East my pleasure lies." It is a reference to Cleopatra, and also it is an esoteric reference to Eastern Sufism. But, where does one's pleasure lie? Where is one's heart inclined? Now we can begin to say realistically that it is where I am. It's not the place in terms of the coordinates of space and time and clock time, but the region towards which my presence is committed or aligned. One can be very far away from a place and from people and still be in the same region with them.

J.W. That also has to do with how one is never really alone, unless one cuts oneself off in some way. If we have a connection with the work — whatever that means — we are always connected with other people, we are never alone. When people feel alone, it is usually because certain procedures were not followed to keep the contact going. In P. D. Ouspensky's novel *Ivan Osokin*, a marvelous story, the hero went back, and he remembered as long as he wished to remember — only as long as he wished to. This brings a different importance to wish.

A.G.E.B. John talks of wish, and I've expressed it in other ways. One thing about it that we must remember, of course, is that it has a kind of form, a shape to it. We experience it in terms of vision, a group, an aim, but we come to this in interaction with the world of space and time. Of course, it is through time that we come to what we align ourselves to; and therefore it has a history to it. We build up something between a group of people which is more than just colliding in space and time and just talking and doing things together, but the actualities through which we have gone have enabled something to be established which then can be independent. Time spent working together is necessary, but then we are involved in something which is beyond that component and can be semi-independent of it.

J.W. Very much so. Recently I met somebody with whom I'd been in a group in 1950, and it was as though it was yesterday. He thought Bennett was mad, and he has nothing to do with it any longer, but there was that component which he couldn't deny and neither could I. It was there, because we'd been through a certain event together. It was beyond time completely.

A.G.E.B. This is time out of time.

J.W. And it's always there, that contact.

Q. I've noticed that with childhood friends also. Someone that I've known since I was about one or two years old; I'd call him on the phone, just like it was yesterday.

Q. The experience I had last night was one of a few similar experiences I've had — something about the 'right time'. Last night I just knew it was right to go out, and I knew I needed to go out and have fun, I mean, just kind of blow energy. Then the lecture was changed to the afternoon, and a lot of things just worked out. At the same time I also had pictured myself washing the dishes after dinner. When I asked people if they wanted to go to the track, they said they would go earlier than I envisioned, and somehow without planning it, it got turned around so I wasn't pushing myself as it originally seemed to be; thus I was still free to wash the dishes. I don't know, it was a very strange thing: I went in the kitchen and I was still going to go right after dinner, but no one was washing the dishes. It was as if I just looked at this, and: "Wow, I really did picture myself here, and it's just sitting there waiting for me." I washed the dishes and then I went to the track; it just felt that there was something very right about it. I had this feeling that as long as I stayed within certain bounds I was really safe. There was a certain feeling of rightness about it, and I knew I could get as caught up in the races as I wanted, and I had the feeling I didn't have to worry about that. When I came back I sort of blew it. I went down to work in the kitchen at the house which I hadn't envisioned myself doing. There was something really positive about going to do that. I really felt that was the right thing to do, but while I was working there, I just blew a lot of energy. There was a party atmosphere going on for part of the time, and I got really caught up in that. Could you say something about this feeling of the right time? It's very strong when it's happening.

A.G.E.B. I must preface this by saying that this is a very, very important question for me, and I remember asking Mr. Bennett about observations in connection with this kind of experience you've had. He gave a certain explanation at that time which I've been thinking about for three years now, and I'm trying to see it more clearly. But it is awkward to talk about it in a proper way. I'm going to approach it like this and say that I think we'll all recognize that in our ordinary experience everything is helter-skelter.

There's always some sort of conflict, or things impinge and interfere with each other. It is that kind of world we live in, and it makes it messy, untidy, and incoherent. It's difficult for us to learn in those circumstances, because we don't see anything clearly, we don't experience anything fully, we don't complete things, we're not awake to when things begin. One thing robs from another so that everything comes out imperfect and distorted. This really is a world which is there in our experience having that characteristic. If you like, it corresponds to the world in which there is the 'law of accident', using Gurdjieff's terminology. The thing he means by this is not that some tile is going to fall off a roof and kill you, or your car is going to go into a fence, but that things will happen in an accidental way; that is, what happens doesn't have any relevance to what there is. If it's a person, it bears no relevance to who he is. If it's a job, then the inherent nature of the job is obscured. It's a world in which we go around doing things, but not really achieving anything.

There is another world corresponding to a world of rightness. This rightness is simply that everything has its own nature, has its own pattern. We have a pattern which has been given to us with which we are born. It gives us a certain character, a certain key to open certain kinds of situations in life. It is something. It is limited, but it is something. It's the same for a chair, for a job; it's the same for mending a motor car or making a meal. Everything in that world has its own nature; so that if we take a practical activity, it's not a matter of people looking at the job with subjective attitudes about how it should be done or not be done, or treating it as an excuse to show off, or to gain reward. All these are second-hand things which belong to the first world. Simply: there are jobs, there are tasks, there are beings, there are situations, there are events, and it's a much cleaner kind of world. It is really another world.

I feel more and more convinced about this; the depth of it must be extraordinary. Ordinarily we touch only fragmentarily on its surface, for example, in the phenomenon of significant coincidence. We happen to think of somebody, and we meet him around the corner. It happens in times of strife that our feelings become awake at that moment, and there comes some sort of sense of meaning. People can get very trapped at the lower level of this kind of world, and they may study numerology, for example, and chase up correspondences of numbers and become identified with that. It produces another kind of dream which is fixed at a low level. I say that this depth must be extraordinary, because it's the beginning of this timing, the right timing of things that's connected with being in a world where things are what they are. And this is for us a very extraordinary world. It's extraordinary for us, because we're not used to it. I remember Mr. Bennett saying time and time again, "This is the natural world for man." It's simply because historical artificialities have come about for various reasons, and so we do not live in this world. We imagine that very young children naturally live in this world and then lose contact with it, so that the whole character of our experience is distorted.

You can talk about experiences and still get this association of subjectivity about it, but there's more to it than that. It really means that the *kind of events* that can happen are quite different. You have a quite different sort of events in this second world compared to the first world. It's often said that two people, seemingly in the same place at the same time, are really taking part in quite different events, and possibly only the one in the second world will be aware of it. The one in the first world won't recognize that there's another level. That is why if there is group action at any moment, there are people who go through a significant event without even being aware that it is significant, because they were not themselves in the second world. There is in our lives this sort of division. It is the division between the quick and the dead. Of course, in your example there's a certain concentration, because there has been a certain containment, a kind of focusing, which builds something up which can momentarily gain us access into the second world. We don't know very much about how to handle things there, because when these first experiences come to us they are so much more rich, deep, and fulfilling than anything we ordinarily have. They can absorb us into them, because there must be another kind of world beyond that which is deeper in another sense. You just begin, I think, to grasp that in the second world. Things are what they are, and in order for them to be what they are while involved in actualization, there has to be *timing*.

By the way, before I go on to what I will say next, it should be mentioned that there is one very fundamental thing which is spoken of in the New Testament particularly, which one can't get hold of in the English translations. I came across this when I made a book review of a work by a German theologian on *Christ and Time*.[1] This whole book was devoted to the teaching on time that is in the Gospels which you can only appreciate in the original Greek. There is this word there, 'Kairos', which is the 'propitious time'. It's misunderstood, you see, and it's only now that I begin to grasp how it is misunderstood. People take this notion of the propitious time in the wrong world; you see, the time is propitious only in the second world. If you're in the first world, it doesn't matter in what time you are. There's no such thing as a propitious moment in the first world. This only arises if there is something alive to do with the second world, then the opportunity can be taken. This opening which is there, this encounter, whatever it is, is to manifest at that moment. There is the danger of being disoriented by those experiences which for us are very precious and valuable. Now what is beyond that is really to do with the wholeness of things; that is, in the second world everything can enter into itself. A human being in this world can begin to enter into his own nature, experience the depth of himself; but it will not go further than that in this world. It will not go beyond himself. It will not go beyond the particular nature of a particular thing.

But there is something beyond. There is not, for example, true communion in the second world. There is communication, there is synchronicity, but there is not this interpenetration.

Q. How does this relate to the domain of harmony?

A.G.E.B. Yes, it is rather like the domain of harmony, to do with realization and making real; but this second world doesn't have the power to make real, to make something possible to come through. At the moment this word gives me a meaningful image; that is, Gurdjieff said that the true seat of conscience is the 'Kesdjan body', the inner body. Conscience cannot operate in a physical body. The physical body in the second world is too insubstantial to survive conscience. The physical body in the second world is exactly like the material of flatland, a completely two-dimensional world taken into a three-dimensional world. If you take something which is only two-dimensional into a three-dimensional world, it crumbles, but in its own world it is strong. There can be warriors, kings, wars, moons, sciences, and logic in a two-dimensional world, but taken into a three-dimensional world they'd be just like tissue paper. It is the same with our bodies. Our bodies cannot contain experience corresponding to conscience. This is why conscience in us is fleeting; it is put in the perspective of the physical world. Some events to do with the second world make it possible to have a moment of remorse, and then it passes. I see the second world very much as *the gate*. In that world one has positive emotions, conscience, and also what Gurdjieff called objective reason.

This is an extraordinarily difficult thing to appreciate. I remember Mr. Bennett said that for him this was best expressed in C.S. Lewis' book, *The Great Divorce*. For those of you who haven't read it I'll describe it to you. C.S. Lewis presents an image of the hereafter. There's a set of people queuing up for a bus, and they're in a smog-polluted city. They're arguing and bitching about everything, and then the bus comes. They trouble about where it's going, why it's going; and they fight about which seat they're going to be in, and they fight with each other. They get taken to another world. In this other world as they get out of the bus, the light is so strong it makes their eyes ache. They begin to encounter beings who are of a higher level, and each one of these higher beings approaches one of the people and gives each one an opportunity to realize their situation. Of the party of twelve only one accepts to see. In this world, besides the light which is making these people's eyes ache, there is grass which they try to walk on, but it cuts into their feet, because their bodies are not strong enough to withstand these blades of grass. The blades of grass do not bend under their feet, instead they pierce them, because the grass of this world is so much more substantial than the bodies of the people. The higher beings explain that this is an intermediary world, "This is as low as we can come, and for us this is darkness. There is hardly anything here, we can hardly see, you are like ghosts." But for the beings who come from below, the darkness of this other world is an intense brilliant light and the grass is like steel. It is an amazing picture. We have these ordinary associations of what going to another world is like — floating off like a fairy, passing through walls, and so on. Maybe something has been completely inverted here. You pass through the wall, not because one has become so vapor-like, ghost-like, but because in that world the walls are ghost-like. Walls in the deeper regions of the second world are hardly there.

There is a clue about understanding the relationship between worlds which Mr. Bennett showed to us. It is a very important one which I've tried to present to some of the students here. Of course, you've really got to work at it until you see it. It is the thought experiment in which you imagine yourself tying a knot. I think everyone can concretely imagine himself tying a knot. Now you represent to yourselves tying a knot in four dimensions. Don't worry about what the fourth dimension is; treat it as another degree of freedom. Now, try and tie a knot. For a moment you can get it. Don't think about it, just go straight into it. You have to let the image operate on you. In this kind of visualization you are not projecting pictures out in front of yourselves, you have them coming from within yourselves. You can see that you cannot have knots in four dimensions.

We may not see straight away that what we call a material body cannot exist in a higher world. The cohesive energy which locks things together, such as the crystals, corresponds to a knot; but this gets undone in a higher world, and therefore constructs made of the material energies do not exist in the next world.

We have come a long way from washing up dishes!

Q. If I'm talking about what you've been talking about, it seems to me that events are recognizable by their meaning: they form a whole experience which has a certain meaning. They seem to me to be the building blocks that go against time and space. I have a specific number of events that I can return to, each of which gave me a moment of meaning or perception of what I saw as the truth. It seems that these things add on to each other, so that there is a constructing process of some sort, and it's in something that isn't time and space. Is there something in this way of seeing things from your viewpoint? Can you say something about that?

A.G.E.B. Very much. This belongs to a domain about which I remember Mr. Bennett talking to us. When I first heard about this I was so amazed. Let's see how we can talk about it.

There are things that happen that are events, which, far from fading away or perishing or becoming dead, locked in the past, so to speak, not only appear to endure or to live, but even to grow or to deepen in their significance. This kind of change belongs, indeed, to the second world; there it is possible, but not in the realm of actualization, space and time, which belongs to the material energies where the past is dead. Let us say that the inner experience belonging to the event is capable of evolving in its own time and of communicating with other such moments. The general term we give to this is the 'living past'. We know there is a past that has been left behind, like debris; and there it lies, behind us. But there is another kind of past which is with us. But, of course, our possibility of experiencing this, recognizing or seeing it, depends on the state we're in. Usually, it is when we enter into one real event that we come again into these other events; isn't it? You say you come into a kind of meeting of these events. This is why there is Eliot's line, "History is a pattern of timeless moments." Much of the *Four Quartets* is about describing this very thing. You come to a significant moment, and again you enter into the same region as other corresponding significant moments. There is a co-presence of these different events, and they have a wholeness of enlarging significance.

There is also the possibility of going into events, and this is related, in fact, to something that S— suggested in his first question. For me it's only a vague possibility, something that at times, perhaps, I have come close to. This is the possibility of really entering into the past of man, into the historical past. It does happen, I believe, in the case of extraordinary men such as Bennett. He could do it, and at times I could recognize when he was really doing it; at other times he was just drawing on the material of his studies and past experience. At times he would really go to an ancient city and be there. There are certain events in which he actually did participate. Many other people such as Steiner have done this. Toynbee, the historian, has done this a few times and reported on it in his *Study of History*. I believe that all of us participate in this; it belongs to what we call the unconscious — but what Gurdjieff calls the true consciousness.

The consciousness in us is not our property. We make many barriers for ourselves. As John was saying, the properties of the sensitive energy are barriers to true consciousness. One has to do much to tame the sensitivity, to culture the sensitivity, to enable the consciousness to enter. We say, "I am conscious," and we believe we can claim consciousness for ourselves. But consciousness is a universal energy and cannot be brought down into the kind of location which we have in our sensitivity based on attachment, reaction, emotionality, and so on. It is something that we can share with all men; we even probably share it with all life, because there is consciousness in a species of animal. The subtleties of connection within this region are quite beyond our minds which work on a sensitive level.

As one gets older, besides the decay of certain powers, there comes a certain freshness and the possibility of an enlargement. This enlargement is an enlargement of significance. Life gets bigger by having more connections in it; which means that any event within that expanding whole, if it has reached the status of being aligned, is aligned within the larger whole. It is from its participation in the larger whole that evolution can come.

The same thing happens in history. Mr. Bennett used the example of the French Revolution. At the time when it happened some people in England such as William Blake were very excited by it and saw it as a chance of a new breakthrough in human society. Other people saw it as a threat to civilization and stability. The Parisians went rushing about the streets of Paris bringing people to the guillotine left, right, and center. The participants were dreamers moving about at random, rushing around full of crazy ideas, dreams, fantasies, and nightmares. All Europe was in agitation about this. What was it about? What is the significance of the French Revolution? You read the account of people taking part in it, and it doesn't make sense to you. How could they have looked at it in this fashion? They must have been completely caught up in it. But from where do you look at it? You look at it, however crudely, from the point of view of an expanding present moment, of a present moment which goes back into feudal times and forward into our modern industrial civilization; it takes all of that into account. The French Revolution is itself evolving in its own time. It is becoming more what it is.

Now that phrase that I just used, 'becoming more what it is', leads me to something that I had wanted to introduce here. Earlier this week we began talking about three kinds of time. Now, again, I want to talk about three kinds of time, but in a slightly different way.

J.W.   This is very important; this sensitivity somehow being able to withdraw itself to allow the consciousness to take over. We were talking about how we have to perform a task for a period of time, and how we go through all the tricks the sensitivity can play until it is tired or ready to surrender. If you look at it on a historical level, you see that humanity has to go through all the tricks, and the sensitivity has to play itself out before something else can enter. But it is not just that.

A.G.E.B.   It is extraordinary how we can make a connection between the two hours scribbling on a piece of paper and the French Revolution! This is what is needed for work on understanding. Look at what John said about sensitivity. The concentration and dispersion of sensitivity is a big clue, a very big clue. It gives a way of finding our place in the second world which I have been talking about. It is very important to see how the sensitivity is distributed in an experience. We will come back to this, hopefully tonight, when we talk about history.

Q.   I just wanted to ask a question about this 'going the other way' into the future, and what that has to do with possibilities.

A.G.E.B.   You stated it so directly that we'll take this historical example. First of all, our modern industrial civilization and the post-world-war civilization is in the future of the French Revolution. What is being born now is entering into the French Revolution. Remember the lines of Eliot warning us against disowning the past. You see, we have never got beyond the past! All of that is still reverberating around us. We can say, as an approximation, that the past is within us and we have to redeem it; otherwise, we will not be free. That is why we talk about serving the future, preparing for the future, and so on. We have to see and admit that *we are only the past of the future*. In order for this enabling from the future to enter us, we have to serve by preparation. This is the reciprocal maintenance between the future and the present. We are the past of the new age.

Did any one ever see the fantastic, French, science-fiction film called *La Jetée*? It's about a time in which civilization had suffered from atomic warfare, and there were people living underground, divided into masters and slaves. Survival is threatened, so they begin to experiment with time travel. They find a technique of training people who have a great capacity for mental imagery. They train a particular man to enter, first of all, into the past, and then finally, into the future. He asks the future for the wherewithal to save the present.

Q. Nine years ago I wrote my senior paper in college about the first of the *Four Quartets*. There was this line "Garlic and sapphires in the mud," and it haunted me. I couldn't get rid of it and I couldn't get hold of it. When you were talking about the intensity of events, I saw what those words mean, just the intensity of the flavor of garlic and the blue of the sapphire admidst this fudge of ordinary experience.

A.G.E.B. You don't suppose you wrote that thing nine years ago because of now!

Now we need to orientate our minds towards the three kinds of time in a slightly different terminology. I want to talk about 'functional time'; that is, the time in which there are processes; and nearly all that we know is about such processes, things happening step by step. This is itself a very important kind of time, because we certainly have to be intelligent in it to live and do our business in the world. We can be more or less intelligent in it, and there is certainly an enormous complexity of processes.

Then let us think of *a being time*. We have touched upon this being time. When one is bored, time seems to pass slowly. If time is passing slowly, this enables me to do something. Boredom *can* be a threshold. I often repeat a marvelous remark by Krishnamurti. A man came to see Krishnamurti and said, "I'm so upset about myself; I've got all this money, and I follow these high ideas and pursuits, and I find myself constantly in the state that I am bored." Krishnamurti said, "My dear fellow, *be* bored." There are important states brought about in music such as the Gregorian Chant. I remember Simone Weil, a most extraordinary woman, writing that this is music which is so monotonous that it is almost unbearable. It brings one into a time which is clearly not a process time but can be talked about as a kind of time.

It came to me a couple of days ago in one moment when we were working in the back yard. There was one genuine conscious breath, and I clearly saw that what was there could not be described in functional time. There was nothing happening. Yet it was a time, because there was a life there, that moment of attention in the breath belonging to being time. Quite possibly when Ouspensky got hold of the idea that time is breath, he originally had this kind of intuition; but then there is always the temptation to put it into something we can easily visualize. We get the idea of comparing the duration of breath of a man, of an insect, of a planet, of a solar system. This is a significant and valuable idea, but it also can mislead us, because we fall again into clock time or functional time. Being time is unmistakable in our experience, because being time is what we can call 'truly experienced time'. Truly experienced time does not happen. It is in this domain that we can talk about events evolving and significance deepening.

Then there is this third kind of time which is 'will time', which is the most extraordinary time of all. Somebody asked about attention and what it has to do with choice. Are we aware of the moment of choice? What we are ordinarily aware of is in functional time. The moments when we are aware of our experience as such, belong to being time. Now, in the genuine act of attention, there is much to do with being in it. But in the act of attention there is something beyond. Not only does it not happen, but it *is not*. We cannot visualize the act of attention. The content of a visualization is almost bound to be something happening. Very rarely can we visualize something which genuinely has to do with experiencing experience; where we live in ourselves, in our own time, where we enter into living time, being time.

We talk about a spiritual world and think that the spiritual world interpenetrates this world. What is the proper time, the time of the spiritual, the really unconditioned which is beyond consciousness? It is 'act' or 'will time'. This is probably the dimension of decision, and it is not what we are aware of.

We must do what we can to get hold of the relativity of time. Remember this morning I turned the pentad into the essence classes: germ, animal, man, demiurge, and the cosmic individuality. Now I want to translate it into five qualities of time. What is the significance of time? We start with the easiest which is the animal level. This is the time of 'duration'. This is the time in which our bodies accomplish something. It can be small or it can be large, and also it can be experienced in a variety of ways. It can seem to pass quickly or go slowly. If it's passing quickly or slowly it has to do with a linkage with other components. There is a genuine and obvious meaning to time as duration: something lasting so long. We made a lot of experiments with Susan connected with learning about our sense of duration. You can clap your hands in a certain rhythm and then have a period of silence corresponding to the same duration. You can learn how to do this exactly. It comes from our physical body.[2] It is what we put into the design of our clocks.

Now I'm going to look at the kind of time equivalent to the demiurge. As far as I understand it at the moment, it is connected very much to the reading we had from *Hamlet's Mill*. 'We live within a time.' This sense was very clear in ancient times and has come back again with the popularization of the idea of the Age of Aquarius. It is not impossible for us to grasp it. What age are we in? What does this mean? Goethe, at the beginning of the nineteenth century, introduced the word *Zeitgeist,* the spirit of the age, (*Zeit,* time; *Geist,* spirit), 'Time Spirit'. Instinctively one feels this means something. 'We live within a certain time'; everybody talks in this way, but let's look at the significance of it. There is something which ancient people represented by the great cycles of time. Sometimes they gave them a name, and they were represented as gods or higher principles. They were known as the *Aeons.* I always wondered why an age as such could be identified with a spiritual being. Now it begins to make sense to me. It is because it signifies a time within which we can have living time. So if I talk about the ages, it corresponds to the demiurge and means such things as the 'epoch'. This is why Bennett associated the cycles of the epoch with major acts of demiurgic intelligence — not of the supreme God, but of demiurgic intelligence — and the idea that they somehow enabled a new age to come through the mind of man.

Henri Bortoft, at one time a fellow research worker at our Institute, taught me much about this, as he insisted time and again that it's hardly possible to enter into the mind, the time-mind of past epochs; we're so much within our own age.

I suddenly realized today that the middle term, to do with the essence of man, is 'psychokinetic time'. It is a time associated with transformation. It's easy enough to remember that the animal time of duration does not change what a man is; it does not change his being. The whole pentad emerges out of looking at the genuine moment of choice. In this time the moment is unique, but unique in a way that does not separate itself from other moments. In fact there is a uniqueness that is far more capable of integration into other moments than events in ordinary time. This is the whole character of psychokinetic time. Here we come to the most incredible meaning of the term psychokinetic — the movement of the psyche. It must be something like that; it's only when there is the psychokinetic that you have a man. In the psychostatic realm, there is no coming into the essence of man, into the potential of man; it is 'marking time'. Between the psychokinetic and the ages there is evolutionary time.

Now you say, what can possibly be beyond all this? The best way in which I can put it for the lower term is the time of *chance.* We talked a few days ago about hazard, and how it is connected with the way in which opportunities arise so that a step could be made. But the material of these openings, the material that is to be used, comes out of something which we feel is random. It's very difficult to pin this down, because if you ever try to pin down what is random you get nowhere. People imagine that computers generate random numbers, but this is not true. It is impossible to get a computer to generate random numbers: as G. Spencer Brown points out it can only produce something random with respect to a certain concept of order. There is no such thing as pure randomness in mathematics. But there is something corresponding to our intuitions about randomness, about chance; something which gives sense to there being the erratic, the uncontrollable, in our lives. It relates to what I mentioned the other day, briefly, about the elementals, the material spirit forces. This is important, because it means that the material world in which we exist is not simply a clock-work mechanism; there is something coming out of it which is to do with randomness. For instance, without all kinds of accidental shocks happening in my perception and to my associations, I'd die. They tone up my nervous system and are necessary to my existence. But where does this come from? This is the level that I'm trying to get at. We can hardly be directly aware of it, so we tend to give it names such as randomness, chance, and so on. Whenever you try to make sense of it and to bring it in to a concept, it eludes you again. We'll see this happening also in the top term. If you'll forgive me, I'll use the term 'chance' and associate it with the germinal essence.

At the top is something that I do not understand. I was reading about it this morning in Bennett's *Dramatic Universe*, Volume IV. What is the time of Christ? This was given at one time the name 'parousia'. The parousia is the time in which the act of Christ penetrates the creation, that is, the act of love from God towards the creation. It then becomes interesting to say that the 'Second Coming' is now upon us. This has to do with the triangle between the psychokinetic, the ages, and the parousia. But the parousia penetrates all regions of time and cannot be reduced to anything such as: "Christ is going to appear on the earth in 1984." It also points to the fact that we may use the word Christ, and we only have an image of this, and a Mohammedan may use another word, a Hindu, still another word, but all mankind like all life, like all creation, has a place in it.

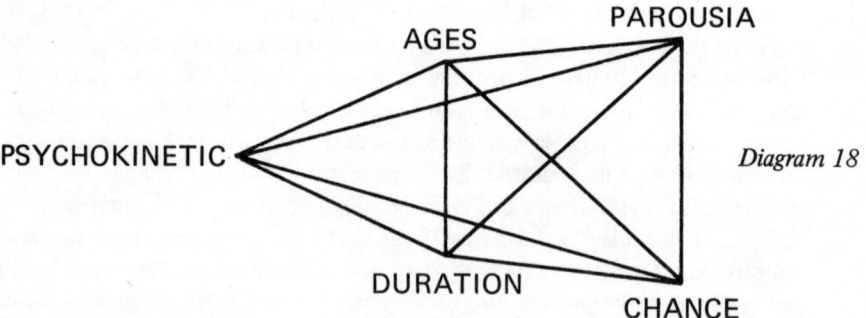

Diagram 18

The Qualities of Time

Bennett describes the action of the higher intelligence or demiurge in terms of the cycles of 2-2,500 years; he called them epochs. He relates the influence of Christ, or the energy of Love, to cycles of 24-26,000 years which affect the evolution of man as a species. But the upper part of the pentad of time involves *creative energy*, and this means that is is associated with *acceleration*.

There is a Sufi tradition in which it is asserted that once the psychokinetic action has been initiated, the various steps succeed each other in an increasingly rapid way. The psychokinetic action depends on an act of cooperation with the 'enabling powers' — represented in the diagram by the upper triangle. This region is the region ahead of time, the region of freedom.

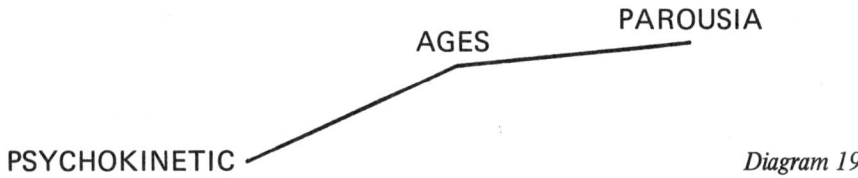

Diagram 19

The region defined by a connection with duration time is the region of the epochs and great cycles which influence mankind as a whole.

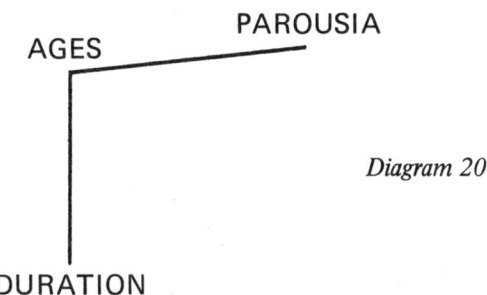

Diagram 20

The region connected with chance represents the totally unpredictable background of our existence, out of which 'miracles' can come.

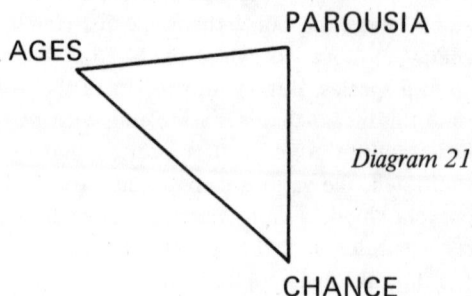

Diagram 21

These remarks are simply suggestions to stimulate you. To say any more would turn into nonsense. The true nature of *Systematics*, which is exemplified in this five-term structure or pentad, is to enable us to contemplate our experience and knowledge; it is an instrument of active search, not a formula for conclusions.

I begin to feel more deeply that there are different kinds and qualities of time. Many people have felt this, but then they have been tempted to describe it in a closed and sometimes even quantitative way, even Rodney Collin falls into this temptation. It is useful to have some picture to think about, but eventually this even gets in the way of direct contemplation of experience.

The taste of psychokinetic time is so important. We have the phrase 'waking up', but this is usually very inadequate. We think of it as some kind of change in self-feeling. I certainly did when I first began to study these ideas. But changes in self-feeling are the *precipitate* of the significant action. What is essential is that something can be done in a way that otherwise is not possible. *There is the time to do something real.*

It is interesting to reflect on the basic idea of the pentad time: man feeds on chance and is food for the coming of Christ.

Q. May I ask something? It's always puzzled me, and I think I have some feeling of this in a sense, going from the top down to the bottom — it's a circle.

A.G.E.B. Yes.

J.W. It's not just a flat picture.

A.G.E.B. Yes, so true. We speak about levels and imagine there is a sort of ladder.

J.W. So that randomness is another form of what we call freedom.

Q. You hear everybody at the right time, that's what it is. We're here because we hear what you're saying at the right time. Do you know what I mean? It's synchronized; it's really incredible.

J.W. Tell her the Mullah Nasser Eddin story.

A.G.E.B.   Mullah Nasser Eddin went walking in the night by a graveyard, and he saw some horsemen in the distance. He got terribly frightened so he jumped into an empty grave. The horsemen seeing this man behaving like this went alongside the grave. They looked over and said, "What are you doing in there?" Mullah Nasser Eddin said, "Well, it's a little more complicated than you think. You, you are here because of me. Me, I am here because of you."

Living Time

Everything living has its own time. Many years ago I read in one of Ouspensky's books that "a tree is a diagram in four dimensions." I often wondered what that meant. It is an extraordinary experience to enter into the time of a tree.

There is a time for every creature, whether vegetable or animal. Try to enter into this, when you look at something living, or become aware of it, open yourself to *its* time. Success or failure does not matter; they do not mean anything here.

Something alive lives in its own time. There harmonization of all the times is in the intelligence of the biosphere.

If you can do something about recognizing the time of living creatures during the day, then perhaps you can contemplate this question: what is the time — the *normal* proper time — for a man? What is its special character?

There is a clue to this in what John was saying just before this meeting. He spoke about bringing something into manifestation. What is to be manifest cannot really belong to this world. This is a difficulty. There is something to be born into this world that comes in the time of a human being. Every living creature has its own time; but man's time can be something more than his own.

I say again that in exercises like this, we must have a very positive and calm attitude. The exercise is not something that we can do, but it is something that is there. Our feelings about success and failure have to do with the functional time of before and after. This is another kind of time. Simply put your attention on the living creature and open your creative imagination to what is there. Take a positive attitude. Do not force anything. We are not going to fake it, we are going to project images onto things; but we will *accept from ourselves* that everything that lives lives in its own time. It is there whether we are aware of it or not.

One is what one is; one does what one can. This can only be seen in being time.

Making Progress

There can come a time in undertaking something when the undertaking begins to undertake us. It is no longer a working of our functions that comes from our functions. You see, we are bound to believe that we are beings who have come together to learn something and do something here; but there is only one thought setting other thoughts in motion, one piece of function leading to others.

At the beginning we think, "I am doing this." We feel that there is an 'I' or 'self' which is substantial and out of which the action comes. This feeling is itself a fact and does exist, though only in a certain world — the world of personality, world 48. In less conditioned worlds it cannot exist; it is like a knot.

We confuse the shape and limits of our personality with the integrality of the inner world. We confuse thoughts with essence perceptions. It is very interesting and important to consider this idea carefully: that in world 48 we cannot tell the difference between the genuine inner-life and the sham pretense of the personality. In world 48 there is no difference. When, for a moment, we are free of twenty-four of the laws, in that state of liberation a different perception and a different experience is tasted and known. The different worlds are in their very nature different in perception and knowledge. It is out of the different orders of perception that our kind of experience is derived: but 'we' are nothing apart.

So, at the beginning of an undertaking, we believe ourselves to be the doers, and also that the coherence and substance of the world comes from us as beings. This is only illusion when you are free enough to see that it is an illusion; a point that is not widely understood.

We are undertaking something and it is in our charge. But, as we go on, we come into a region where it is different. We see that it is the undertaking which has substance and *is*. Our functioning is drawn into it rather than making it up. There is a flow, because now identity does not come from separation, but from mutual relevance.

Out of this comes a more synchronous experience, which simply means experience relatively free of the disordering effect of time and space, but often idolized as the world of the paranormal. We need very much to cultivate our sensitivity to the range and depth of synchronous experience. It cannot be attained, however, by thinking about it or by trying to bring it about.

Synchronicity and a different order of concentration have associated with them values of significance, insight, and understanding. These values are integral to a world of natural relevance, a world relatively free of the conditioning of separation and succession. Names, things, and personalities vanish as discrete entities. Friendship exists here. Ideas exist. There are no ideas in world 48: only words, formulae, and associations.

There can be a sudden release of experience. We speak crudely of 'letting go' and things 'coming in'. There is, what we suppose, a blending of the workings of the centers, which we experience as a sense of meaning in everything we look at and take part in, even in our thoughts. Thinking, feeling, and moving come into the same world, and some possibility is released. We can lose the balance and become excited, intoxicated, and begin to masturbate in our self-feeling.

It seems that we leave the world of having a direction, having to do things, having to get somewhere. 'Here it is'; but it is an everlasting that will perish. There is a world yet to be made, but in a way quite unlike our images of doing. It will not come of itself. It is not existent. Yet it has a special power, because it is much less conditioned. It feels to us like nothingness. The second world is relatively silent. The third world is relatively void. What remains in it is the need to create.

The undertaking becomes the work. The work is primary. It is not a purpose but a source of purpose. There must be purposes for the balance of the whole.

What is needed of us? It is to say, "Let there be this undertaking. Let us be a particle of the undertaking." Neither submission nor action: nothing but adherence to the impossible.

We can so easily forget — not that at the beginning we knew and later did not know. What we have forgotten lies in the void of the future.

What enables us to make the journey worthwhile? When we set out to do something, invariably we tend to close our options. We say, "We shall do this," implying that we will not do all the other possible things. It has to be like that. And if there were not a source of action of quite a different character, we would remain in a world of constant frustration, because all our efforts would have to go into preventing what we do not want to happen. We can begin to understand this from considering our visual perception. The organ of the eye as it works with the brain is designed for selection and fixation, but there is a power of seeing without which the organ is useless.

As we enter into an undertaking, we must gather things together. What is gathered together may be knowledge, people, and materials — depending on the nature of the enterprise. If we persist in aggregation, we will reach a point of saturation. Without making room, nothing new can enter. But emptying is of no use unless there is something. A container requires walls.

Therefore, we must have both gain and loss; and the art of enterprise is in their balance and timing. This principle goes all the way: "What does it profit a man to gain the whole world but lose his soul?"

The interplay between the conditioning of our setting out and the deconditioning that enables us to progress gives a changing meaning to the ingredients of gaining and losing. But the four elements form an integral system that determines our state of harmony and balance in the various worlds.

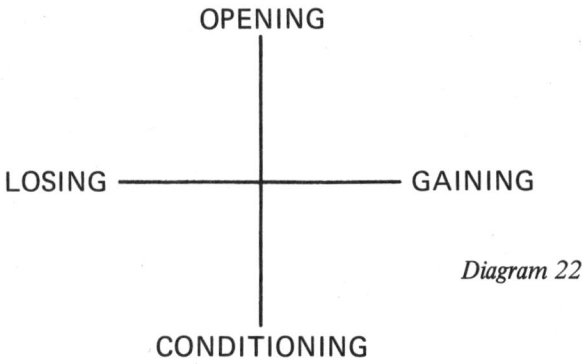

Diagram 22

(See, also, final chapter.)

The, so-to-say, rules under which we operate are the rules of existence. These apply differently at different levels. What is common in these rules are the 'cosmic laws'.

We have been trying to deepen our understanding of time. We have been drawn towards the contemplation of the degrees of conditioning to which we are subject. This has brought us close to what Gurdjieff called the 'fundamental cosmic laws' — which are the way through which time can be conquered. When we first encounter a description of these laws, we treat them like anything else: we think about them, we ask for them to be demonstrated before our eyes, and we expect to sit back in our chairs and have them explained to us. But these are the laws through which the work of our minds is made possible. They cannot be turned into objects of study. Gurdjieff often spoke of them in a way reminiscent of ancient accounts of great gods.

This was not anthropomorphic. In our ordinary way of thinking there is just inert, passive material-existence and human personalities, or minds. The fundamental laws refer to what is not subject to the limitations of either mind or matter. They are the laws of 'world creation and world maintenance', and mind is only one aspect of the conditioned worlds.

To be able to understand these laws we need to reach the point at which *they see through us*. Bennett emphasized this a great deal in the last years of his life. He regarded nearly all of the material on the laws written by people other than Gurdjieff himself as hopelessly misleading. In what I have done, I have avoided as much as possible giving you an explicit definition of the laws. Together, we are going through in action the working of the laws, and the action is faster and deeper than our available capacity for thought. When we come to see something, the laws are manifest in that seeing. It is useless to think about a verbal definition of the laws and then apply these ghostly thoughts to what we know. All that is putting ourselves further and further away from the world in which the laws are manifest. The requirement is *to see*: but this is not at all that 'I' should see. Nor is it a matter of seeing lofty spiritual things as if they were something separate in a very special far away region. No! seeing is more concrete, here and now, than ordinary knowledge. Gurdjieff portrays this by stories such as the one of the shepherd who observes the seven-sided crystal forming out of the milk extract.

In seeing, the fictional 'I' disappears and so does the usual belief in separation and the need for some supposed interaction between the fiction of the 'I' and the fiction of the 'external world'. But when there is seeing, we are in a different world: no subject and object, but something of a different kind. Observation goes.

Make no mistake, though, I am not talking about having way-out experiences which lead us to complain about the inadequacy of words. When seeing is total, words can be an integral part. The words say precisely what is seen. If you doubt me, I recommend you to study *Revelations of Divine Love* by Julian of Norwich, who was one of the inspirations behind the *Four Quartets*. It is always a test of authentic seeing that it is articulate.

MAKING A BEGINNING – WHAT MAKES THE FUTURE?

All of us know about undertaking something, of attempting to understand something, to accomplish something, to become something. Maybe it appears in the form of an outward task, or of self-development, or of a step of understanding, or of the creation of a work of art. Whatever it is, we wish to make progress, and we begin by setting off in a certain direction. This direction can only be that which has the form of something that we know, which is already crystallized in our experience. The reason for this is that we cannot specify anything except in terms of what we know. If we say, "I want to acquire a soul," fine; but the way in which we set out on this acquiring of a soul has the form of what we know about soul formation. In all probability the soul has very much to do with what we do not know. The form of our search or efforts must be based on what we know and is therefore conditioned.

There is at the beginning of a true undertaking, not only a setting out, but a *calling*. This is why it is said that in the first doh, the second doh is sounded. We talk sometimes about having a good sounding of the first doh (making a good beginning), but it is more tricky than it appears. "At what moment do we begin?"

I talked some days ago about the beginning of this seminar. Now, when did it begin? I announced that it would begin at five o'clock last Thursday, but the day already was underway before that, and all the activity of preparing for it was before that, and the conversation I had with Pierre was before that. I talked of the idea that came to me last September and the commitment that I felt. I could have gone back twenty years ago when I sat on the downs in Bristol, and for some reason the image of *The Dramatic Universe* came to me when I was trying to define my aim. And I can go back before that. If I look for it in time, where do I place the beginning? Gurdjieff says, "Search back even as far as your grandmother." And since my gradmother is dead, I can't ask her how it was or how she started it. But we have the requirement of specifying something beginning at a time and place. This requirement is both arbitrary and not arbitrary. If there is an undertaking, it has a shape on many levels, including that of space and time. That is why drama is so informative. We are at this place, at this time. The action begins to unfold. But what begins the action is not in space and time; rather, it endows a certain time and space with a significance that enables us to say, "There and then it all began."

Just put into your minds the question, "When and where did man begin?" This seems to be the question that Dr. Leakey and his son have done much to answer. But their answers are not at all to do with origins, but with working back along the traces of time. The evidence they have uncovered has put into question previous beliefs about the time period in which the distinctively human strain of hominid appeared. But they will not find the origin of the beginning.

Very much is at stake in finding the beginning of man. Part of it is the discovery of what is distinctively human in physical terms: what is the kind of body which permits a human experience? When Mr. Bennett wrote *The Dramatic Universe,* Vol. IV, the current belief was that Australopithecus stood on the road to modern man, Homo Sapiens Sapiens. This is no longer so. The Leakeys have uncovered more probable regions of beginning, more likely candidates for the evolutionary step in which we were formed.

The widespread attitude towards this work is that we will discover the various steps in the emergence of man and be able to explain them. This is typical eternity-blindness. In the psychological field we can realize that creative steps are characterized just by the fact that they do not come out of the past. It is only *in retrospect* that we can order the traces in time to give a convincing picture of inevitable progression with one thing leading to another along the constrained paths which characterize our sense of time.

Of course, it has been a great blessing to have got rid of old ideas about a special creation, some act that completely ignores the constraints of space and time. Such beliefs have held us back for thousands of years; current scientific beliefs will hold us back for hundreds of years. In these beliefs there is retained a kind of magical thinking centered on the fiction of chance. We are presented with ideas such as that of 'random mutations'. Theorists like Jacques Monod turn chance into a god.[1] When we spoke about the pentad of time, we saw that chance was an important aspect, but only one out of the five influences. The core of significant change lies in the hazardous moment. If Richard Leakey progresses in his work, he will uncover a region of extreme unlikelihood; but it will be difficult for him and other scientists to put aside the attitude that since man has actually happened, he cannot be all that unlikely!

There are two factors I would like to introduce in our looking at the beginning of significant change. One of these is potential: there is present in the region of the beginning an influence that is not actual. The power to see is present before the eye is formed. The energies which work in man were already present in the transition into the actualization of a human body. The other factor is intelligence, which has more to do with the will. Will makes connections which reverse the influence of time.

In Bennett's account of the evolution of man, he posits the working of a higher intelligence. The important property he ascribes to this intelligence is the power to embrace a far greater present moment than that of a human mind. Because of this power to embrace, such an intelligence can act *from the future towards the present* as far as any smaller present moment is concerned. Such a view presupposes that we can understand something about the relativity of the present moment and can see that what we call our 'minds' is only one form of the present. Practical studies have been made in business organizations into what is called 'time-span capacity', which relates to one dimension of the present moment which can vary between individuals.[2] The possibility of totally different orders of time-span capacity is hardly ever entertained.

But make no mistake about it; the current rejection of old forms of belief is very helpful. The denial of higher powers is forcing us to come to new modes of expression and new undertakings which the preservation of old forms would not have allowed. Similarly, many people strongly feel that the death of religion is making it possible for people to return to God.

The relativity of the present moment within ourselves gives a firm foundation

Making Progress 157

to the notion of self-development. It all depends on what we take seriously. Gurdjieff, for example, says in *Beelzebub's Tales* that only a constant awareness of our own death can rid us of egoism. To make the total present moment of our lives a reality for us requires the will to do so and the energy to sustain such an experience. Herein lies all the substance of practical religion; for example, prayer is a certain kind of expansion of the present moment, which can be described as a 'communication' with higher intelligence.

At the beginning is the question: "What is the present?" There is another question also; "What is making the future?"

When there is a present moment, the time out of time concentrates experience so that a beginning is possible. Time and place have a quality which lifts them out of the amorphous medley of actualization and separation. The dream place and the actual place coincide. This is the sounding of the first doh.

But in the sounding of the first doh, there is the presence of the second doh; this is within the dream. What we have to do is already here.

The calling of the future is not a shout from a distant place, but a whispering in the ear. Utnapishtim, the Sumerian Noah, listened to wisdom, Ea, whisper to him by the wall. He harkened to the future that he would have to create, and he began to build an ark. Ea is the greater present moment in which both the facts of the causal world – the destruction to come by flood and the way out of danger, the ark – can be experienced. If we look honestly at ourselves and the world, it is easy to see that we neither experience the facts of the determined future nor the opportunities of the unconditioned future. That is why we say that communication with higher intelligence is *neccessary* for our survival and progress.

Something calls us. What calls us? It is the end. When Eliot said, "In my beginning is my end" and "The end is where we start from," he was talking very concretely about the beginning originating from the end. We have sometimes referred to Rodney Collin's image of the death moment as a release of energy through which we are conceived. This is the same thing. But we do not have to excite ourselves with poetry or the thought of death to see the point. We have only to see that at the beginning we do not know the end; yet, we can have confidence in starting towards it, because it is really there, though *in a different world*.

The creative power we have gives us the possibility of making a beginning. We must surely know that the operations of the creative energy are beyond our awareness. But we can have a certain kind of confidence that what we are seeking is to be found, even though we do not know what it is. This is a genuine calling and had often been reported by scientists and artists. Creative action is not problem seeking or anything like that. Even the problem has to be created.

We have to begin *as if* we knew what we were going to attain. It is a mode of conscious fiction which is very important to our work — after all, we say that we must endeavour to act as if we had 'I'. If we do not, then either we become identified unconsciously or give up and drift. The act of conscious pretense is the spirit in which work must be approached, because it can save us from mechanical delusions. The act of conscious pretense is inherent in *real aim*.

In a genuine beginning we start to enter into an action, the significance of which we do not know. It is absurd that people believe they know what it is to gain a soul. I remember being heckled by a well known writer whose first book introduced me to Gurdjieff's ideas, because I was saying that the psychokinetic way is a journey of unknowns. He actually believed that Gurdjieff had mapped out the path, and all one had to do was to apply will power and one would get there!

Nearly the whole of our culture is devoted to the removal of the unknown in action. We demand to know in advance what result we will get. This is the antithesis of having aim.

Probably all of us here have been touched by what we call the 'need to search'. What initiated this search in us? I know for myself unmistakenly that it was not of my own choosing; I had to assent to some impluse that arose in myself. I knew that I did not know what was entailed. I could not say that suddenly the clouds rolled back and a voice cried out to me from heaven.

I began to search. But I realized more and more that in one sense my searching has been the very thing which has got in the way of the truth. Expectation is such an enemy.

Rumi has a marvelous story in the *Mathnawī*. A man has persisted in calling on the name of God, "Allah!" He has cried out and wrung his heart. One day Iblis, the devil, comes and says, "Look, what answer have you ever received? What is the point of crying out and asking if there is no answer?" The man is bewildered by the logic of the devil's speech. In a confused state he wonders in himself. Then God speaks to him, "Oh, Man! You think that *you* have been calling My Name. And hence you expect an answer. Do you not realize that all the time there has been the answer! The answer is the cry you make, *Allah*! It is I who cries out in you."

We have been trying to understand time. Why? Where can we reach? Where have we reached? Just look at the efforts we believe we have been making. Do you really think that these are getting us anywhere? Important ideas have come out. We have all seen things in a different way. An action has been present today such as we heard in Elan's playing of the piano that fills us with wonder. But is this what it is about?

Sir Isaac Newton was probably the greatest enemy that the release of human understanding ever had. He was one of the greatest scientists, and his powers were extraordinary. His influence is immeasurable, but his conceptions of space and time have made a cage for human thought for hundreds of years. Do you see what I am getting at?

We are called, but when do we begin? This is the big question. Time and again we start out on the path of progress to end only in the same region as we began. The new idea rapidly becomes a prison.

Gurdjieff in his 'toast of the idiots' depicts the development of a man up to 'enlightened idiot', who knows what to do but is not able to do it. There he is faced with the need to *descend* with conscience back to 'ordinary idiot', the normal human being. The beginning was not right.

This same theme recurs in writings on the work. Rodney Collin gave us the image of the moment of death originating the conception of the same life: a cycle to be gone through repeatedly until one becomes able to bear the energies released in dying — able to lose one's life. His intuition was connected with the events surrounding the death of Ouspensky and with the telepathic contact he had with him at that moment.

Always in our work we have to begin again. Always it is a question of beginning, not of carrying on from where we left off. Our suffering is to find a beginning.

There is the well known joke of the American asking an Irishman the way to Killarney. "Well," he says, " if I were going to Killarney, I wouldn't start from here."

You will have heard the idea that the past can be changed, and maybe this has excited your interest or strained your credulity. Very rarely do people take such ideas and dig into them and find out what they can mean practically. Changing the past is finding a better beginning. We have many illusions about change and getting somewhere. We believe that if we start off any-old-how, then something comes out of it; but if you really look, you will see that nothing has changed. What we go through in our struggles and strivings and journeys is to enable us to accept the beginning that is right. How many stories there are of people searching for love, for truth, for wealth even, far and wide, to discover that what they needed was in their own backyard.

The Buddhist theme of escaping the 'wheel of samsara', the cycle of birth and death, is that of discovering the real beginning, the beginning in which there is the end. That is why many spiritual teachers pour scorn on all our ordinary notions of making efforts and searching as forms of delusion. One Sufi method is to find ways of distracting the pupil's attention so that his fragmentary efforts do not interfere with the real development.

But none of this is absolute. We make beginnings in a muddled way, of course, but it is not all useless. The truth is compassionate. If we can accept that we have only opinions, images, of the way, we can remain open.

There are some very simple things we can do. Before we begin something, we can *listen*. We must pause and bring ourselves into as quiet a state as possible. We bring together our force of intention, but then, let it be. In the active quiet we make a small act of submission; we need not know to what. There is not a thing we submit to, not a being we listen to. This quiet is for attunement to the time in which we can live, the time in which a higher order can operate. The plant has its roots in the soil and draws on the elements, but it also opens its leaves to the sun. The radiation of the sun is a source of order. It is by drawing on this that life can maintain itself.

Inshallah! God willing: not just the words but the acceptance that the journey or task will be real, only if it is so in a higher world.

We have to understand it in a way that corresponds to the size and content of our own present moment. Our material for understanding is the limited experience of this seminar. We began our study from certain perspectives in terms of what we knew and what we were interested in, from all kinds of associations, circumstances, and so on; we thought that we were going to gain something and know something more about time. One can never expect the unexpected, one can never know the unknown, one cannot look towards anything except what one has already seen. Yet, it is also true to say that there can also be a sense of something other which we cannot even qualify or circumscribe. A step in understanding is really such a thing, but we do not know what this means before it comes about. The connection with the unconditioned is not even like knowledge; it is not like experience either.

UNDERWAY – SPACE, TIME, AND EXISTENCE

In the beginning is an incredible tension between value and fact, between the unknown and the known, between the future and the past. The real sounding of the first doh is the experience of that tension; it is not really a moment in time, that is, duration time. An action comes out of it. First of all, a process begins – but in fact, many different processes. For example, even in cooking a meal, we have to do things such as bring in the foodstuffs, make sure the pots are clean, and work out a menu. These are all in different parts of oneself or amongst different people. Similarly with this seminar, one begins with bringing in different kinds of activity, different ideas, and different people come in at different points. This we call 'getting underway'. It produces a certain *configuration of actualization* that has a significance in it. We have to bring a number of people together in a building for a certain time and do various things. At the beginning we can feel it is all silly, because what we are doing is not at all like where we hope to reach. These exercises and practical work and talks are not changing our understanding. Things go on here, things go on there — what does it matter? At this stage there is no real cooking, but what is being done has to be done.

It is sometimes called setting the stage. At the beginning of a dramatic work of art, there are devices for introducing the different characters and setting up the situation so that the audience can share in what is going on, get a picture of it, and be engaged in it. A scientist in undertaking a line of research does setting up for his experiments: reading papers, doing calculations, and so on before he touches a piece of apparatus.

EMERGENCE — THE FORM OF A HAPPENING

After a time there will be another step. The audience will feel that they have got an idea of what is going on — the plot emerges. The kitchen activities will begin to converge towards specific dishes. The scientist will begin to assemble his experimental rig. There is a change in the coherence of the action. There emerges a quality, or qualities, which is more than we can directly know. Bennett spoke about this in terms of Laws of Synchronicity. I will briefly mention two of the laws.

First, the Law of Mutual Adjustment. When various things are together in a spatial region, their regulative influences mutually adjust so that a common pattern can be experienced; in other words, things come to fit together for more than can be expected. All of us people have been thrown together for a period, each with our own quirks, but the situation has not fallen apart. We tend to take this for granted, but in factual terms it is not to be expected.

Second, the Law of Common Presence. By existing together in space, not only a common pattern emerges but also a common presence. This means that a situation begins to exhibit a direction of its own that has not very much to do with the separate inclinations of any part of it.

We see in this stage of every enterprise, including our own, a certain degree of harmonization or blending-of-tempo. This makes possible a shared undertaking. Things begin to work out and go in a certain direction, in a certain way. But nothing has been changed. What has happened is that a shape has emerged that is beginning *to give the undertaking its own character*.

TIME OUT OF TIME

In the discussion this afternoon some people talked about a common attitude we have towards working within a fixed duration. Being confronted with a fixed duration seems to be a threat to our freedom, and we resent it. It is different when we experience a deadline, which is the experience of 'running out of time', that can so often radically change the quality of our efforts. Deadlines are one device for bringing ourselves into being time. An activity prescribed within certain limits is different; we have to find our own challenge.

We have had various exercises that evoked boredom. Then we found that on occasion we could accept that what has to be done is simply what is here and now. This may seem a weird thing to say, because one is doing things; the point is, though, one is not doing things. There is activity, even harmonized activity, but there is no *being time*. For there to be being time there has to be an act of giving oneself to the situation, not that we can reach into ourselves and take something and hand it over. It is sometimes described as letting go and has to do with a deeper level of commitment. The characteristic of it is doing what is here and now, not something else and not being attracted towards something else. In ordinary language it is called 'having one's heart in it' — not in an emotional way because one is attracted or stimulated, but because one's blood is given.

It is coming into a world where 'a spade is a spade'. And strange to say, (and more and more I am convinced about this), ordinarily we do not live in a world where a spade is a spade. We are not aware of the spade. For us the spade is an awkward thing, or 'my spade', or not there at all. We are doing something, but we do not see what we are doing.

When we are simply doing what we are doing, we are aware of what is there. The step is at first difficult to recognize, because it has to do with being time. Nothing has happened which is any different, but there is a real change. There is a rightness.

Sometimes we come to that point through a crisis. It is connected with the separation of consciousness and sensitivity. Nearly always the sensitivity has to go through all kinds of tricks, blind alleys, and useless experiences in order to get tired of all that. This tiredness is the sensitive side of disillusionment. It has to do with abandoning what the consciousness in us *already sees* as useless.

But the sense of reality is still incomplete. We are substantially engaged in an activity in this physical world, and a depth is opening up. We are aware of what is going on and see in it a significance far greater than before. But there is a further barrier. It is like the exercise of the third dimension: when the depth of what is there opens up to us, we come to the point of seeing the whole thing as insubstantial. What is lacking is a certain power of *act*.

There is sometimes the feeling of the parallel worlds, one a dream and the other an activity, which are incompletely related together. Remember that the true experience of consciousness is not the enhancement and stimulation of sensitivity, but something that gives us the realization that we *are asleep*, not simply that we *have been* asleep.

HARNEL-AOOT – THE MOMENT OF CHOICE

The activities carry the past with them, but now there is something relatively free of the past. The question of the future changes. We *see* that something different is needed, but we do not know what to do. We have separated from old doing, that is, activity, daydreaming, planning, but have not yet found a new doing. Everything that we can look at belongs to the past. We realize that it is unable to change; we realize that we do not know how to change. We have to carry on with consciousness of our blindness. Many of you will know that this stage was referred to by Gurdjieff as the Harnel-Aoot and describes the point of tension in the middle of the way.

It also describes the psychokinetic dilemma: we become to some extent free of the past, but we have no firm connection with the future. I have gone through this many times during the seminar, reaching the limit of my understanding of Bennett's ideas and seeing some of their intrinsic limitations, but having no awareness of where to go.

One of the roles of psychokinetic people is to bear the experience of this maximum uncertainty. Because the pull of the future is very weak, we have the conditions for a free commitment, a leap of faith. It need not be dramatic. It can be very quiet and unobserved: simply that we go on. But our going on is right, only if we have realized our helplessness. It is not a matter of despair – here, despair keeps us back. It is a matter of confidence in what is beyond our awareness, which we cannot have unless we have come to the middle of the way and have seen that we have done nothing.

In certain exercises we do, derived from Naqshbandi sources, (the first written record of them traces them back to Samarkand in the thirteenth century and the influence of a remarkable anonymous Buddhist shaman[4]), we practice the opening up of positive feeling through the 'latifas'. In terms of human structure rather than process, the latifas stand in 'the middle of the way'. You will remember that the positive feelings are not directed towards any object or image, but are awakened through acceptance of the unconditioned world.

We have to let hazard enter our heart. It is not a matter of making a mental commitment. The real act of commitment comes like a thief in the night. If it were mental, this would bring us back into the conditioned world. What does enter the mind is the thought, "How astonishing! I find myself going on, not knowing where or how."

It is at this point that we make the kind of payment which enables us to participate in the whole event. Instead of chasing along a part of the circle, we can come into contact with the whole of the circle. There is even happiness in it to do with enjoying our own difficulties and dilemmas. We come to accept them as friends — realizing that we do not have to like our friends all of the time! The release we have is in ceasing to demand and expect things of the world, including ourselves. It is then that the power of another world can enter.

THE MALLEABLE DREAM – TIME THAT DOES NOT PASS

In previous discussions we have talked about the second world and the power it can have in the first physical world. The second world is where things are what they are, where non-causal modes of communication are possible, and where ideas exist. When a right balance has come about in ourselves between these worlds; that is, between 'inner' and 'outer', some of the characteristics of the inner world can be made manifest externally. This does not happen by taking thought.

Dreams are a weak form of this linkage between the inner and the outer worlds. When we have worked and come into a harmonization of our energies, the linkage can be very strong. In our ordinary state of disharmony, there is still a linkage but it can be of a destructive kind — which we describe as being in world 96, the world which includes negative laws.

The linkage is intimately connected with what we call the *power of imagination*. Gurdjieff called it 'piandjoëhary', the fifth step in the transformation of the foodstuff. In the disharmonized state, piandjoëhary destroys our possibilities. In the harmonized state, it helps to create possibilities. There is also an in-between state of relatively harmless self-indulgence which simply degrades the quality of energy without negative consequences. It is through this power that we can create.

Today I found myself with new ideas, a whole flood of ideas; everything became connected with everything else. One can wish to have more and more of these; and a very difficult step it is to leave that behind. It comes in its proper time, the time of release. Then it has to change.

It is probably the same in meditation. We go through certain stages until we can really accept being in the meditation; then the *dhyanas* start, the 'absorptions', as they are called. These absorptions belong to the same realm as that in which we do what there is to be done, which is here and now, in practical activity. Then we come to the stage of bewilderment where, in meditation, ordinary thought ceases. In our state of inarticulateness we can be attracted back to having some form in our minds, but we must remain steadfast. There is a contradiction here: we have to persist even though it is not something that we can do. The act of persistence, in which we are involved in the struggle with our body and with many other things, is an act that we make, and it has to be made at a time when there is not strong experience; otherwise, it cannot be genuine.

Whenever there is in us a strong experience, it is almost impossible for us to be free. This is why new possibilities for us have to be opened up in subtle ways, and it is useless asking anybody, even Jesus Christ, "What do I do to be saved?" Whatever answer He gave, it would not help.

FREEDOM — THE UNCONDITIONED FUTURE

Why is it that the sense of bliss that comes in meditation is sometimes referred to as Mara, the evil one, the very epitome of temptation? In this region one is under a pattern, one's own pattern. I saw this today, and I reached a point in myself when I could hardly stand upright or walk anywhere or do anything. A particular something happened, and I still can't understand why. It came very clearly, not as a flash, not as a revelation, but very, very simply that there is a wider reality than this. This is the interesting point, because here we get into a realm beyond excitement, beyond *hal,* beyond state, beyond having ideas. And I said to myself, "Well, what happens next?" I have no idea. What is beyond this? I really have no idea. Let it come." There in front of me was simply the fact: it must be different, whatever it is. It is not more of the same. If I held onto this state, it would deteriorate into all kinds of negativity and confusion. In Shakespeare's plays nearly always, just at this point, the process is left and the curtain falls. "The rest is silence." At the moment of death, when you can face it, all that has come about and has been done is nothing at all.

Now we can ask, "Why did we begin?" What was there at the beginning to do with there really being a destination? And here, still, the rest is silence. But there *was* a calling. Something comes to call us to search, and though it remains hidden, it is there nevertheless. But maybe it is not hidden all the time. I remember when I spent some time with Mr. Bennett looking at the structure of the theatre or drama. In looking at certain great plays, we saw how they reached towards a sense of destination that requires us to give up even our form of experience. It is only in comedy that the dramatist will reach beyond the silence of Hamlet to some form of unexpected reconciliation.

It is not always like this. We look at *Peer Gynt*, an extraordinary play. Peer Gynt blows every single opportunity. He uses up all his potential and thrashes around in all sorts of blind alleys, always believing in his own reality and power to do. Peer Gynt is strongly associated with the power of the piandjoëhary. When it is exhausted, he is helpless. But then a hand comes out of heaven through the woman who prays to the Virgin for his salvation. The Button-Molder wants to take Peer Gynt and melt him down like an old button to be used again to make new buttons. The Button-Molder says, "Well, Peer, your time is come." Peer Gynt protests, "I've been such a good person, how can you melt me down?" The Button-Molder brushes that nonsense aside and explains, "You had something in you which you did not develop, a pattern which you did not bring to fruition." So Peer tries another tack, "I've been so wicked, so terrible, and so black." But the Button-Molder is remorseless, "Oh, if you'd been black enough, it would have been all right. You can escape if you're either a positive or a negative, but not if you're just a muddle." Peer Gynt pleads for a little more time. He wanders back to his old home, and there, now blind, is the woman who loved him, who is praying still to the Virgin for him. She takes him to her as a mother takes her child, because she is the channel of grace. There is a very strong, sacred image in Christendom of the Virgin gathering those in need under her robes. We can be gathered there, she can accommodate us there, because she is utterly pure. In the silence, beyond the power of making forms, there is the reality of compassion.

Even being time in a way passes, because it has a pattern. It passes away, because there is a creation, and all that is made must be unmade. It is only in the third realm of will time that there is no unmaking. This suggests that in every genuine act of progress the final realm is associated with failure, with the recognition that one has no power of one's own, and all that which produced the strength, the perception, and the power, are, so to say, borrowed. This passes through us and cannot remain in anything limited, in the way in which our pattern limits our experience and possibilities. In the end we can say that this which lies beyond must be something of the immortal. In an historical event it is the fulfillment of the destiny. In our lives it is the fulfillment of our destiny. The fulfillment of our destiny is done through this world, but the fruit of it is not in this world.

It is this that makes the world also sacred and why the image of the Virgin is so important. She is a natural creature but can pass without difficulty into the unconditioned world.

The critical question we have to ask about every aim is: "Is it for real?" remembering that reality cannot be given limits defined for our own safety and lack of perception.

THE BEGINNING OF THE END

At the end there is the marriage of the beginning and the calling. It is symbolized in the *Divine Comedy* of Dante. The Beatrice of flesh and blood glimpsed in the street becomes the guide to the place of union.

But remember that a progression is not a step by step process leaving the earlier steps behind. In being time, they co-exist. In will time, they become one.

We have to talk about stages sequentially, but we can get a taste of their co-existence when we have time to see.

I have talked about progress against the background of our experience of this seminar. I think we can recognize something about how things have worked out in correspondence with a structure. It is of course the structure of the *octave*. I wanted to present it in a way which did not bring us back to the same old thing that I have heard over the years: people talking glibly about 'second conscious shocks'; I have so long been convinced that this is quite wrong. I can remember some nut case at Coombe Springs who went around giving people 'conscious shocks' by hitting them in the eye. The octave has to do with the interpenetration of events, with the kinds, the qualities, the species of events of transition and of state. There is a unity of action between them. In each of the stages there is a kind of event in which some realization of freedom is possible. I speak about the unknown hand out of heaven, but how does the hand out of heaven come? Not as it's portrayed in the movies. But if it is totally invisible, then what use is it? That is why I chose the image of Mary; that a creature of this earth can really be a channel of grace is very important. The intervention of what is higher is concrete.

We may fail to recognize the culmination of our progress, because we are not purified enough to accept reality without distortion and judgment.

We see that progress has a much vaster range of meaning than we ordinarily give it credence for, because each of these stages or transitions, as I have described them, could be taken as a meaning of progress. In earlier stages you get something done. In the middle region you begin to touch upon what people think about as evolution, where what is entering is something about what things are. We speak about emergence of higher levels, higher forms of life. Bennett's account of human evolution deals with the first half of the structure of progress. The other half is often referred to in a non-historical way. People can get trapped into this and say that the cosmic redemption is out of time and cannot take place historically. There is something incomplete here, because there is more than eternity. The spiritual is more than eternal. Eternity is too small for God. The point about eternity is that it is fixed. It is fixed in allowing a certain pattern of potential. That is not good enough. In this notion of progress we come to something which is deeper than any ordinary picture we have, for example, of evolution. It is, to put it more strongly, like the making of reality, and this is not by going elsewhere, but by going deeper.

It is partially intentional that I have spoken about three kinds of time, five qualities of time, and then of the sevenfoldness of progress. It is not a matter of more complication, but of arriving at the point where everything can find its place. This everything finding its place, fulfillment, is something which is ultimate. Let us call it fulfillment, truth, *haqq*. What is this? You see the growth of a plant, you see the emergence of life on the earth, a work of art is created, an idea is seen, a group of people learn to love one another. What is common to all of this, and what is it all? The point is to enter them in such a way that the real diversity of the world is experienced. Do not reduce everything to the same kind of thing. The growth of a flower, a group of people learning to love one another, and all the myriad things are *the meaning of time*. We can speak of the Creator's time and the work of the Good Spirit or of Ahura Mazda or of His Endlessness. This work is in the face of the Merciless Heropass. What the Heropass is is probably utterly impossible for us to see. It is the absolute, beyond God. All we know is that what we call progress, and which we witness everywhere according to our nature, is for us a *sign of our Creator*. When we say this is one, that there is one meaning of time, this is the same as the declaration of faith, "There is no God but God." When people are touched by this, perhaps they begin to speak in a confused way about the end of time.

Unstuck in Time

Freedom

I intended to call this talk "Freedom" when I planned the seminar a week ago. As with many of the titles I then wrote down for myself, I am going to stick to it. The titles have been a thread for me. It was not that I knew what I would talk about, it was not that I knew what the words, such as 'freedom', meant; but, somehow or other, having these titles gave some form and some direction to something very difficult. They helped in finding my way through. Now, when I look at it, I am really surprised that this talk is called "Freedom". It is so very appropriate that it is uncanny. Often it is like that. One sets up something in what seems to be a very primitive kind of way, and it serves very well.

It is very good to have to talk about this theme of freedom now, because I myself have hardly any energy to do so, and as far as I can see, all of us are moving away from the heart of the event in which we came together into the realms of disintegration. So maybe we can learn about freedom. The question of freedom is really here in our midst.

I make this observation, because we need the material of the experience that is here. We are after real understanding, and this needs what is most truly here and now.

Whenever there is an occasion, on whatever scale, in which there is a 'manifestation', then something is brought into expression or into being which is not of this world. There comes a climax or culminating event, some kind of experience some kind of insight, some kind of product. Then it seems that it all fades away — or that we pass away from it. But, really, in this period of passing away, when we feel that the energy and connectivity are going, it is possible to enter into something different and deeper.

History is full of this: people come up to something, it appears to be working, and there is a concentration of sensitivity. And then it appears that the whole thing is a failure or just moonshine. It happened, for example, in the French Revolution; a vision of democratic society entered into people and it worked up to its crescendo. Then it became excitement and craziness: the guillotine and the witch-hunting of the aristocracy — a reign of terror. All kinds of persecutions along with the struggle for power came out of it. Brother turned against brother. The vision became a nightmare. This kind of thing is found again and again.

It is found in the biggest event of all: in the coming of Christ and the extraordinary events of the crucifixion and the resurrection. The resurrection was the great manifestation. It was the proof of the Word. Then, at Pentecost the enabling power of the Holy Ghost came down so that people could speak in tongues and manifest the charismatic powers. Then what happened? They set up an organization! In the very first state they were actively waiting; for 'tomorrow' they would 'wake up' and the Kingdom of Heaven would be upon them. But it did not seem to come. They began to develop different sects, schisms, practices, beliefs, rules, and poor St. Paul had to rush around trying to sort people out. He had to write explanatory letters, get things organized, and keep things going. When you read these letters, you can so vividly picture what a chaotic scene it must have been and the sort of anguish he must have gone through at seeing what he believed to be the essential truth being covered over and confused — let alone what happened later, the way it was taken into martyrdom and into withdrawal from life and community in the deserts of Egypt and Libya.

Then came the institutionalization of Christianity through Constantine. And there appeared theologies, churches, and bishops, until it produced an authoritarian structure that soon was responsible for very much brutality and death. Every event in human life has this kind of failure in it.

If we look at this along the direction of linear functional-time, the inevitable conclusion is that history is a pattern of failure. Islam was the call of Muhammad to all to make the proclamation of faith in one God. Jew, Christian, and Zoroastrian had only to make the declaration, "There is no god but God," that only God is to be worshipped. They would not do it. Those that did became righteous fanatics, and Islam is typified in world history in terms of the *jihad*, holy war.[1] Islam has become one of the major political forces in the world. There is in it a violence, a separateness from other beliefs, and one of the most rigid orthodoxies that exist. Everything has this pattern of the crescendo to the dramatic moment — as in the invitation of Muhammad to Medina and the entry into Mecca — from which in time there is a fading away of the light and a coming again of the darkness.

Even in our own limited scale of experience it is like that. Our difficulty is to see what we do not see in events: how they begin and how they end. Yesterday I said that the true beginning is invisible to us. It is the calling of what has to be fulfilled. If we look at our own search — which has brought us here together — we fool ourselves greatly if we assume that we know what began it. Mr. Bennett had a study made of the people who came to Sherborne. Everyone was asked to write their life story and say how they came to the Academy. At the bottom of these stories there was always something inexplicable. People can be brought up by parents interested in these ideas and these ways and they can have all the opportunities in the world, but nothing happens. Others, whom you might think have no chance at all, have come into connection with it. This sort of thing we can study through our own experience of the beginning of important ventures. Never does there appear to us what is in the beginning.

Of course, there may be a moment of experience when a voice comes, or something like that. I know for myself that my experience of death was the moment in which I recognized the work. But I did not know anything because of this experience, and I did not know what had gone before to bring me to that personal moment of terror and joy. We know the beginnings have something deeper behind them: the beginning of the beginning. There are visible starting points, visible changes of fortune, visible changes of direction, but the beginning of the beginning we do not see. How does the beginning *come about*?

The 'real' beginning may be considered one event or many, both, or neither. There is no way of knowing, but we can look at it and give our attention to it. We do not need to know anything or imagine anything.

Let us take again the example of Christ. There is the Annunciation and the moment of acceptance, 'fiat mihi', of Mary. She is pictured as being visited by the archangel Gabriel. There is the Transfiguration, an event belonging to higher worlds totally incomprehensible to ordinary men and women. Christ is described as speaking with Moses and Elijah. Then there is all the preparation going back over the Aeons to prepare the mind of man for such a revelation. In one direction it is hidden in the angelic kingdom; in another, it is hidden in the act of 'Will of Mary'; in another, it is hidden in the higher worlds; and in another, hidden in the depths of the past. Angels, 'will', higher worlds, and the depths of the past are all hidden from us. It is the same for us in our lives. There is no doubt that all of these mysteries are in our origin and foundation, but we see nothing of them.

It is the same for the ending of things. What is the 'future of the end'? What is the ending of Christianity? We see it as the petering out of the waters of love in the desert of man's heart. If we look around, there is nowhere evidence of any more love than there was two thousand years ago. Perhaps some of us believe in the *Parousia*, the Second Coming of Christ, and the doctrine of *Revelations*, when time will have an end. People talk of this as they talked about the beginning, in terms of angels or some unimaginable miracle, and so on. They really consider the last two thousand years to be a colossal failure, and, like the very first Christians, they live in hope of miracles which will banish the agonies and brutalities of our human life. Can it ever really be like that? On the one hand there is the actual past, what men have been through — a nightmare — and on the other hand, hope of a miraculous intervention which will wake us up. What happens if the miracle comes, and we do not even notice it? Can we really ever hope to 'wake up tomorrow'? Can any future state be any different *for us?* What really happened in the last two thousand years?

You see, some people will say that we are getting into a muddle here, because the spiritual action is really outside of time and Christ is in all time. But that is not good enough. What is all this struggle and suffering and bearing and searching of people? What is it that we ourselves are going through? Maybe we can never say what it really is. That does not matter. What matters is to give our attention, to care about the whole of it. I know how 'blissfully delightful' is this image of an eternal state, but I also know that it is poison.

We must face it, Christianity failed. Islam and Buddhism and the other religions also failed. The spectacle of a religion of love becoming an agent of exploitation, massacre, intolerance, narrow-mindedness, and hate is almost unbearable. Here is something very extraordinary. Gurdjieff always used to say, "Everything turns into its own opposite;" and Christianity seems just another example of this law that one can also verify in one's own experience. But it is not the last word to be said. There is the turning around of the hope to the despair, the virtue to the vice, the vision to the dream, in which something we do not ordinarily see also happens. I say that this must be so; otherwise, all of this life is a charade, and what is done here has no meaning. We do not even have to believe in progress to see this. The play of opposites is as mechanical as the play of gravitation and radiation, pressures that keep the stars in balance, or the play of expansion and contraction in the whole universe. If there is only that, it is all meaningless. We must abandon the visual images of evolution and progress to get the feeling of what is more than this mechanical play.

Dialectical materialism is useful, but too naive. Some religions are incredibly stupid about real life with its ideas of renewal in another world. Look at every image we can possibly have of this thing we are after — all the images invented by people who were in the business of persuading other people! Where do they go wrong? It is not even that they are wrong; dialectical materialism is fine. The problem is that we ordinarily have no contact with what is beyond the image. This itself is the clue.

Mr. Bennett gave a hint about this concerning Christianity many years ago when he wrote in *The Dramatic Universe*, Vol. IV, that the significant thing to look at in the last two thousand years is that enough experience has accumulated for at least a few people to realize that man as he is is *not able to accept* the gift offered to him. Something has been offered to us, and we have not been able to bring ourselves to accept the gift. Here is the failure of all religions. In this failure there is an action which we can call *humiliation*.

We know that we cannot do what is set before us, even though we know that it is right. I am not just speaking about morality; it is deeper than that. It has to do with the deep, inner torment of our lives. It does not exclude what many say that if you really *see*, then you *will* do, because to see is the whole question, and how to help man see is the problem hidden in religion.

Bennett, in *The Masters of Wisdom*, went further to say that humiliation is *the key*, because this general humiliation of mankind over the last two thousand years is a pale but real reflection of what the disciples of Christ went through. Even those few who were with him in the Transfiguration and witnessed what He really was would reject Him. They would have to go through the horror of rejection — Peter went through it and also Judas and James and John; because, until they went through it, they would still believe themselves to be something. You see, love cannot come if you believe yourself to be something.

We have an image that in some higher region within ourselves or 'on high', there is a certain reality, there is love. This has happened through Christ. But we keep something separate, which is ourselves in the ordinary world. Somehow or other the truth has to come even into the ordinary world. But this is impossible: this world is so built that in it we believe ourselves to be something, and we are *full* of ourselves; that is, we are a construct of images, or imagery. This impossibility can only be resolved by an extraordinary kind of action that we ordinarily do not accept or even notice. It is this action that Bennett gave the name humiliation.

Here is the true meaning of *the end*. We can begin to see here and now together, that what is involved is totally different from our ideas of evolution and progress and getting somewhere. What could be more real and important than the coming of love? This requires the extinction of the imagery, for the imagery cannot do.

This extinction was carefully examined and researched by the Sufis. In Sufism there is the term *fanā*, which means annihilation. The Quranic basis for this idea is the injunction, "Die before you die!" The annihilation is the ending that extinguishes the inevitability of failure. There are distinguished various degrees of *fanā*.

The first *fanā* is the *fanā-i akhām*, which means annihilation of entanglement in the conditioning of the physical world. *Akhām* is derived from *hukum*, laws. This annihilation has to do with becoming disillusioned with trying to change things from outside, which means in the world where everything is outside everything else. This is required if we are to enter into what I have been calling being time. It sets up the possibility of entering into life. We can have a taste of this; there was the exercise we had practiced today and all the other simple exercises. We come to see that when we simply do what is in front of us, when we go through the barriers of boredom, when we have got tired of trying to do imaginary things, then something different can happen. The very same thing is constantly repeated by people who have made, what is called, a creative step — which is really a transition into the world where everything is what it is!

The next *fanā* is the *fanā-i afāl*. This is very important for us. *Afāl* is the plural of *fīl*, action. The extinction here is of the belief that it is in our power to do things or to change what things are. It enables us to live in life, to be aware in being time.

The third *fanā* is the *fanā-i sifat*. *Sifat* means attributes. Here is the realization that one does not have anything of one's own; we do not even have our own mind. The material of mind is borrowed from a collective source. Our reality is not that of mind, nor any kind of awareness; awareness is secondary. In coming to some insight or realization, it is very important to be able to see that the material for this is all borrowed. Everything is temporary and partial, no matter how deep and strong it appears. To see this is a very high thing, and in Sufism this *fanā* is said to be the gateway to sainthood. It has to do with passing beyond the image to the reality, even when the image is sacred — and the realization that whatever the image, it is only an image. This is a much tougher image proposition than it sounds.

The Sufis go on to speak of the *fanā-i zāt*, annihilation of essence. I have no idea at all what this means. It makes me feel the creation trembles!

Spoken about in the usual way, it seems that the doctrine of *fanā* is simply a religious psychology. This really misses the point. The *fanai* are actions involving different worlds. They are not locked up inside people. In the higher worlds, the insides of people are very much an outside. This is the meaning of higher energies.

I am going to say that we should look at the *fanai* as manifest in history. If they are not manifested, then all that is just another psychological dream. The possibility of this manifestation can be called 'religious history' as long as we do not confuse this with the history of religions. The idea of this probably came in with the Israelites and their prophets and messengers who taught that real history, real events, were a manifestation of God's *time*. Really, this is the only straightforward meaning of the sentiment expressed as, 'God is with us'.

It is very difficult to understand. As I have said, in the past because of limitations of language and the nature of the cultures of these times, nearly all expressions about spiritual attainment were associated with eternity or the a-temporal. But eternity is the being time; it is the time of paradise. We can see this is quite literally true when we get a taste of entering into the time of life: it is exactly like a taste of paradise or heaven.

By and large, people think of the 'perennial philosophy', as Huxley did, as something eternal and unchanging, fading in and out of human life. There is also the deeper insight expressed in Sufi teaching that the world of functional linear time is too restricted for the 'will of God' to operate. This means that there is a great divorce between will time and function time. But it is for this reason that there are special constructions such as man — that is, three-centered beings — in which the three kinds of time can be unified.

For me there is a genuine sense in which we can affirm that history and the historical actions which we refer to as evolution go towards God. But how impossible it is to say anything sensible about it! I so much agreed with Mr. Bennett's sentiment that the Vatican council did well to put Teilhard de Chardin's books on the index. We really do go astray and get these things wrong by being satisfied with cheap pictures. De Chardin draws a straight line between molecular attraction and union in love and invents a theory of increasing complexification. It is all done with the highest of motives, but it is a slavery to the inherent disease of the mind to seek gratification through spurious images. We do like to imagine that we understand! Feeding this desire has become a major human activity.

My aim has been throughout not to give any more theories and any more explanations of images, but simply to keep our attention on the facts. We are trying to *see what we know*. There is something in history that is really other, that cannot be contained in what we know or think or imagine. Our path towards this entails our going through the region of experience, the being time, which is not itself the reality. That is why this time, in which our experience is failing, is so very valuable. Here is the most difficult region of all, the crossover point from image to experience to the truth. There is help which comes through the very structuring of the world which makes what we call "failure" possible.

The real world is so different from the picture we are almost bound to have of some piece of intricate clockwork, whether we consider this clockwork as glorified machinery or boring machinery. It is so different from any belief that all good things get somewhere in a visible way. We do not see and appreciate the facts of the situation: something is built up which is difficult and arduous and requires labor, and which is wonderful and exciting and liberating, and then it all goes to pieces. In the end it is all taken away. We can fall into despair, or we can fail to remember how it was, because we get entangled in functional time, and then we are not able to remember. But this failure and how it really is, is what we need to remember. In remembering this, we have a true liberation. Can we not be glad that "the Lord giveth and the Lord taketh away"?

We can look and say, "What is real in all this?" You can picture the 'experiencing material' concentrated together in a 'good event', and then fragmenting again, dispersing, with all the pieces flying around, getting in each other's way. We are all soon going out into different places. Our associations are diverging. There is something painful in seeing this, but it is better than not seeing it.

What was it that was coming to presence in us? Without blasphemy one can speak of this in the same breath as saying "What was it that came amongst the disciples three days after the Crucifixion?" Or maybe we cannot, I do not know. There *is* a definite experience of the coming into manifestation. It may be part of the 'domain of harmony' that John asked about two days ago — the region where spiritualization of existence and the realization of essence reside. We may play a part in this, but we miss the real step of progress in it. It remains simply an experience. It is not an *act of objective reason* for us.

The act of objective reason must visibly appear to us as nothingness, but we do not have the power to make this nothingness in us. It must come by participation in events. It is this which comes in the middle. Rightly or wrongly, I have no idea, but I picture it as coming in the middle of the event which is the reality. We can see this when there is a large enough perspective, as there is in historical events of the past. We see a leading up to and a going away from; we do not see the center. But we realize that it is true that time is going backwards from the center and forwards from the center. In our own experience of events, we see that we are drawn towards the center and pushed away from the center. This is an image, only an image, of what I am meaning by the third kind of time, the time of *will*. In the visualization exercises prepared by Mr. Bennett that John gave to you, you came to something very difficult at the end. It is exactly the same as what is in the question: "Where is god in history?"

We must look and ask this question, "Where is God in history?" It is a much stronger question than, "Where is the time of life?" I feel it is quite possible to develop an organ of perception sensitive to being time by means of the exercise we have been following. We can come into the time of living creatures and see that life lives in its own time. The question I am trying to get at now is much deeper than that.

I can say that God is in the beginning of events, in their center, and in their ending. This is to make the same mistake that de Chardin made and reduces it all to linear functional-time. Nothing can happen in that time. Nothing can get anywhere. And in being time, nothing has to get anywhere, because it *is*.

When there is manifestation, the three kinds of time are coalesced. That is the theory of it. But to attain any real seeing, we have to get hold of the fact that *there is not time*. The real event of manifestation does not take place in time; it is the *creation of time*. This is what I called, 'God's time'.

We speak of doing things and of having to do things. This is an image like all the other things we look at; but it is an image of God, because there is nothing within us that is not derived from God. Real events are *doing*. There is more than life. We come to this only indirectly through our being thrown away from life into darkness by our thinking, through being aware of death, and through the failure of all that we strive to attain. We see it in the negative way, but the seeing is not at all negative.

What can we see hidden in every real event? We can approach this by contemplating what in Christianity is called the 'communion of saints' and in Sufism the *be'it* or abodes. The communion of saints is the same as the communion of events. They cannot be separated. Each is utterly individual, but each is utterly with the others. We know this too; it is not far away, nothing can be very far away from us. God cannot be far away from us, even though there are barriers; it is not like that.

When we touch each other in the will, when we encounter who we are, not as an experience but as a recognition of the totally unexpected, it is utterly mutual. There is one tremendous act. Perhaps it is love.

The Greater Present Moment

Q. Mr. Bennett said in a letter that it was his feeling that one of the problems that people were experiencing with the Gurdjieff Work was that they were so afraid of losing sight of their own nullity that they neglected a positive approach towards the higher powers. One of the things that Mr. Bennett thought we could learn from Sri Aurobindo was his way of having a fresh, open, positive orientation towards the supra-mental or higher powers. I wonder if you can say anything about what we can do to keep that in mind? I think a lot of the time I'm so busy with the orientation of getting rid of the garbage in me so that something can come in, that I forget what I'm doing it for. Is there anything, perhaps, you can say about how we can live with this a little better?

A.G.E.B. I'm so easily tempted to say that I can't say anything at all, because this is so high, but that itself is an example of what you're talking about. We must not assume that we can't see anything, know anything, or say anything about important matters. I'll tell you what I can. The first thing is to believe in the higher powers, which is to accept them. To find some way of doing this one needs to find a corresponding image for oneself, because we seem to lack direct perception. For example, during this seminar we talked about the higher powers in terms of a kind of time. We live in the time of the higher powers, but only in the higher part of ourselves. This is what Sri Aurobindo means by the supra-mental. To tune into that we need to accept that we are in their time and living within their action. I can take an image such as this — being in their time — and it is useful to me. Whenever I have contacted it in the past, it has opened something in me. I think this side of believing and coming to accept the higher powers is aided by that sort of thing. At a place like Findhorn, for example, there are very strong images about the action of the higher powers which they share. And because they share them, they really do something.

Let us think about participating in events. Significant events have to do with the intersection between our personal lives and the history that is being made. We can say that the higher powers are our meaningful history, rather than looking at them as beings. They are primarily a mode of action which affects *all* people. No matter how blind one is to what's going on, it is *here*. The crises of uncertainty which now exist among nations, among all people, intersect with one's own uncertainty. When there is an intersection of the big scale and the little scale, something can open.

It came to me yesterday or the day before, something very simple to do with nature. There is something very important in what I crudely described as the time of living things. Life lives in its own time. Another way of talking about this is having respect for nature; but, ordinarily this is taken as an emotion rather than as a perception. I think there is some kind of perception to be developed. It has to do with an attitude towards nature, a perception of the time in which nature herself lives, which we can approach only through the creatures which are around us. When I find this in my experience, it seems to enable me to come into my time, my human time. Then I become aware that this time is being worked on. It is not something which is there; it is not me or anything like that. There is a whole. I become aware of a chain of orders of time. When we come into a relationship with the time of life, what is more than life begins to come into a relationship with us. This is the beginning of an experience of synergy, cooperation.

J.W. About acceptance. First of all, I accept that perhaps there was a purpose in life. I remember when I was very young that it was very crucial for my future existence that I find a purpose. If I didn't find a purpose, I was going to finish my life; it was as simple as that. I found some sort of purpose which was vague but acceptable for the moment. Then I found that an acceptance of what was in front of me came about. Through an acceptance of that, there eventually came an acceptance of myself for what I am. Through that came acceptance of other people and of a greater whole. Then came an acceptance that there were such things as higher powers. It seemed to be a circle for me, a series of acceptances, one within the other that led back to a deeper acceptance of the fact that there were higher powers, whatever they are.

Q. Is there a danger in that we would think we could be active towards higher powers?

A.G.E.B. We do all sorts of silly things, of course, such as people going around invoking the higher powers. It all gets muddled and it is bound to. We have to accept that as well. My way of working involves very much an acceptance of muddle; that everything which is me, or in a human being, *is in its very foundation muddled.* I remember being so relieved when I found out that Bennett had said that to exist is necessarily to be confused, because to exist means to be under such limitations that it is not possible to see the whole. We expect too much of ourselves. We can operate only with what is limited and incomplete. Wholeness cannot be contained in something that exists. All that is required is to be "sufficient unto the day."

The Greater Present Moment

Q. Ever since I can remember, I've had this feeling that I was isolated and rather painfully lonely in spite of a somewhat gregarious exterior. That feeling has diminished here, and with it has come an acceptance of what John and you were talking about self. But now in terms of time, I've had this constant feeling, "I must do something with this acceptance that I've been given." I don't know in which direction to go. I don't know what a good starting point is for me.

A.G.E.B. I'd like to hear what John says about it. What I see is that if there is acceptance, what it leads to is taking certain things seriously, giving them a weight which one did not before. This, of itself, deepens and reveals what is to come. There is acceptance and then a deepening of what is duty. Duty becomes different.

J.W. It's an understanding of: "Render unto Caesar the things that are Caesar's, and unto God, the things that are God's." Each domain has the tax that we have to pay. The world of function is the world of doing. The world of being is the world of being. The world of will is almost unfathomable. But we have to learn when we have to do and when we have to be. We have to be sensitive to what is the appropriate mode of conduct. But if we start doing when it is time to be, then we create problems. It is possible to develop a sensitivity towards this. It is very much bound up with duty, because we have a duty to these various domains or worlds, and this duty has to be met if we wish to become efficient servants of them, but it does require that we develop the power of seeing what is necessary at any one moment. You know, with children, how sometimes you have to do something about them, while at other times you have to *be* something. It is the same with yourself and with God, and with everything else; they are not very different.

Q. Would you have a moment to say anything on the relationship between cycles and time?

A.G.E.B. I've been waiting all week for you to ask this. I can just say what I can see and it is not all that much. There is a marvelous phrase that I learned in London from Charlotte Bach, a woman of great genius who is a truly original thinker on time: *acausal synchronicity*. This phrase describes how the actions of beings are connected. Charlotte presupposes that every entity, high or low, is a focus of intentionality and reaches out into its environment to complete itself. What we call causality is simply the static common denominator of all this medley of intention; but you must understand that she is really talking about living time, the time in which things are what they are. With everything reaching out to everything in its own way, there has to come a harmonization, or the world could not be stable and would cease to exist. When I gave the talk on "Making Progress," I briefly referred to the stage at which synchronicity becomes a dominant factor.

You are interested in the strange fluctuations in food productivity and prices, emotional states, lunacy, disasters, wars, all kinds of things which enter into human life. You want to know what is producing these. Why does it have to be so? In recent years the world has generally been having strange weather conditions. Some people try to explain it in terms of an up-dated astrology. The basic notion we need to look at is that of synchronization.

Things come together in rhythms, in times, and seasons. The cycle of time, you see, is the visible part of what you can call 'the act of the being'. There are cycles in human life and this expresses what we are. Picture that everything is in some way becoming. There is the transition between the potential and the actual in us. So we grow old and die, we do things of greater and lesser intensity, there are different levels of action, and so on. This is expressed outwardly in space and time through various motions. But we do this in an environment. It has to be coupled with the other contents of that environment, with other people. For example, if you are going to do a task with others, then you have to couple what you do with what other people do. This also applies to the non-human environment. If you do farming, you have to gear in with what is happening in the soil, in the weather, in the seasons, in the seeds. Without this coupling of action you couldn't live in the same world as other beings.

We have here something which is very close to what I said about space. Space is the condition of outer relationships which is to do with the separation of bodies so they can exist apart from one another. Cycles are the way in which there can be an actualization of different kinds of things in the same region, without which there would be chaos. The coupling of actions has to do with hyparxis, the third kind of time.

You have a manifestation of it in music. Where is hyparxis in the music? Hyparxis has to do with where the music is going. Let us use this strange phrase, "Where is the music going?" It is close to, "What is it for?" but not quite the same.

Everything that is has will; or, will lives through everything. It takes a certain form in man, a certain form in an animal, a certain form in a rock, a certain form in an angel. What is will? It is this going somewhere, this act, this going towards meaning, or the creation of meaning. Everything in the universe has a kind of going, or a kind of coming, and everything in the universe has to adjust to the coming and going; otherwise, there could not be a universe. That is why you have giving and taking as the principle of the universe, the 'Trogoautoegocrat' and the transformation of energies. Everything arises from everything and again enters into everything. The coming and going in time adjusts itself to form cycles and rhythms. When a man is effective in a task, he has a rhythm.

Do you know this story about Steiner? When the Anthroposophists were

The Greater Present Moment

building the first Goetheanum, they employed some Italian woodworkers who were very skilled craftsmen, and the kind of design they had to do in wood around these windows was very complex and difficult. Steiner liked to work with craftsmen and talked to them a lot. One day he was with them and said, "It is a question of rhythm, let me show you." He executed the carving in an amazingly short time.

Some people are interested in cycles, because they want to make money, as in commodity buying and selling. As Maurice Nicoll said, "Each one buys what they can afford from their pocket".[1] The hard step is to accept that everything has a kind of reach out, or intentionality. Mr. Bennett called it 'hyparxis'. Hyparxis is an extension into intentionality, the power of intention, the power of direction, the power of making a direction, the power of choosing. It is an alignment in time and eternity. In any world epoch — which means any present moment for the human race — everything striving to get somewhere will have reached an equilibrium, a time equilibrium. This time equilibrium is cyclic, and there are greater and lesser scales of it. This does not mean that these cycles are in any way absolute. Even the procession of the equinox, which is associated with the divisions of the Great Cycle of approximately 25,000 years, probably came about by some geophysical event or some major cosmic event at one time. Cycles are the static side or the passive side of the becoming time. The other side of it is evolutionary, totally directional. When this enters, everything has got to adjust around it. This is a very curious thing to visualize. People say such things as when Christ came on earth, the minerals on the earth had to change. Why? Because the time is different. Events in whatever 'great time' there is, relative to the event you are looking at, change the cycles, and thus the equilibrium is disturbed. This is why it is difficult. Astrology seems to deny, as it does, evolution, progress in ourselves. What there is from the astrological cycles is the passive side of our lives, and there's another side which is dynamic.

J.W. Do you know Gurdjieff's story, of the wise bird who tried to eat a long snake? Every time he gobbled it down, the snake came out the other end. He kept gobbling it down, and it kept going out the other end. So he thought and started to gobble, and he put his head by his ass and said, "Circulate, circulate."

Q. Every time I try to get a handle on hyparxis it seems to want to blend with eternity. I keep thinking of eternity as the storehouse of potential and hyparxis as the flesh and blood of the ableness to be. But I can't keep them separated.

A.G.E.B. There is the famous parable of the talents in the Gospels. The servants were given a certain number of talents — this is potential. What they did with them is the actualization. But the degree of being a good or useless servant is to do with hyparxis. Everyone had the same talents: one went and buried it in the field, one bought some material with it, and one invested it and made more. The difference is in their hyparchic power. They have the same apokritical interval — the talents. With an increase of potential the number of options becomes more complex; therefore, you can say that the responsibility becomes more. What is responsible? Who is responsible? What is it to get somewhere? Or, what is the measure of getting somewhere? It becomes a question of progress. There is income, there is expenditure, but what comes out of it? If you rest with either the potential or the actual, it collapses back again, because you have to keep taking it further.

Meditations and exercises can be similar to burying our talents in the field. We never start living differently. Yet, if we get results, these are actualizations which fix and limit our possibilities. We need to invest in an action that increases our possibilities. This is the principle of our work. It is sometimes expressed as: "The reward of work is the opportunity to enter into a deeper kind of work."

All these words — potential, eternity, income, resource — if you keep them still, if you fix them, you miss the point, because hyparxis is the source of the dynamic. You're trying to make a static picture of something that is the very epitome of dynamism. "He who kisses a joy as it flies, lives to see eternity's sun rise." My favorite image is the shaman. To get to heaven there is the ladder of arrows. You shoot the arrow, you stand on the arrow, you shoot the arrow, you stand on the arrow, you shoot the arrow, you stand on the arrow — that is hyparxis. That is will time. Any one arrow is at a certain level in eternity. John?

J.W. A man was told that the gates of heaven were opened once every hundred years, so he sat and he worked on himself. As it got near the time to the hundredth year, his eyelids for a moment fell shut from weariness, and the doors opened and closed.

A.G.E.B. Do not take it entirely as Mr. Bennett expressed it: 'ableness to be', because you will see it only in a narrow personal sense. There are also such things as ableness to serve, ableness to be at the right place at the right time, ableness to be useful. Getting with it is hyparchic.

J.W. The sly man . . .

A.G.E.B. The sly man is hyparchic! You see, the monk, the yogi, and so on; they are all looking at eternity. The monk is looking up and hoping eternity comes and visits him. The fakir is pushing at time, against time, to get up there. But the sly man is slipping around them all through hyparxis, which is the quick way, because you do not have to move in hyparxis.

Q. What is our relationship with that?

A.G.E.B. Our relationship? What's this, our relationship? You think of yourself as something in time. It is not like that. There is being time, and then

The Greater Present Moment

something is possible. If something more than a dream comes out of this, there is will; whereas, states and so on are intermediaries. They do not get anywhere; they are resources. To have the right knowledge in the right state, this is hyparchic, and something can come out of it. There is no question of *who*, unless there is an act. Then there is an act of servantship or service or progress. This may not change anything outwardly at all; it may consist of an act of acceptance in that moment.

Would you tell them the story about death, John?

J.W. Once upon a time there was Hasan, a servant of a Sufi, and he had been to the market to buy things. When he came back, he saw his master talking to death, and he was so frightened that he jumped on his horse and rode to Bukhara. Death was talking to the master and said, "How is your servant Hasan?" The master said, "He's out fetching vegetables." "That's funny," said death, "I have an appointment with him in Bukhara tomorrow."

A.G.E.B. This is a very good illustration of the connection between hyparxis and hazard, and how this wrong understanding of doing puts you in the net, puts you into the state where you are ineffective. The understanding of doing is connected with hyparxis. It does not matter if you do not like the word hyparxis. Please forget it, never use it again. But something is there which influences our relationship with events. I was talking to some people about the predictions that people make about catastrophes, especially here in America. Some are no doubt ridiculous. Some, like Cayce's material, is to be taken seriously. But if you *react* to the prediciotns, either scientific or those of clairvoyance, you are liable to get into negative time like Hasan. You are going to rush off and go to the very place where disaster can strike you, and this happens time and time again, because you do not see. There's some lack of seeing here about what it is that we can do.

You could sum up the whole thing in these terms: there is confusion in the world between hyparchic time and actualization time. Some people, of course, have become disillusioned with this rat race and all the absurdity of what is imagined to be 'doing'. One escape route is in being time: states, experiences, ecstasies, whether through drugs or meditation. Art sometimes can be such an escape. Beauty is a temptation. But there is the way of understanding. The sly man is the one who understands events and what is really going on. We need to confront ourselves with what we see or what is being seen through us, and not make pretty pictures for ourselves. If we enjoy them, all right; but let us leave them alone, not drag dead ideas around with us which we do not need.

The Cosmic Present Moment

My last offering to you just came to me today. It is based on the Sufi Octad which I found a drawing of at the beginning of the seminar. I felt that the symbol would prove to be important, and so it did.

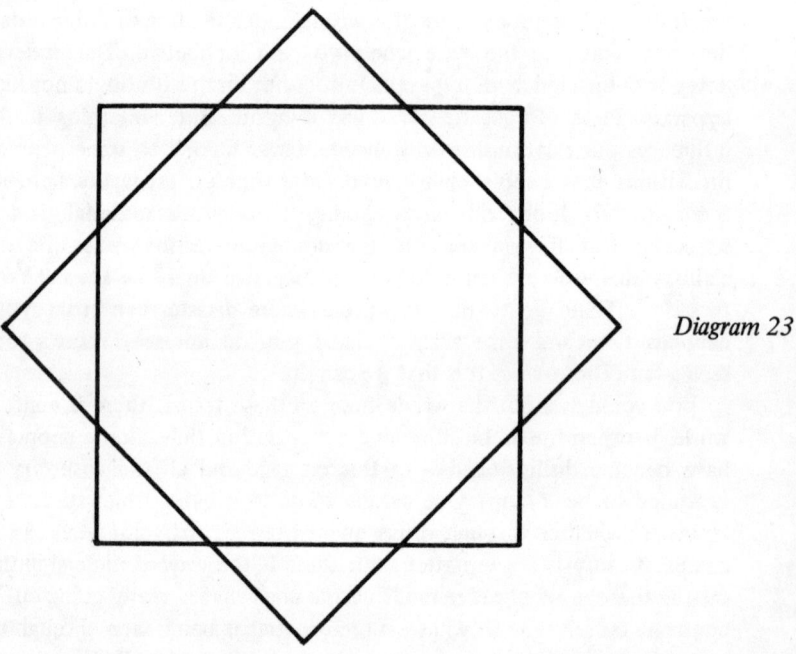

Diagram 23

You will remember that the first square symbol I put in front of you had the terms: eternity, space, time, and hyparxis. These four conditions apply to everything that exists, but they do not go beyond the factual. They say nothing about what makes our experience, or parts of it, significant or valuable.

The Cosmic Present Moment

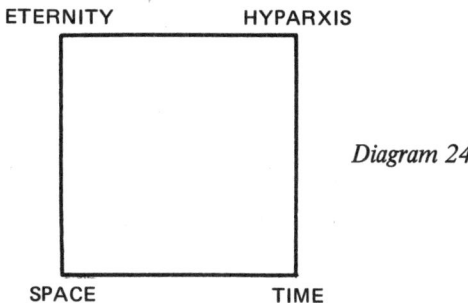

Diagram 24

Our experience has a significance because of the possibilities of freedom in it. This has to do with the ableness to make an independent contribution to the whole. What can we say about this?

Firstly, our mode of freedom is influenced by our experience arising between the spiritual and material worlds. The spiritual region is beyond and ahead of time and can be placed above the line of eternity and hyparxis. The natural region is contained by the laws of actualization and separation and can be placed below the line of space and time. What comes from the spiritual and material regions we do not really know. But in some way they must shape the form of will that is possible for us or for any other autonomous existence.

Secondly, we have two sides to our freedom. On the right hand there is something suggested by the line hyparxis-time. This is the line of doing in all its ambiguity. So on the right hand, we put the active will, which I am going to call *interfering*. This may seem a very strange word to use, but I want to remind you that we are not talking about our fondly imagined mechanical universe 'working like a pianola', but about the real world. Man interferes with nature, with other people, and with himself. This is necessary. Remember, too, that Beelzebub himself was banished to the solar system because he poked his nose into affairs that did not concern him. Out of this came very important results for the benefit of all intelligences.

On the left hand side there is the line of eternity and space. These are the conditions of potential and absence, and they suggest that here is the place of the passive will. I am going to give it the name *allowing*. It is so important to the world that we are able to allow things to happen and not interfere. It may seem strange to speak of this as an element of will, but only because we have become conditioned by very sterile images of masculine doing. It is so important to get a feeling of what comes through allowing. It is not passivity in the sense of being weak but in the sense of freely permitting an action to take its course. This was the way of the Mother with people who came to Sri Aurobindo's ashram.

The spiritual and the material factors can then be called the *enabling* and the *limiting*. The spiritual world does not make us free, but it enables us to be free. The material world does not really limit *us*, it is rather that it is 'recalcitrant'.

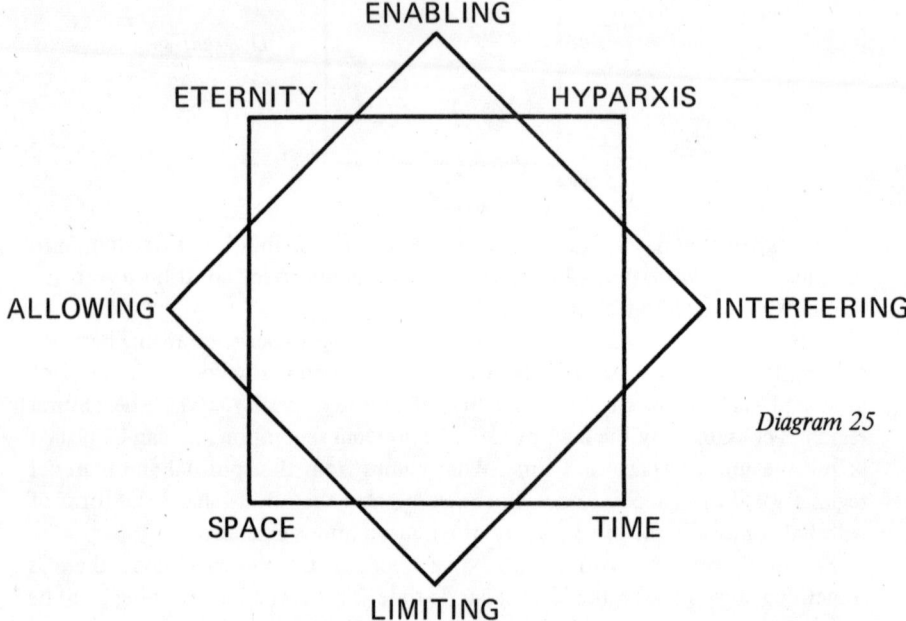

Diagram 25

So far we have the composition of our human world. But this is within the cosmic world. We need to see the human octad as nested within a cosmic octad.

To begin with we can take the four great Images of God as they have been described by J.G. Bennett. These images are really great beings in their own right and have led to nearly every conception we have of ourselves and our world. These four images I will connect with a larger 'diamond' that contains our octad.

At the top is God the Creator — but I am going to use the greater name of God the *Father*, because creation is a subsidiary power of Him.

At the bottom is the depth beyond material form. This is not death, but a kind of plenitude which we can hardly imagine. It is the Great *Mother*.

In the conception of life on the earth, the sun is the Father and the earth, the Mother. It is not simply that the sun is 'higher' than the earth. Each provides something needed for the new life. For all the creativity of the sun, without the immeasurable power of response of the earth, nothing could have happened.

On the masculine side of the will there is the *Savior*, God the Savior. On the left is the Great *Spirit* or the Holy Ghost.

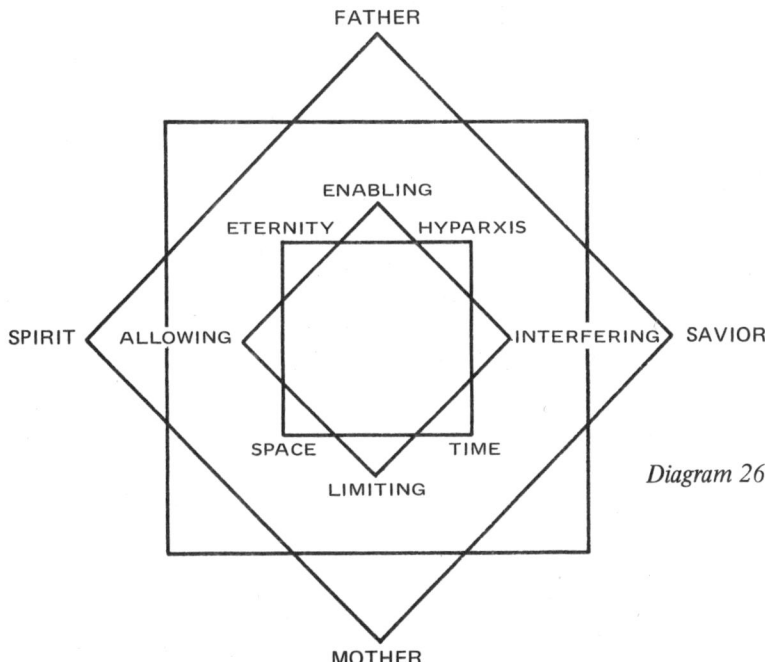

Diagram 26

The Savior towards time becomes the *Hero*. Towards hyparxis, the *Redeemer*.

The Mother towards time is the Bearer of Children. She is *Fertility*. Towards space She is the *Receptacle*, as you find in Plato's *Timaeus;* or she is the Great Matrix.

The Spirit toward space is the *All-Pervading;* towards eternity, the *Ever-Lasting*.

The Father towards eternity is *Dharma*, the law of the Will of God, the rightness of the will, impersonal. The Father towards hyparxis is the *Creator*, personal and individualized.

If you look through all the records and conceptions of God, from those of paleolithic man through those of early civilizations, through those of the great religions and through those even of contemporary man, you will find that all of them are covered by these great ideas. You will begin to see why the Hero comes to marry the Mother and why the Redeemer is sometimes thought of as creator of history.

190   A Seminar On Time

For the final part of the picture, we turn to the cosmology of Gurdjieff as he presents it in *All and Everything*. This we will place on the big square that so far has not been labelled.

In Gurdjieff's account of the coming into being of the world, there are four main protagonists. He talks a great deal about triads, but three-foldness is not absolute. The triad is just one form of understanding.

There is the 'place' of God: the *Holy Sun Absolute*. This is the region of the ultimate laws in their pure form. It is the source of *dharma* and all the cosmic laws.

The Holy Sun Absolute, in its character as the ever-lasting, is threatened by the *Merciless Heropass*. The Heropass is beyond God. It is the unthinkable reality behind the action of time.

The awareness of the results ensuing inevitably from the Merciless Heropass gives rise to the decision that entails a creation. This decision is called the Word-God, the *Theomertmalogos*.

The Theomertmalogos emanates into the 'space surrounding' the Holy Sun Absolute, called the *Etherokrilno*.

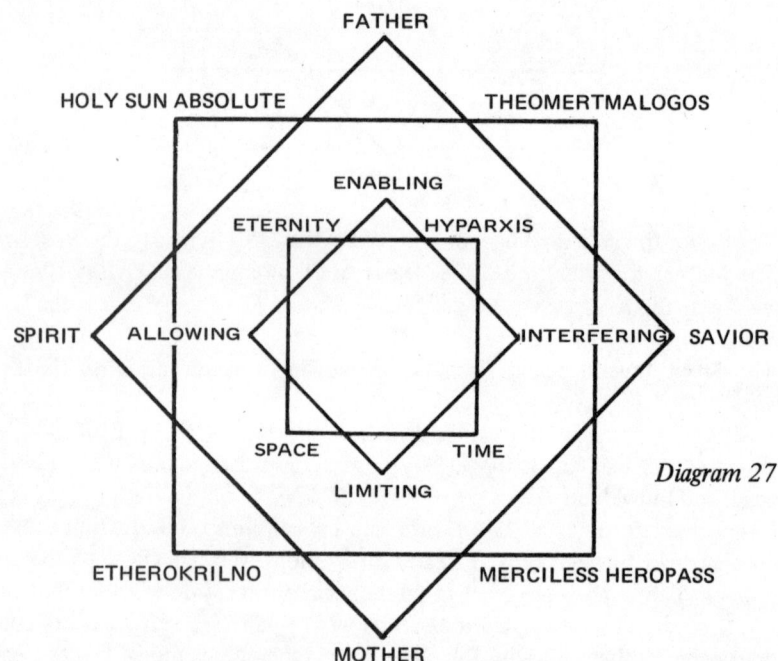

Diagram 27

The Cosmic Present Moment

His Endlessness is the wholeness of the Names of God and is not represented here in any one place. Neither do I represent the human being in any one place. Please take note of this and try to understand why.

Every point of intersection has a meaning. You see, it would be quite wrong to combine the four squares into one. Each one rotates out of line with the one proceeding. There is no end to it. There are no absolutes. All we have here is a symbol of our moment of understanding embedded in the present moment of all human understanding.

At the center is the cross where there can be an act of reality. But we will never be sure whose act it is!

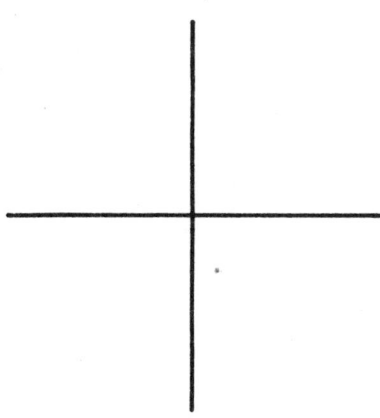

Diagram 28

Notes

Notes to Chapter 1, Part One.

1. Gurdjieff, *Meetings with Remarkable Men,* p. 36.
2. Santillana and Dechend, *Hamlet's Mill,* p. 297 and passim.
3. Bennett, *Masters of Wisdom,* p. 61. (And at the present time the religious language is being abandoned.)
4. These quotations come from *The Epic of Gilgamesh,* translated by Sanders.
5. Bennett, *Gurdjieff: Making a New World,* p. 276.
6. Shah, *Thinkers of the East.* This is a paraphrase of the author's story.
7. Gurdjieff, *Meetings with Remarkable Men,* pp. 90, 161-2, 239; Bennett, *Gurdjieff: Making a New World,* passim; Bennett, *Masters of Wisdom,* p. 59.
8. Heidel, *Babylonian Genesis,* p. 46.
9. Heidel, loc. cit.
10. Ibid.
11. Ibid.
12. For the reader who reads books backwards, the property of catalysis belongs to eternity, and intelligence to hyparxis.
13. A. R. Orage, *On Love: wtih Some Aphorisms and Other Essays.* (New York: Samuel Weiser, Inc., 1974), p. 55.
14. For a detailed exposition, see the chapter on "The Merciless Heropass" in Bennett's *Talks on Beelzebub's Tales.*
15. Gurdjieff, *All and Everything,* p. 23.
16. Ibid, p. 124.

Notes to Chapter 2, Part One

1. E.g. Professor John Taylor in *Cosmology Now* (London: BBC Publications, 1973).
2. Cf. D. Bohm, *Causality and Chance in Modern Physics.* London, Routledge & Paul, 1957, p. 163.
3. This is described in *Existence* by Bennett.
4. Though I never referred to it and hardly read it, Merleau Ponty's *Phenomenology of Perception* has had a big influence on my thinking. It is only excelled by the work of Gurdjieff and Bennett which takes into account the three centers of man. A 'center' is a center by virtue of its image.
   Cf. J. G. Bennett, *Deeper Man* (London: Turnstone Books, 1978), Chapter Three.
5. Reciprocity and self-determination are the two faces of hyparxis, the third kind of time.
6. This is of vital importance for understanding the idea of Reciprocal Maintenance and why there should have to be a complex chain of transformation of energies to maintain the universe.

Notes to Chapter 5, Part One

1. See Bennett's *Deeper Man*, Part II.

Notes to Chapter 6, Part One

1. Henri Bortoft, J. G. Bennett, and K. W. Pledge, "Towards an Objectively Complete Language," in *Systematics*, vol. 3, no. 3.

Notes to Chapter 7, Part One

1. Cf. J. G. Bennett, *Creation*, Studies from The Dramatic Universe, no. 3 (Sherborne, England: Coombe Springs Press, 1978), Chapter One.
2. Cf. G. I. Gurdjieff, *Life Is Real Only Then, When "I Am"* (New York: Privately printed by E. P. Dutton & Co., Inc. for Triangle Editions, Inc., 1975), pp. 144-6.

3. J. G. Bennett, *The Crisis in Human Affairs* (New York: Hermitage House, 1951), p. 184.
4. Cf. J. G. Bennett, *Sex,* Transformation of Man Series, no. 3 (Sherborne) England: Coombe Springs Press, 1975), p. 8.
5. The sides of the square are very interesting. In old language they are to do with 'archangels'. cf Rudolf Steiner, *The Spiritual Hierarchies,* Anthroposophic Press, New York, 1970."
6. This is the real substance of St. Anselm's syllogism on the existence of God.

Notes to Chapter 11, Part Two

1. The term *acausal* is taken from the work of Charlotte Bach, who is referred to in Chapter 18, Part Two.

Notes to Chapter 14, Part Two

1. A.G.E. Blake, review of *Christ and Time* by Oscar Cullman, trans. F. V. Filson, in *Systematics,* vol. 3, no. 4, p. 361.
2. Our physical body, not that of animals. Our bodies allow a connection with awareness that animals do not.

Notes to Chapter 16, Part Two

1. Jacques Monod, *Chance and Necessity.* (New York: Knopf, 1971).
2. Cf. A.W. Low, *The Systematics of a Business Organization, Systematics,* Vol 4, no. 3.
3. This is the burden of the production-line worker.
4. Cf A. Bausani, "Religion under the Mongols", in *The Cambridge History of Iran,* Volume 5, Cambridge University Press, 1968, pp 545-6.

Notes to Chapter 17, Part Two

1. People may object and point to the wonder of Islamic art. But what has great art to do with God?

Notes to Chapter 18, Part Two

1. Nicoll, *Living Time*, p. 234.

Select Bibliography

Original Works:

Bennett, J. G.   *The Dramatic Universe,* 4 vols., reprint. Sherborne, England: Coombe Springs Press, 1976.

The Masters of Wisdom. London: Turnstone Books, 1977.

Gurdjieff: Making a New World. New York: Harper & Row, 1974.

Talks on Beelzebub's Tales. Sherborne, England: Coombe Springs Press, 1977.

Hazard, The Dramatic Universe Series, no. 1. Sherborne, England: Coombe Springs Press, 1976.

Existence, The Dramatic Universe Series, no. 2. Sherborne, England: Coombe Springs Press, 1977.

Collin, Rodney.   *The Theory of Eternal Life.* New York: Samuel Weiser, 1974.

Eliot, T. S.   *Four Quartets.* New York: Harcourt, Brace and World, Inc., 1963.

Gurdjieff, G. I.   *All and Everything: Beelzebub's Tales to His Grandson.* New York: E. P. Dutton & Co., Inc., 1964.

Meetings with Remarkable Men. New York: E. P. Dutton & Co., Inc., 1963.

Nicoll, Maurice.   *Living Time and the Integration of Life.* London: Watkins, 1959.

Santillana, Giorgio di, and Dechend, Hertha von.
Hamlet's Mill: An Essay on Myth and the Frame of Time. Boston: David R. Godine, 1977.

Shah, Idries. *Thinkers of the East: Teachings of the Dervishes.* Baltimore: Penguin Books, 1971.

Shakespeare, William. *Sonnets.*

Sumerian Sources: *Enūma Elish* (When on High). Trans. Heidel, A. *The Babylonian Genesis.* Chicago: University of Chicago Press, 1951.

The Epic of Gilgamesh. Trans. Sanders, N. K. Baltimore: Penguin Books, 1960.